Machine Learning

OrangeBooks Publication

1st Floor, Rajhans Arcade, Mall Road, Kohka, Bhilai, Chhattisgarh 490020

Website: **www.orangebooks.in**

First Edition, 2025

ISBN: 978-93-7426-852-0

MACHINE LEARNING

DR. A.J.K. PRASAD
DR. GOWRAMMA G.S. | DR. REDDAPPA H.N.

OrangeBooks Publication
www.orangebooks.in

About the Cover

The cover of this book has been designed to visually represent the core themes and progression of machine learning for undergraduate learners. At the top, a series of symbolic icons illustrates essential components of the field—ranging from artificial intelligence, data processing, decision-making systems, pattern discovery, and networked learning. These icons highlight how machine learning integrates diverse concepts to build intelligent computational models.

The central title, *Machine Learning*, is presented in a bold and modern typeface to reflect the dynamic and evolving nature of the discipline. The tagline emphasises that this edition is tailored exclusively for undergraduate students, offering clarity, accessibility, and comprehensive coverage.

Below the title, a five-node conceptual diagram forms the heart of the cover. Each node represents a major pillar of the book:

- **A:** Introduction to Machine Learning and Learning Styles
- **B:** Data Analysis and Feature Engineering
- **C:** Similarity-Based Learning and Regression
- **D:** Probabilistic Models and Neural Networks
- **E:** Clustering Algorithms and Reinforcement Learning

These interconnected modules visually communicate how the topics in machine learning are interrelated and build upon one another—mirroring the structure and flow of the textbook.

The background features subtle digital and geometric patterns symbolizing algorithms, computation, and the underlying mathematical foundations of machine learning. The clean layout and futuristic design convey clarity, precision, and innovation—qualities that the book aims to instill in its readers.

Overall, the cover encapsulates both the spirit and the structure of the book: a clear, systematic, and engaging introduction to machine learning for undergraduate students.

Preface

It gives us immense pleasure to present the first edition of *"Machine Learning"*, a comprehensive textbook designed to bridge the gap between theoretical foundations and practical applications in the rapidly evolving field of machine learning. This book emerges from our collective experience in teaching machine learning to undergraduate students and our recognition of the need for a resource that balances mathematical rigor with accessibility.

Machine learning has transformed from an academic curiosity into a driving force behind technological innovation across industries. This textbook aims to equip undergraduate students with the fundamental knowledge and practical skills necessary to understand, implement, and innovate in this dynamic field.

The textbook is organized into five carefully structured chapters, each designed to build a strong foundation while gradually introducing advanced topics. Our pedagogical approach emphasizes conceptual understanding supported by mathematical foundations, ensuring that students develop both theoretical knowledge and practical intuition.

Special attention has been given to including relevant illustrations and tables that enhance understanding and provide visual clarity to complex concepts. Additionally, each chapter concludes with a set of thoughtfully curated questions categorized into short answer, medium answer, and long answer types, encouraging students to reflect on and apply what they have learned.

Key Features of This Edition:

1. Comprehensive Visual Learning Aids: This first edition includes 61 figures and 58 tables, meticulously designed to simplify complex concepts and support visual learners. We have ensured high-quality visual appeal with clear, informative graphics and simple table formats. Black and white figures are provided in both hard copies and e-books.

2. Structured Learning Framework: Each chapter begins with a concise overview, providing a clear roadmap of the topics covered, and concludes with a comprehensive summary and reflective thoughts to reinforce learning outcomes. This structure helps students navigate complex topics systematically and consolidate their understanding progressively.

3. Active Learning and Reference Features: To support active learning and critical thinking, a comprehensive set of theoretical review questions has been provided at the end of each chapter, categorized into short, medium, and long answer formats. These are designed to deepen conceptual understanding and encourage analytical thinking. An alphabetical index and glossary are included to ensure ease of reference for both students and educators.

4. Practice-Oriented Appendix: Appendix A provides chapter-wise numerical problems with solutions, Python code implementations, and graphical representations. This section is intended to strengthen practical understanding and enable learners to connect theoretical concepts with computational applications. We believe this appendix will empower students to confidently tackle real-life problems encountered in their professional journeys, encouraging them to explore new challenges and develop effective problem-solving skills.

Chapter Organization and Content:

Chapter 1: Introduction to Machine Learning

(*10 figures and 17 tables*)

This foundational chapter introduces students to the fundamental concepts of machine learning, tracing its historical development and establishing its position within the broader landscape of computer science and artificial intelligence. Students explore what constitutes a "machine" in machine learning, the compelling need for machine learning in modern applications, and the knowledge pyramid that illustrates the progression from data to wisdom.

The chapter clarifies that the term "machine" refers not to a physical device but to algorithms or statistical models capable of learning from data and improving performance autonomously. It also examines advantages, limitations, and relationships with related domains such as statistics, data mining, and artificial intelligence, along with a comprehensive taxonomy of learning paradigms.

Chapter 2: Data Analysis and Feature Engineering

(06 figures and 09 tables)
This chapter focuses on the essential aspects of data preparation and analysis. Students learn bivariate and multivariate analysis, multivariate statistics, and mathematical foundations necessary for understanding complex datasets.

It also covers feature engineering, dimensionality reduction, learning system design, and fundamental learning theory concepts, enabling students to effectively preprocess and model data for machine learning applications.

Chapter 3: Similarity-Based Learning and Regression

(*12 figures and 05 tables*)
This chapter introduces intuitive learning methods based on similarity and regression techniques. Topics include nearest-neighbour algorithms, weighted k-NN, nearest centroid classifiers, and locally weighted regression.

Comprehensive coverage of regression techniques such as linear, multiple, polynomial, and logistic regression is provided. Decision tree learning principles are also introduced. The chapter clarifies that a regressor refers to the independent variable(s) used to predict the dependent variable.

Chapter 4: Probabilistic Models and Neural Networks

(*09 figures, and 10 tables*)
This chapter presents the probabilistic foundations of machine learning along with the computational paradigm of artificial neural networks. It bridges classical statistical approaches with modern machine learning techniques.

Students gain insight into probabilistic reasoning and neural network architectures, enabling them to understand both traditional and modern approaches to data-driven modelling.

Chapter 5: Clustering Algorithms and Reinforcement Learning

(*25 figures, and 17 tables*)

The final chapter explores advanced paradigms of machine learning, including unsupervised learning, neural computation, and decision-making systems.

It begins with clustering techniques, covering hierarchical (agglomerative and divisive) and partitional methods for discovering hidden patterns in unlabelled data.

A significant portion of the chapter is devoted to **Artificial Neural Networks (ANNs)**, discussing their biologically inspired architecture, including input, hidden, and output layers, along with weights, biases, and activation functions. Learning mechanisms such as forward propagation and backpropagation are explained, highlighting how neural networks learn complex nonlinear relationships. Applications in image processing, speech recognition, and predictive analytics are also discussed.

The chapter concludes with **Reinforcement Learning (RL)**, where agents learn optimal behaviour through interaction with an environment using rewards and penalties. Key components such as states, actions, rewards, and policies are introduced, along with Q-learning as a fundamental model-free algorithm.

A Note to Learners and Instructors

This textbook serves as both a comprehensive learning resource and a practical reference guide. Students are encouraged to engage actively with the material, work through examples, and solve end-of-chapter questions to deepen their understanding. Instructors will find the structured approach suitable for semester-long courses, with flexibility to emphasize topics based on course objectives.

Machine learning requires both theoretical understanding and practical experimentation. Readers are encouraged to complement their study with hands-on programming and real-world applications. The journey into machine learning is challenging yet rewarding, opening doors to innovation across diverse domains.

We hope this textbook serves as a valuable companion in your learning journey. Constructive suggestions for improvement are welcome and will be incorporated in future editions.

Authors

Acknowledgements

Firstly, we express our gratitude to the Almighty for blessing us with the opportunity to write this book. We extend our heartfelt thanks to the management of Don Bosco Institute of Technology and the Rajya Vokkaligara Sangha, Bengaluru, for their unwavering support and encouragement.

We would like to sincerely thank **Dr. B.S. Nagabhushana**, Principal of Don Bosco Institute of Technology, and **Dr. Vijaya Prakash A M**, Principal of Bangalore Institute of Technology, Bengaluru, for their guidance and motivation throughout this endeavour.

Dr. Gowramma G. S. expresses her sincere gratitude to her family members, **Mr. Basavaraj N. Nashipudi and Akshata Nashipudi,** for their support and understanding. But for which accomplishment of bringing this book to present shape is not possible.

Dr. Reddappa H.N. expresses his deepest gratitude to his family members, **Mrs. Dharani S**. and **Diganth R**., for their unending support and encouragement.

Dr. A.J.K. Prasad is profoundly thankful to **Venkata Lakshmi**, **Aparna**, and **Jyotsna** for their continuous support, encouragement, and understanding throughout this endeavour.

We extend our indebted thanks to our colleagues for their invaluable encouragement and timely support. We also acknowledge Mr. Kushal for his assistance in creating some of the illustrations featured in this book.

We sincerely appreciate the developers and promoters of OpenAI, Sonnet Claude AI, Perplexity AI, Grok AI, DeepSeek AI, and iMathEQ.com for their invaluable tools that significantly aided in clarifying complex concepts, generating SVGs, and providing Python code for visuals and equations. Their contributions have been indispensable to the success of this project, and we extend our heartfelt thanks to all the team members behind these remarkable platforms.

We express our sincere gratitude to OrangeBooks Publishing (Orangebooks.in) for publishing this book in such an elegant format. Our special thanks go to Madhavi, Payal Ghosh, Preeti Shetty, and their team for their editorial support and dedication.

Dr. A.J.K. Prasad

Dr. Gowramma G. S.

Dr. Reddappa H.N.

Dedication

This book is dedicated to our teachers, whose guidance and wisdom have shaped us, and to our students, whose curiosity and enthusiasm inspire us to remain focused and committed to lifelong learning.

About the Book

Machine Learning for Undergraduates is a comprehensive guide designed to make the complex world of machine learning accessible to beginners. This book introduces foundational concepts, starting with the need for machine learning, its relationship with other fields, and its diverse applications. Through a structured exploration of essential topics, readers will gain a clear understanding of data analysis, including univariate, bivariate, and multivariate statistics, as well as techniques like feature engineering and dimensionality reduction.

Building on these basics, the book delves into core machine learning methodologies. Topics include similarity-based learning, regression analysis, decision tree algorithms, and Bayesian learning. The chapters also introduce artificial neural networks, explaining their biological inspiration, architecture, and applications. Advanced subjects such as clustering algorithms, proximity measures, and reinforcement learning—covering Q-Learning and SARSA—are presented with clarity, ensuring a thorough understanding of each concept.

The enhanced second edition covers a description of learning paradigms that covered in chapter-1 batch and online learning approaches, along with advanced few-shot and one-shot learning techniques. Learners explore how models adapt to different data scenarios—from processing complete datasets to learning from just one or a few examples—using various learning styles, including metric learning, meta-learning, prototype-based methods, and attention-based approaches across diverse applications in healthcare, robotics, and computer vision. In chapter 3 polynomial regression is elaborated. **Appendix A** dwells on several numerical exercises for the learner to practice.

About the Authors

About the Author

Dr. A.J.K. PRASAD

With nearly four decades of experience in industry, research, and teaching, Dr. A.J.K. Prasad holds degrees from prestigious institutions like Andhra University, IIT-BHU, the University of Strathclyde, and Visvesvaraya Technological University. He is a professor at Don Bosco Institute of Technology, Bangalore, specializing in AI and ML. Dr. Prasad has published extensively, holds a granted Indian patent, and has mentored Ph.D. scholars. Certified in AI, ML, and Python for Deep Learning from IIIT Jabalpur, IIT Kanpur, and NPTEL, he continues to innovate and teach AI to undergraduate students. Dr. Prasad co-authored a textbook titled "Artificial Intelligence for Undergraduate Students" with Dr. Reddappa.

About the Co-Author

Dr. GOWRAMMA G. S.

Dr. Gowramma G. S. received a Bachelor's Degree (B.E., Electronics and Communication Engineering) from Kuvempu University (1997); a Master of Technology (M.Tech. in Computer Science and Engineering) from Dr. MGR University (2007), and a Doctor of Philosophy (Ph.D.) in Artificial Intelligence & Machine Learning from Visvesvaraya Technological University (VTU), Belagavi (2023). She has more than 22 years of experience in teaching and research and 5 years of software development experience. She is presently working as Professor & Head, of the Department of Artificial Intelligence and Data Science at Don Bosco Institute of Technology, Bengaluru, during which she has groomed budding computer scientists and data scientists. She is guiding Ph.D., M.Tech., and B.E. projects.

Certified in Python for Data Science, Machine Learning, Data Mining, Introduction to R Language, and Patent Drafting for Beginners in NPTEL. She has national and international research publications and IPR to her credit. Participated in and organized several conferences and workshops. She is now into writing textbooks for undergraduates.

About the Co-Author

Dr. Redappa H.N.

Dr. Reddappa H. N. received a Bachelor's Degree (B.E., Mechanical Engineering) from Malnad College of Engineering, Hassan, University of Mysore, Mysore (1996); a Master of Technology (M.Tech.) in Production Engineering and System Technology (2000) from National Institute of Engineering, Mysore; and Doctor of Philosophy (Ph.D.) in Composite Materials from Visvesvaraya Technological University (VTU), Belagavi (2013). He has more than 23 years of experience in teaching and research and is presently working as an associate professor in the Department of Mechanical Engineering, Bangalore Institute of Technology, Bengaluru. He guided PhD, M.Tech, and B.E. projects. He has national and international research publications and IPRs to his credit. He is into the Artificial Intelligence and Machine Learning field. Dr. Reddappa (with Dr. Prasad) published a textbook titled "Artificial Intelligence for Undergraduate Students", and "Machine Learning for Undergraduate Students."

Contents

List of Figures

List of Tables

Chapter - 1

Introduction to Machine Learning

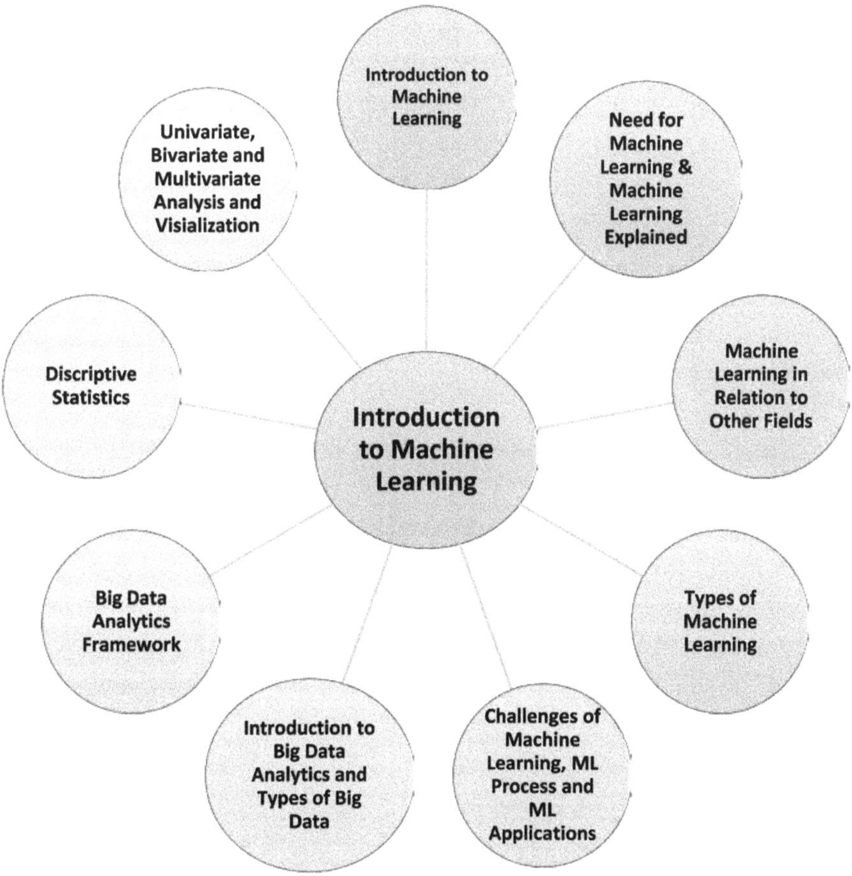

Chapter Overview

This chapter presents a comprehensive introduction to machine learning, emphasizing its growing significance and usefulness in today's data-rich environment. The chapter delves in the evolution of machine learning as a field, its distinctive position within the broader domains of artificial intelligence and data science, and how it can be applied to complicated/challenging real-world problems. Various kinds of learning (supervised, unsupervised, reinforcement, and emergent paradigms like self-supervised learning) were discussed in detail, providing a solid theoretical foundation. The challenges of ML, such as overfitting, computational constraints, and data quality issues, were highlighted to prepare readers for practical considerations. The machine learning process has been explained, illustrating how data moves through multiple stages to generate meaningful insights. Finally, the chapter discusses big data and its symbiotic relationship with machine learning, demonstrating how contemporary tools tackle the enormous amount and complexity of today's data environments.

1.0 Introduction to Machine Learning

Machine learning is present in numerous areas. This observation appears to become increasingly accurate over time. I struggle to think of any facet of life that could not benefit from in one way or another. For tasks that involve repetition or analysing data to draw conclusions, machine learning proves beneficial. In recent years, the field of machine learning has experienced significant expansion owing to increased and the widespread availability of data collection to highlight a few uses of machine learning: recommendation systems, image recognition, text processing, autonomous vehicles, spam detection, and medical diagnosis... and many more. Perhaps you have a specific aim or field where you aspire to create a difference (or perhaps you are already doing so!). It is highly probable that machine learning can assist you. The word "machine" in Machine Learning is used in a figurative sense and signifies the algorithm or model that acquires knowledge from data. It does not represent a tangible machine or robot but is instead a collection of computational strategies that enable systems to enhance their efficiency over time without direct programming. This clarification is vital for grasping the nature of Machine Learning as a subset of Artificial Intelligence.

1.1 Need for Machine Learning:

In today's digital age, we are witnessing an unparalleled data explosion, spurred by the growing popularity of digital communications, the internet revolution, and the widespread use of social media platforms like Facebook, X (formerly Twitter). Individuals, organizations, and devices all over the world generate, transfer, and store enormous amounts of data every second! From social media interactions and e-commerce transactions to Internet of Things (IoT) sensor data and corporate operations, the sheer volume of data is astonishing. This data contains significant insights, but manually analysing and employing it for decision-making is not only impractical, but also nearly impossible!

Traditional methods of processing and analysing data depended mainly on manual labour and rule-based programming. While these strategies worked well for small-scale or organized datasets, they struggle to handle the intricacies of modern data streams. Modern datasets are generally unstructured and complex. Moreover, the data is constantly changing, necessitating the adoption of dynamic and scalable strategies for data manipulation. For example, pattern recognition in photos, predicting/forecasting client Behaviour, and recommending personalized content are beyond the scope of manual or conventional programming. This rising gap between data availability and making useful insights from such big data has necessitated to the development of automated techniques, paving the way for machine learning (ML).

Machine learning addresses the above issue by enabling systems (see explanatory note of machine in machine learning in the following section) to learn from data and improve over time without necessitating explicit programming. Machine learning has democratized data analysis by developing complex algorithms while additionally rendering tools like Python and R more accessible. These technologies allow researchers and businesses to Analyse vast datasets, identify trends, and make reliable predictions. Machine learning algorithms can detect fraud in real time, offer products (also services) based on consumer preferences, and even predict diseases using medical images. Machine learning relies on the ability to process, Analyse, and provide important conclusions from vast quantities of data, making it extremely important in an information-driven world.

Furthermore, the incorporation of machine learning into modern industries has changed how firms operate. Machine Learning powers / propelles predictive analytics for better informed decision-making, automates repetitive tasks to enhance productivity. On the consumer sector especially I e-commence platforms and entertainment segments such as OTT platform analyses user behaviour to provide customer-centric solutions. Whether it is improving supply chains, enhancing cybersecurity, or transforming healthcare diagnostics, the uses of machine learning are reshaping industries. With the rise of big data and technological breakthroughs, machine learning is no longer a luxury; it is a requirement for remaining competitive in a quickly changing digital market.

1.1.1 Evolution of Data-Driven Decision-Making

Development of Data-Driven Decision-Making Historically, organizational decision-making was mainly reliant on intuition, manual analysis, and static reports created from limited datasets. However, with the digital revolution, the volume, variety, and velocity of data grew/swelled tremendously. Modern firms are overrun with data, that includes customer transactions and social media activity to sensor readings and website traffic logs. The abundance of data has paved the way for data-driven decision-making, in which decisions are driven by actionable insights gained through data analysis rather than subjective judgment. Businesses may now use advanced analytics and machine learning to figure out patterns, predicted outcomes, and optimize processes in real time, making decision-making quicker and proactive.

1.1.2 Limitations of Traditional Programming

Traditional programming is based on clearly establishing rules and logic for every possible circumstance, making it rigid and inappropriate for complex, dynamic contexts. This technique suffers with unstructured data tasks including picture recognition, natural language interpretation, and pattern detection in large datasets. Furthermore, manually programming systems to react to new data or changing situations is time-consuming and often impractical. For example, constructing a spam email filter using traditional approaches would necessitate an extensive collection of spam patterns and rules, which would quickly become out of date. Making it essential for addressing new, data-intensive challenges, particularly those involving patterns and insights in unstructured data—a key focus of unsupervised learning.

1.2 Machine Learning Explained

Machine Learning in Relation to Other Fields Machine Learning (ML) is a subfield of Artificial Intelligence that focuses on enabling computers to learn from data and improve their performance without being explicitly programmed. Instead of following fixed rules written by humans, a machine learning system identifies patterns and relationships within data and uses them to make predictions or decisions. For example, rather than programming a computer with thousands of rules to identify spam emails, a machine learning model can be trained using examples of spam and non-spam emails to automatically learn the distinguishing features.

In machine learning, learning takes place through algorithms that build mathematical models from training data. These models are then used to Analyse new or unseen data. The quality of learning depends on the amount of data, the features selected, and the algorithm used. Machine learning systems are widely used because they can adapt to changes, handle complex problems, and improve accuracy over time, making them suitable for real-world applications such as image recognition, speech processing, and recommendation systems.

1.3 What is a Machine, in Machine Learning Context?

The phrase **"machine"** in the context of Machine Learning is used figuratively and represents the algorithm or statistical models that acquire knowledge from data. It does not denote a tangible device or a robot; instead, it describes a set of computational methods that enable systems to enhance their efficiency progressively without the need for direct coding. Recognizing this difference is vital for grasping the fundamental nature of Machine Learning as a segment of Artificial Intelligence.

1.4 The Knowledge Pyramid in the Context of Data and Machine Learning

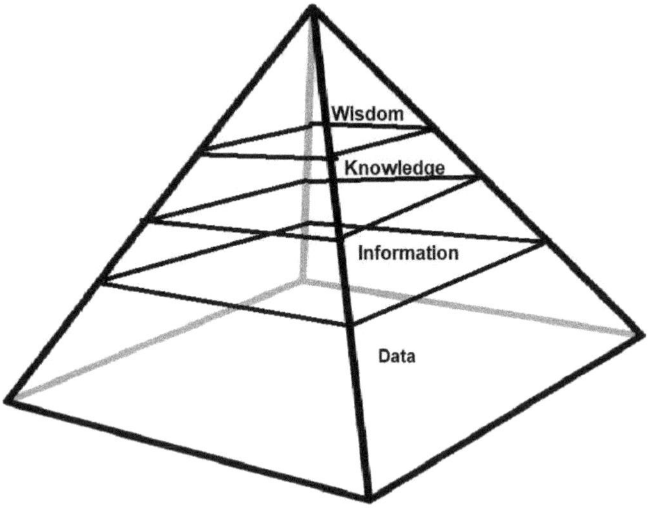

Figure 1.1: The Knowledge Pyramid (Claude AI generated Figure)

The Knowledge Pyramid—also known as the Data, Information, Knowledge, and Wisdom (DIKW) Pyramid—is a structure with levels that outlines how raw data is transformed into actionable insight. This concept is vital in data science and machine learning (ML), as data is the base and the foundation to develop intelligent systems, Figure 1.1.

Data is the base of the pyramid. Data can be considered/defined as raw, unstructured facts or observations that lack intrinsic meaning or context. It is the primary input for machine learning systems.

Examples: Sensor readings (such as temperature and humidity) from any industrial system are examples of machine learning. User activity records/logs (such as clicks, views, and timestamps) are another example in the context of machine learning. Raw files contain images/photos, audio, and text.

Role in machine learning: Raw data must be pre-processed a pre-requisite. Data preparation/preprocessing are the initial stage in every machine learning pipeline. Uncleaned/unprocessed data leads to non-reliable predictions.

Information: Data that has been processed or arranged to convey meaning or context. It exposes patterns or relationships within the raw data.

ML instances involve aggregated values, such as the average temperature during a week.

The frequency with which users perform specified tasks of any website whose data analytics is in consideration.

Tagged datasets (for example, labelled photos) are used in supervised learning.

Role in machine learning (ML), data is extracted through preprocessing techniques such as feature engineering and transformation.

Information is the foundation for model training.

Definition of Knowledge: Deriving meaningful insights, trends, or patterns from examining information.

Examples of Knowledge in ML include analysing the impact of weather on snack sales (e.g., "rain increases bajji sales").

Predicting client attrition/churn out employing past data.

In machine learning, data is extracted using techniques namely employing algorithm s such as regression, classification, and clustering.

Wisdom: The Top of the Pyramid.

Definition: Wisdom is the effective application of knowledge for decision-making, which includes contextual understanding and human judgment.

Some instances of ML include personalized product suggestions (refer to chapter on Recommender System in this book) based on user preferences and contextual data.

Dynamic pricing models for e-commerce.

Self-driving automobiles make autonomous decisions.

The role of machine learning is to apply predictions to real-world issues and gain wisdom. It includes ethical issues, justice, and domain expertise.

In Table 1.1 we present the mapping the knowledge pyramid to machine learning workflow from this table one can grasp the relation between DIKW and ML

Table 1.1: Learning-Based Reflex Agent

DIKW Layer	Machine Learning Workflow Step	Example
Data	Data collection and preprocessing	Collecting images, removing noise, normalizing pixel values.
Information	Feature engineering and exploratory data analysis (EDA)	Extracting edges for image classification.
Knowledge	Model training and evaluation	Training a neural network to classify images as "cat" or "dog."
Wisdom	Model deployment and decision-making	Recommending pet products based on identified user preferences.

Challenges in the DIKW Pyramid

1. **Data Quality:** Raw data is often incomplete, inconsistent, or biased.
2. **Contextual Understanding:** Information without domain knowledge can lead to incorrect inferences.
3. **Model Interpretability:** Black-box ML models hinder understanding and trust.

4. **Ethical Concerns:** Decisions based on ML must align with ethical and societal norms.

Thus, the DIKW Pyramid provides a conceptual framework for understanding how data evolves into actionable insights in the context of machine learning. By leveraging data, extracting information, building knowledge, and applying wisdom, ML systems enable informed decision-making and intelligent automation.

1.5 Machine Learning in Relation to other Fields

Machine learning (ML) is often viewed as a subset of artificial intelligence (AI), though it has roots with other fields such as statistics and data science. Understanding its relationship with different disciplines provides insight into its breadth and relevance. This section explores these relationships, emphasizing the distinctions, overlaps, and synergies. In figure 1.2 we present a picture depicting the relations between artificial intelligence (AI), Machine Learnings (ML), Deep Learning (DL) and Datas Science (DS)

1.5.1 Machine Learning vs. Artificial Intelligence

Machine learning is an essential component of artificial intelligence. While AI aims to simulate human intelligence in machines, machine learning (ML) focuses on allowing systems to learn from data and improve over time without requiring explicit programming. For example, a chatbot uses machine learning models to interpret and respond to user inputs, but it also relies on other AI techniques, such as rule-based systems, to provide programmed rather predefined responses. Table 1.2 compares the relation between AI and ML.

Table 1.2: Comparison of Artificial Intelligence and Machine Learning

Aspect	Artificial Intelligence	Machine Learning
Scope	Broad, encompassing reasoning, planning, decision-making, etc.	Narrower, focused on data-driven learning.
Techniques	Includes ML, expert systems, rule-based logic, etc.	Primarily algorithms like supervised, unsupervised, and reinforcement learning.
Application	General problem-solving systems like robotics, virtual assistants.	Specific tasks like image recognition, recommendation systems.

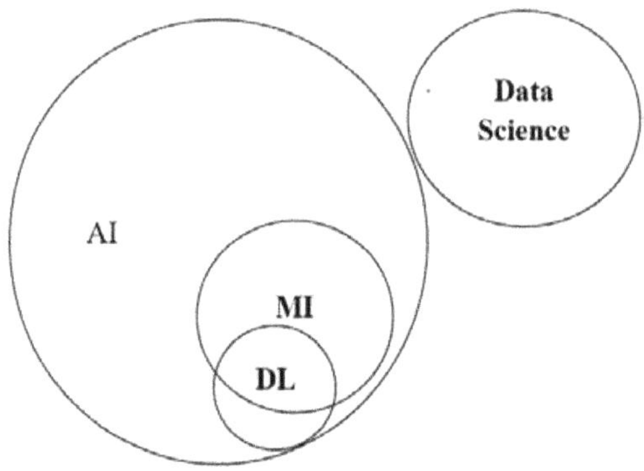

Figure 1.2: A Venn Diagram showing the overlap between Artificial Intelligence, Machine Learning, and Deep Learning.

1.5.2 Machine Learning vs. Data Science

Data science is an interdisciplinary field that focus on data collecting, cleaning, visualization, and analysis. Machine learning is one of the methods used by data scientists to make predictions and derive meaningful insights from data. While data science encompasses business intelligence and exploratory research, machine learning adds value by automating analytical model building/development. Table 1.3 shows the comparisons of data science, and machine learning.

Table 1.3: Compares of AI, data science, and machine learning.

Aspect	Data Science	Machine Learning
Focus	Data preparation, visualization, statistical analysis.	Developing algorithms to make predictions or automate processes.
Tools Used	Python, R, SQL, Tableau for visualization.	ML libraries like Scikit-learn, TensorFlow, PyTorch.
Outcome	Understanding and interpreting data trends.	Automating and optimizing tasks using data-driven models.

1.5.3 Machine Learning vs. Statistics

Machine learning and statistics share a common foundation in mathematical analysis and data interpretation. However, while statistics stresses inference and hypothesis testing, machine learning focuses on prediction and automation. For example, regression analysis is a statistical method that has been used in machine learning for predictive modelling. Table 1.4 shows the comparisons & contrasts of ML and statistics.

Table 1.4: Compares & Contrast of ML and statistics.

Aspect	Statistics	Machine Learning
Goal	Understanding relationships between variables and testing hypotheses.	Making predictions and improving model performance over time.
Key Techniques	Regression, ANOVA, hypothesis testing.	Decision trees, neural networks, reinforcement learning.
Focus	Interpreting data in a structured framework.	Handling large-scale, often unstructured data.

1.5.4 Synergies Across Fields

These fields are not mutually exclusive; rather, they work highly synergistic was. For example,

- AI applications, such as self-driving cars (autonomous vehicles), rely on statistical principles which form the basis for building machine learning models.
- Machine learning is commonly used in data science workflows to assess and anticipate trends.
- Machine learning abridges theoretical statistical models and actual AI applications, making it important and integral to both disciplines.

Understanding the relation between machine learning, artificial intelligence, data science, and statistics provides valuable insight into how these disciplines complement and strengthen one another. Each plays a crucial role in solving complex, data-driven problems, with machine learning—particularly the selection and application of ML algorithms for specific data forms—serving as the core focal point

A Brief Note on Historical Development of Machine Learning

Machine learning (ML) has evolved since the mid-twentieth century, when the foundations of artificial intelligence (AI) began to emerge. Alan Turing's key paper, "Computing Machinery and Intelligence," published in 1950, presented the concept of intelligent computers and proposed the Turing Test as a measure of machine intelligence. In 1959, Arthur Samuel, a pioneer in the field, defined machine learning as computers' ability to learn without being explicitly programmed. His work on checkers-playing platforms was one of the first instances of a machine improving performance through experience.

The 1980s saw the emergence of neural networks, which were inspired by the workings of the human brain. This period witnessed the rise of backpropagation algorithms, enabling artificial neural networks to learn complex patterns. However, development lacked /was hampered due to a lack of computational power and data availability. The 1990s witnessed the introduction of increasingly advanced algorithms such as support vector machines (SVMs) and ensemble approaches, as well as greater availability to digital data.

The early twenty-first century ushered the era of big data, coupled by exponential advances in processing/computational capabilities. Breakthroughs in deep learning, coupled by improved hardware such as GPUs and TPUs, have revolutionized machine learning applications, enabling tasks such as image processing, natural language processing, and autonomous driving. Machine learning is now a cornerstone of AI, continually evolving to address complicated challenges in a number of sectors, including healthcare, finance, entertainment, social media data robotics and consumer product recommendations in e-commerce segment.

This historical trajectory highlights how machine learning has grown from a theoretical concept to a practical tool, driving innovation and transforming industries worldwide.

This historical trajectory highlights how machine learning has grown from a theoretical concept to a practical tool, driving innovation and transforming industries worldwide.

Before we delve into the machine learning concepts, it is important to understand the **knowledge pyramid**. In the following section, detailed understanding of it are presented.

1.6 Types of Machine Learning

Machine learning can be classified into different learning styles based on how a model learns from data the input. These learning styles dictate how algorithms process data, adapt, and boost performance over time. The three basic types of learning are

(1) Supervised Learning,

(2) Unsupervised Learning, and

(3) Reinforcement Learning,

each designed to address a certain sort of problem. Furthermore, emerging paradigms like semi-supervised learning and self-supervised learning offer novel ways to use partially labelled or totally/entirely unlabelled datasets.

In supervised learning, models are trained on labelled data with explicit input-output pairings. This approach is commonly used for classification and regression tasks such as recognizing spam emails or predicting house prices. Unsupervised learning, on the other hand, works with unlabelled data, with the goal of uncovering hidden patterns or structures within it. Clustering and dimensionality reduction are excellent examples of unsupervised learning applications.

1.6.1 Supervised, Unsupervised, and Reinforcement Learning

In ***supervised learning***, models are trained on labelled data with explicit input-output pairs. This approach is commonly used for regression and classification tasks such as recognizing spam emails or predicting house prices.

Unsupervised learning, on the contrary, deals with unlabelled data, with the focus of uncovering hidden patterns or structures within the data. Clustering and dimensionality reduction are excellent examples of unsupervised learning applications.

Reinforcement learning adapts a different approach, enabling agents to learn by interacting with the environment and attracting rewards or penalties/punishments for their executed actions. This style of learning is best suited for dynamic, sequential decision-making tasks such as robotics and game playing. Furthermore, semi-supervised learning combines a small amount of labelled data with vast amounts of unlabelled data.

Self-supervised learning leverages inherent structures within data to generate pseudo-labels. These advanced learning approaches push the limits of what machine learning can accomplish, making it more versatile and adaptable to real-world problems.

1.6.2 Supervised Learning

Supervised learning is one of the most widely used machine learning paradigms. In this learning style, models are trained on a labelled dataset where each input is associated with a corresponding output. The objective is to learn a mapping function that predicts the output for new, unseen inputs based on the learned relationships in the training data.

How Supervised Learning Works?

The supervised learning process typically involves:

1. **Data Collection and Preparation:**
    - Collect labelled data with input features (X) and target labels (Y).
    - For example, consider a dataset of house prices with features such as square footage, location, and number of bedrooms, labelled with the price.
2. **Model Training:**
    - Use algorithms to identify patterns in data and minimising errors between predicted and actual outputs.
3. **Model Testing:**
    - Evaluate the model's performance on a separate/new test dataset to ensure it can generalize to new data.

The Iterative Process in Supervised Machine Learning

Supervised machine learning is an iterative process in which the model is refined repeatedly in the training phase. Large datasets usually divide into three subsets: training, testing, and validation. The iterative cycle consists of training the model on the training set, verifying its performance on the test set, validating it on unknown/unseen (meaning not used either in of train, test, validation phases), and repeating the process with new datasets until optimal performance is achieved. When deployed on entirely new, unseen data, a robust model maintains consistent. Figure 1.3 depicts the supervised machine learning workflow.

To understand this iterative nature, let’s re-examine the workflow as given below:

Supervised Learning Workflow

1. **Training Dataset:**
   - **Example:** A dataset containing 1000 emails labelled as "spam" or "not spam."
2. **Learning Algorithm:**
   - **Example:** Logistic regression learns to assign probabilities for emails being spam.
3. **Trained Model:**
   - **Example:** The model identifies spam emails with 95% accuracy.
4. **Prediction on New Data:**
   - **Example:** Classifies a newly received email as "spam" based on its features.

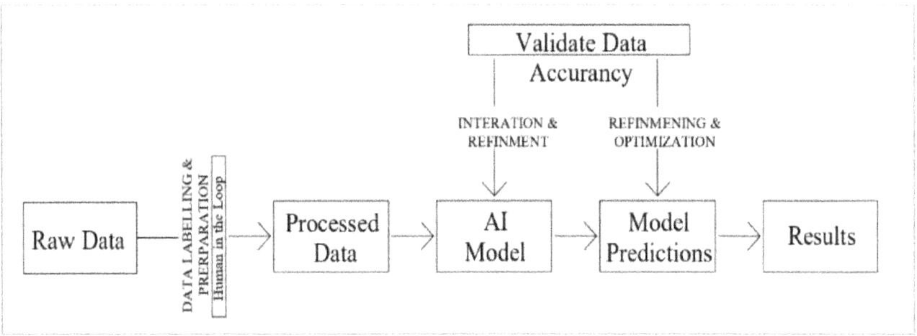

Figure 1.3: Iterative Nature of Supervised Machine Learning

(Flowchart of the supervised learning process (data collection → model training → prediction → evaluation). - Search Images)

Types of Supervised Learning Tasks

1. **Regression:** Regression is a supervised learning technique used to predict continuous outcomes based on input features. It establishes relationships between dependent and independent variables, enabling tasks like forecasting and trend analysis. A detailed explanation can be found in Chapter 3.
   - Used for predicting continuous values.

- **Example:** Predicting house prices, stock market trends.
- **Algorithms:** Linear regression, polynomial regression, decision trees.

The concept of regression is dealt in depth in chapter 3

2. **Classification:** Classification is a supervised learning method used to categorize data into predefined classes. It predicts discrete outcomes, such as identifying emails as spam or not spam. For a comprehensive explanation, refer to Chapter 3.
    - Used for categorizing data into discrete classes.
    - **Example:** Email classification as spam or not spam. Table 1.5 shows a list of some more examples of Supervised Learning.
    - **Algorithms:** Logistic regression, support vector machines (SVM), neural networks.

Advantages of Supervised Learning

- High accuracy when sufficient labelled data is available.
- Direct learning of the relationship between inputs and outputs.

Challenges in Supervised Learning

- Requires large amounts of labelled data, which can be expensive and time-consuming to obtain.
- Overfitting can occur when models memorize training data instead of generalizing.

Table 1.5: Examples of Supervised Learning

Task	Input Features (X)	Output Label (Y)	Algorithm Example
Email Spam Detection	Email content, metadata	Spam or Not Spam	Naïve Bayes, Logistic Regression
House Price	Size, Location, Number of	Price	Linear Regression

Prediction	Bedrooms		
Disease Diagnosis	Patient symptoms, medical history	Disease category	Decision Trees, SVM
Image Recognition	Pixel values of images	Object category (e.g., cat, dog)	Convolutional Neural Networks

Conclusion

Supervised learning remains a cornerstone of machine learning, powering applications across industries. With its ability to predict outcomes from labelled data, it provides actionable insights and automates decision-making. However, the need for labelled data and the risk of overfitting are key challenges that practitioners must address.

1.6.3 Unsupervised Learning

Unsupervised learning involves training models on datasets that do not contain labelled outputs. The goal is to identify hidden structures, patterns, or groupings in the data. Unlike supervised learning, where models are guided by labelled examples, unsupervised learning algorithms work autonomously to uncover insights.

Key Characteristics

- No labelled data is required.
- Focuses on pattern recognition and structure discovery.
- Commonly used for clustering, dimensionality reduction, and anomaly detection.

Examples

1. **Clustering:**
   - Grouping customers based on purchasing Behaviour (e.g., segmentation for marketing).
   - **Algorithms:** k-Means, DBSCAN, Hierarchical Clustering.

2. Dimensionality Reduction:

- Reducing features in high-dimensional data for visualization or preprocessing.

Algorithms: PCA, t-SNE.

Figure 1.4 presents a scatterplot where customer data points are grouped into distinct clusters based on the k-Means algorithm and Table 1.6 compares of supervised and unsupervised learning.

Table 1.6: Comparison of Supervised and Unsupervised Learning

Aspect	Supervised Learning	Unsupervised Learning
Labelled Data	Required	Not Required
Goal	Predict outcomes	Identify patterns
Examples	House price prediction, spam detection	Customer segmentation, fraud detection
Algorithms	Linear regression, decision trees	k-Means, PCA

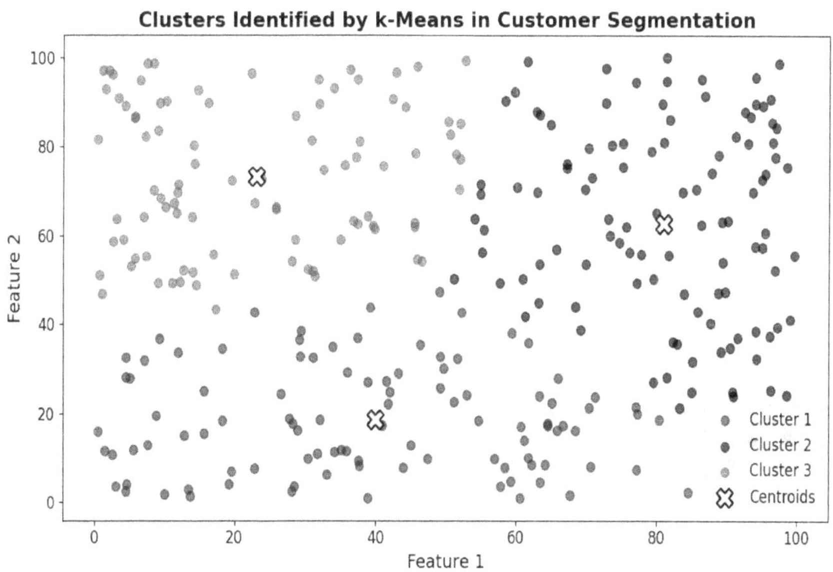

Figure 1.4: A Scatterplot Showing Clusters Identified By K-Means in Customer Segmentation.

1.6.4 Semi-Supervised and Self-Supervised Learning

Semi-supervised and self-supervised learning bridge the gap between supervised and Semi-supervised and self-supervised learning fill the gaps between supervised and unsupervised learning. These approaches use/leverage unlabelled data to increase performance while reducing the reliance on labelled data.

Semi-supervised Learning

Semi-supervised learning involves integrating a small quantity of labelled data with a huge volume of unlabelled data. The labelled data serves as a guide, allowing the model to learn more successfully from unlabelled samples/examples.

Example:

- Predicting diseases using a dataset with few labelled and large unlabelled medical records.
- **Algorithms:** Label Propagation and Self-Training.

Self-supervised learning

Self-supervised learning generates pseudo-labels from unlabelled data. The model learns by solving pretext tasks, such as predicting missing data or understanding relationships within the data.

Example:

- Natural language processing (NLP), models such as BERT can be trained by predicting masked words in sentences.
- Computer vision involves predicting the orientation of images or sections of them.

In figure 1.5 (a) & (b) and in table 1.7 Semi-Supervised Learning Workflow, comparison of Semi-supervised Learning and Self-Supervised Learning are respectively presented.

Table 1.7: Comparison of Semi-Supervised and Self-Supervised Learning

Aspect	Semi-Supervised Learning	Self-Supervised Learning
Labelled Data	Small labelled dataset, large unlabelled dataset	Entirely unlabelled data
Goal	Enhance supervised tasks	Pretrain models for downstream tasks
Examples	medical diagnosis, sentiment analysis	NLP (BERT), Computer Vision (SimCLR)

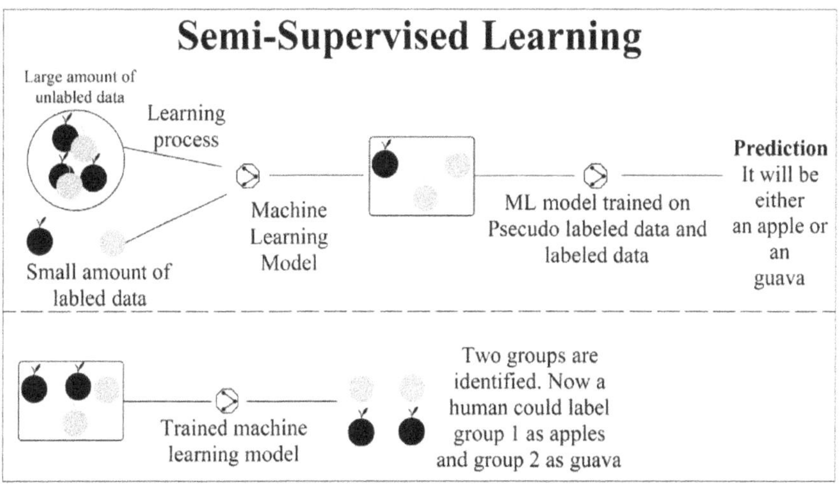

Figure 1.5 (a) Semi-Supervised Learning Workflow

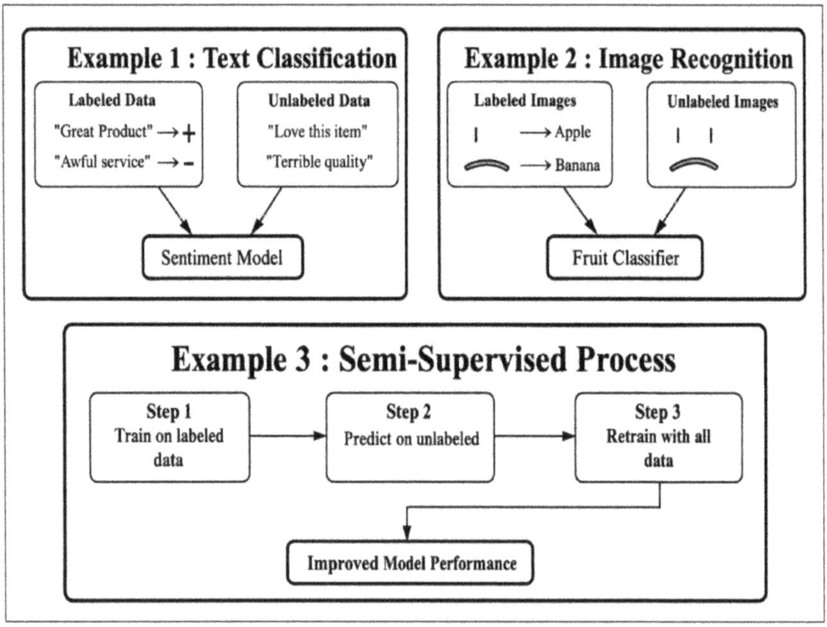

Figure 1.5 (b) Examples of Semi-Supervised Learning Workflow

1.6.5 Reinforcement Learning

Reinforcement learning (RL) is a learning paradigm in which an agent interacts with its environment in order to achieve a certain/specific goal. The agent learns through trial and error by receiving rewards or penalties for its actions then adjusting and ultimately optimizing its behaviour to maximize cumulative rewards.

Key Concepts

- **Agent:** Learner or decision-maker.
- The environment is the system with which the agent interacts.
- **Reward:** Agent receives feedback on their actions.
- **Policy:** A strategy the agent uses to determine its action

Figure 1.6 illustrates a Learning-Based Reflex Agent that improves its actions by updating its internal model based on past experiences. The diagram highlights how the agent uses feedback from the environment to refine its decision-making over time.

Examples

1. Game Playing: AlphaGo uses RL to master board games.

2. Robotics: Optimizing robot movements for tasks such as picking and placing goods at designated places.

Table 1.8 summarizes the key characteristics of reinforcement learning, including agent–environment interaction, reward-based learning, and policy optimization.

Table 1.8: Presents the Characteristics of Reinforcement Learning

Aspect	Reinforcement Learning
Input Data	Observations from the environment
Output	Sequence of actions
Goal	Maximize cumulative rewards
Applications	Autonomous vehicles, game AI

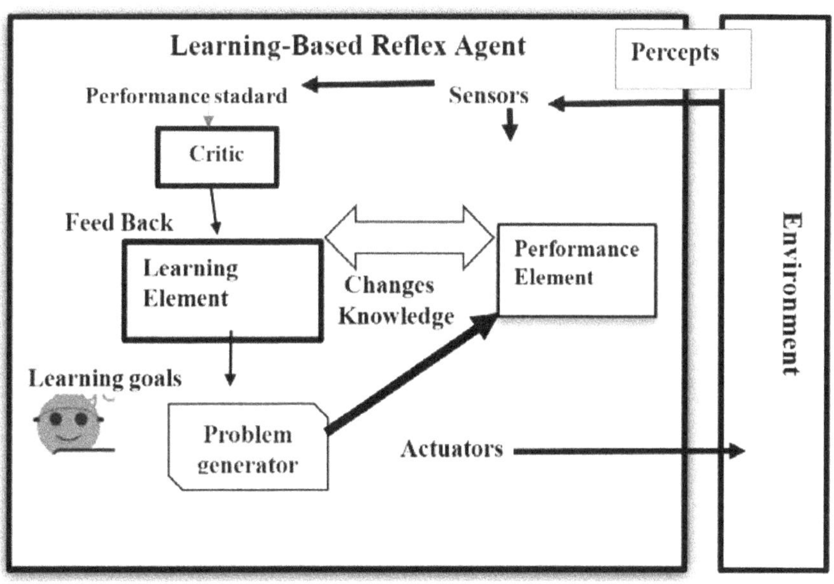

Figure 1.6 Learning-Based Reflex Agent

1.7 Challenges of Machine Learning

One of the most critical challenges in machine learning is striking the correct balance between model complexity and generalization.

- **Overfitting** occurs when a model learns the training data too well, including noise and outliers. This leads to high accuracy on the training set but poor performance on unseen data. For example, in polynomial regression, a high-degree polynomial may fit the training data perfectly but not generalize for new samples. Overfitting can also arise with approaches such as k-Nearest Neighbours (-k-NN) with k=1, where the model memorizes the training points.
- **Underfitting** occurs when a model is overly simplistic and fails to capture underlying patterns in data. This results in low performance across both the training and testing datasets. For example, applying a linear regression model to a nonlinear dataset results in underfitting.
- **The bias-variance trade-off** is a crucial factor in addressing these challenges. High-bias models (e.g., underfitted linear models) fail to account for/capture data complexity, whereas high-variance models (e.g., overfitted complex models) are too sensitive to training data. Finding the right/perfect balance necessitates careful adjustment know as tuning of model parameters, regularization, and the selection of appropriate algorithms.

The concepts of overfitting, underfitting, and bias-variance trade-off are not restricted to regression. They also apply to clustering and -k-NN.

- In -k-NN small k values in -k-NN can produce overfitting, whereas large k values (e.g., near to the dataset size) cause underfitting.
- In clustering overfitting can occur when the number of clusters is too high, capturing noise instead of meaningful groupings, while underfitting occurs when there are too few clusters.

1. 8 Machine Learning Process

The machine learning process involves a sequence of well-defined steps used to build an effective learning model. It begins with data collection, where relevant data is gathered from various sources, followed by data preprocessing, which includes cleaning, handling missing values, and feature selection. Next, a suitable machine learning algorithm is selected and the model is trained using the prepared data.

After training, the model is tested and evaluated using appropriate performance metrics to check its accuracy and reliability. If required, the model is **tuned and improved** to enhance performance. Finally, the trained model is **deployed** to make predictions or decisions on new, unseen data. This systematic process ensures that machine learning models are accurate, efficient, and applicable to real-world problems.

1.8.1 Steps in Machine Learning Pipeline

The machine learning (ML) pipeline is a structure workflow for building, training, and deploying ML models. It consists of a set of interconnected steps that convert (transform) raw data into actionable insights, ensuring that the process is efficient, repeatable, and scalable. Each step in the pipeline is crucial to developing a robust and high-performing model.

Steps in the Machine Learning Pipeline

1. **Problem Definition:**
   - Clearly define the ML project's objective and type of task (e.g., classification, regression, clustering).
   - **Example:** Predicting house prices based on square footage and location.
2. **Data Collection:**
   - Collect relevant data from sources like databases, APIs, and web scraping.
   - Ensure that the dataset being collected is a large and diverse in nature to accurately reflect/predict the problem's complexity.

3. **Data Preprocessing:**
    - Clean up missing values, duplicates, and outliers.
    - Standardize data by normalizing or scaling features to improve model performance.
4. **Exploratory Data Analysis (EDA):**
    - Analyse data to identify distributions, correlations, and patterns.
    - Use histograms, scatterplots, and correlation matrices to discover relevant trends.
5. **Feature Engineering:**
    - Select or create features that significantly impact model performance.
    - Use dimensionality reduction techniques, such as PCA, to reduce computing complexity.
6. **Model Selection:**
    - Select the right/appropriate algorithm for the problem type and dataset size (e.g., decision trees for small datasets, neural networks for large datasets).
    - **Example:** Use logistic regression for binary classification tasks.
7. **Model Training:**
    - Train the model on the training dataset, optimizing its parameters to minimize error.
    - Use techniques like cross-validation to ensure the model generalizes well.
8. **Model Evaluation:**
    - Test the model on a separate validation or test dataset to assess its accuracy, precision, recall, and F1-score.
    - **Example:** Evaluate a fraud detection model using confusion matrices and ROC curves.

9. **Hyperparameter Tuning:**
   - Fine-tune model parameters like learning rate or number of layers to improve performance.
   - Use grid search or random search to systematically find optimal parameters.
10. **Model Deployment:**
    - Deploy the model to a production environment for real-world use.
    - Continuously monitor performance and update the model as needed.

In Table 1.9 Steps in a Machine Learning Pipeline and Their Roles are presented. Figure 1.7 depicts a typical machine learning workflow.

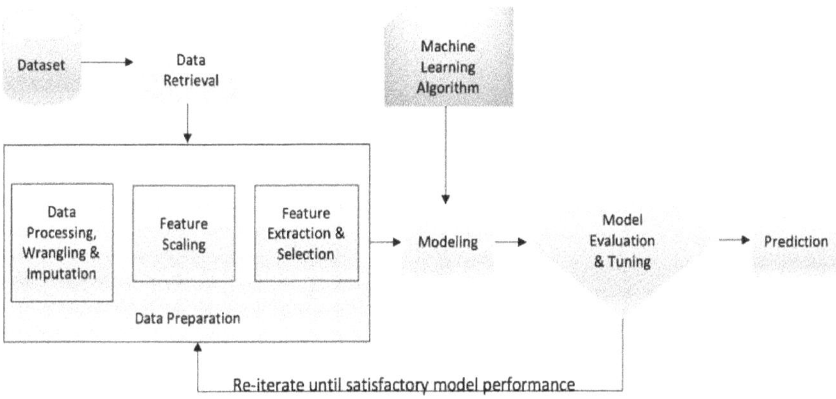

Figure 1.7 Machine Learning Workflow

Table 1.9 Steps in a Machine Learning Pipeline and Their Roles

Step	Role
Problem Definition	Clearly articulate the ML objective and scope.
Data Collection	Gather raw data from various sources.
Data Preprocessing	Clean, normalize, and prepare data for analysis.

Exploratory Data Analysis	Understand patterns and relationships in the data.
Feature Engineering	Create or select impactful features.
Model Selection	Choose the most suitable algorithm for the problem.
Model Training	Optimize the model to minimize error on the training set.
Model Evaluation	Assess ******model performance on unseen data.
Hyperparameter Tuning	Improve model performance through parameter optimization.
Model Deployment	Integrate the model into production systems for real-world use cases.

1.9 Machine Learning Applications

Machine learning has become an essential technology in many domains due to its ability to process large volumes of data and extract meaningful insights. One of the most common applications is in healthcare, where machine learning is used for disease diagnosis, medical image analysis, drug discovery, and personalized treatment plans. By analysing patient records and clinical data, ML systems help doctors make more accurate and timely decisions.

In the field of **finance and banking**, machine learning is applied for fraud detection, credit scoring, stock market analysis, and risk management. ML models can detect unusual transaction patterns that may indicate fraudulent activities and help banks assess the creditworthiness of customers more effectively. This improves security and reduces financial losses.

Machine learning also plays a major role in **e-commerce and marketing**. Online platforms use ML algorithms for product recommendations, customer Behaviour analysis, demand forecasting, and dynamic pricing. Recommendation systems on websites such as shopping portals and streaming platforms suggest products or content based on user preferences and past interactions, enhancing customer satisfaction.

Another important area of application is **transportation and smart systems**. Machine learning is used in traffic prediction, route optimization, autonomous vehicles, and smart city planning. By analysing real-time traffic data and historical patterns, ML systems help reduce congestion, improve safety, and optimize fuel consumption.

Finally, machine learning is widely used in **natural language processing and computer vision** applications such as speech recognition, language translation, face recognition, and object detection. Virtual assistants, chatbots, and surveillance systems rely on machine learning techniques to understand human language and visual information, making human–computer interaction more natural and efficient. Table 1.10 illustrates the applications of machine learning in various fields.

Table 1.10 Applications of Machine Learning Across Industries

Field	Applications	Examples
Healthcare	Diagnostics, personalized medicine, drug discovery, hospital management	IBM Watson Health
Finance	Fraud detection, risk management, algorithmic trading, customer segmentation	PayPal, Goldman Sachs
Marketing	Behaviour analysis, recommendation systems, targeted advertising, churn prediction	Amazon, Netflix
Transportation	Autonomous vehicles, traffic optimization	Tesla, Google Waymo
Manufacturing	Predictive maintenance, quality control automation	Siemens
Education	Personalized learning, automated grading	Duolingo

1.10 Understanding Data

Data forms the foundation of machine learning and plays a crucial role in enabling systems to learn, Analyse, and make intelligent decisions. Understanding the nature, structure, and Behaviour of data is essential before applying any machine learning algorithm. Data can be collected from various sources such as sensors, databases, social media, and online transactions. Proper understanding of data helps in selecting appropriate features, improving model accuracy, and ensuring reliable outcomes.

1.10.1 Introduction

In machine learning, data represents facts, observations, or measurements that describe real-world entities or events. Data may be structured, such as tables in databases, or unstructured, such as text, images, audio, and video. Raw data often contains noise, missing values, and inconsistencies; therefore, it must be cleaned and processed before analysis. A clear understanding of data types, quality, and relevance is necessary to extract meaningful information and build effective machine learning models.

1.10.2 Big Data Analytics and Types of Analytics

With the rapid growth of digital technologies, the volume of data generated has increased enormously, leading to the concept of Big Data. Big Data is characterized by the five V's: Volume, Velocity, Variety, Veracity, and Value. Big Data Analytics refers to the process of analysing large and complex datasets to uncover hidden patterns, trends, and relationships that cannot be handled by traditional data processing techniques.

1.11 Big Data Analysis Framework

Big data analysis refers to the process of examining large, complex datasets to uncover hidden patterns, correlations, and actionable insights. ML plays a pivotal role in making big data analysis scalable and efficient.

1.11.1 Overview of Big Data

1. **Characteristics of Big Data:**
    - **Volume:** The scale of data is massive, often measured in terabytes or petabytes.
    - **Velocity:** Data is generated and processed in real-time.
    - **Variety:** Data comes in multiple forms—structured (databases), unstructured (videos, text), and semi-structured (JSON, XML).
    - **Veracity:** Ensuring the reliability and accuracy of data is critical.
    - **Value:** Extracting meaningful insights from data is the ultimate goal.
2. **Big Data Architecture:**
    - **Data Sources:** Sensors, IoT devices, transactional data, social media.
    - **Data Storage:** Distributed systems like Hadoop HDFS, Amazon S3.
    - **Data Processing:**
        - **Batch Processing:** Tools like Apache Hadoop.
        - **Real-Time Processing:** Frameworks like Apache Spark, Kafka.
    - **Analysis and Visualization:** Tools like Tableau, Power BI, or custom ML models.

1.11.2 Role of Machine Learning in Big Data Analysis

1. **Data Cleaning and Preprocessing:**
    - Automating the detection and correction of errors.
2. **Predictive Analytics:**
    - ML models predict trends and outcomes using big data.

3. **Real-Time Analytics:**
    - Reinforcement learning and streaming algorithms process live data for immediate decision-making.

Figure 1.8 depicts a layered Big Data architecture where data ingestion, storage, and processing pipelines integrate seamlessly with machine learning models. It highlights how ML components enhance analytics by enabling automated predictions and intelligent decision-making within the data ecosystem. Table 1.11 contrasts batch processing and real-time processing based on factors like latency, data volume, and use case suitability. It shows how batch processing handles large historical datasets, while real-time processing supports immediate insights for time-sensitive applications.

Table 1.11: Comparison of Batch and Real-Time Processing in Big Data Analysis

Aspect	Batch Processing	Real-Time Processing
Data Handling	Processes data in chunks	Processes data as it arrives
Latency	High latency	Low latency
Tools	Hadoop MapReduce	Apache Spark Streaming, Apache Kafka
Use Cases	Historical analysis, large-scale ETL jobs	Fraud detection, live recommendations

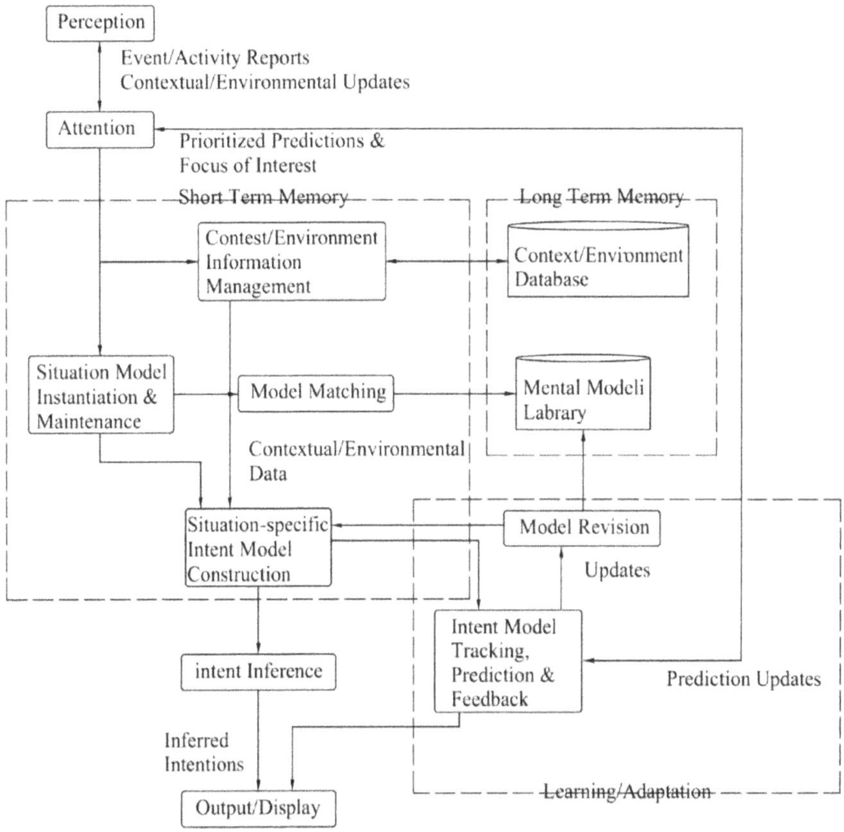

Figure 1.8 Big Data Architecture with Machine Learning Integration

1.11.3 Types of Big Data Architecture

Big data architecture defines the framework and components required to ingest, store, process, and Analyse massive datasets efficiently. Depending on the use case, data flow, and processing requirements, big data architecture can be categorized into **batch processing**, **real-time processing**, and **hybrid architectures**.

1. Batch Processing Architecture

Batch processing architecture processes large volumes of data in chunks, typically at scheduled intervals. It is well-suited for scenarios where immediate results are not required.

Key Features:

- Processes data collected over a period.
- High throughput but higher latency.
- Suitable for historical analysis and reporting.

Example:

- Analysing yearly sales data to identify trends.

Tools Used: Apache Hadoop, Hive, and Amazon EMR.

2. Real-Time Processing Architecture

Real-time (or stream) processing architecture processes data as it arrives, ensuring low latency. It is ideal for time-sensitive applications like fraud detection or stock market analysis.

Key Features:

- Processes data in real-time or near real-time.
- Low latency but may require more resources.
- Suitable for applications requiring immediate action.

Example:

- Detecting fraudulent credit card transactions as they occur.

Tools Used: Apache Spark Streaming, Apache Flink, and Apache Kafka.

3. Hybrid Architecture

Hybrid architecture combines batch and real-time processing to provide flexibility for handling both historical and real-time data.

Key Features:

- Processes historical data in batches and incoming data in real-time streams.
- Balances throughput and latency requirements.
- Suitable for complex systems like recommendation engines or IoT analytics.

Example:

- A recommendation engine that uses batch processing for historical user data and real-time updates for current activity.

Tools Used: Apache Lambda Architecture, Google Cloud Dataflow.

Table 1.12 Provides a side-by-side comparison of different Big Data architectures, highlighting their core components, processing capabilities, and scalability features. It helps illustrate how each architecture supports various analytical needs, from traditional data warehousing to modern real-time and cloud-based solutions.

Table 1.12: Provides comparison of different Big Data architectures

Aspect	Batch Processing	Real-Time Processing	Hybrid Architecture
Data Handling	Processes large data chunks	Processes data as it arrives	Combines batch and stream processing
Latency	High latency	Low latency	Medium latency
Use Cases	Historical analysis, periodic reports	Fraud detection, stock market analysis	Recommendation engines, IoT applications
Tools	Hadoop, Hive, Amazon EMR	Spark Streaming, Kafka, Flink	Lambda Architecture, Google Cloud Dataflow

Benefits of Choosing the Right Architecture

1. **Efficiency:** Matches data processing needs with the system's capabilities.
2. **Scalability:** Ensures the architecture can handle data growth.
3. **Cost-Effectiveness:** Avoids unnecessary resource usage by tailoring architecture to the workload.

1.12 Descriptive Statistics

Descriptive statistics provides tools to organize, summarize, and represent data using numerical measures and graphical techniques. These methods help in understanding the central tendency, dispersion, and overall distribution of data, forming a strong foundation for further data analysis and machine learning tasks.

1.12.1 Measures of Central Tendency and Dispersion

Descriptive statistics provide numerical summaries of data distributions, helping data scientists understand the core characteristics of their datasets before applying more advanced techniques.

Measures of Central Tendency:

Central tendency measures identify the "typical" or "central" values in a dataset.

1. **Mean (μ):** The arithmetic average of all values.

$$\mu = \sum \frac{x}{n} \text{..........} 1.1$$

    - Sensitive to outliers
    - Appropriate for normally distributed data

2. **Median:** The middle value when data is arranged in order.
    - Robust to outliers
    - Better representation for skewed distributions
    - For even-sized samples, average of two middle values

3. **Mode:** The most frequently occurring value(s).
    - May be multiple modes (multimodal)
    - Useful for categorical and discrete data
    - Not always meaningful for continuous data

4. **Weighted Mean:** Mean where certain values contribute more than others.
    - Formula

$$\boldsymbol{\mu(wx = \frac{w_1x_1 + w_2x_2 \text{.........} + w_nx_n}{w_1 + w_2 \ldots + w_n} \text{...........} 1.2}$$

- Used when observations have different importance

Measures of Dispersion:

Dispersion measures quantify the spread or variability within a dataset.

1. **Range:** Difference between maximum and minimum values.
    - Simple but sensitive to outliers
    - Formula:

$$\boldsymbol{Range = Max(x) - Min(x)} \ldots\ldots \mathbf{1.3}$$

2. **Variance (σ²):** Average of squared deviations from the mean.

$$\text{Formula: } \boldsymbol{\sigma^2} = \frac{\Sigma(x-\mu)^2}{n} \ldots\ldots\ldots\ldots \mathbf{1.4}$$

    - Units are squared (makes interpretation challenging)

3. **Standard Deviation (σ):** Square root of variance.

    Formula:

$$\boldsymbol{\mu} = \sqrt{\frac{\boldsymbol{(x-\mu)^2}}{\boldsymbol{n}}} \ldots\ldots\ldots\ldots \mathbf{1.5}$$

    - Same units as original data
    - In normal distributions, ~68% of data falls within ±1σ, ~95% within ±2σ

4. **Interquartile Range (IQR):** Difference between 3rd quartile (Q_3) and 1st quartile (Q_1).
    - Formula:

$$\boldsymbol{Inter\ Quartile\ Range\ (IQR) = Q_3 - Q_1} \ldots\ldots\ldots \mathbf{1.6}$$

    - Robust to outliers
    - Basis for boxplots and outlier detection

5. **Mean Absolute Deviation (MAD):** Average of absolute deviations from mean.

    - Formula:

$$MAD = \sqrt{\frac{|x-\mu|}{n}} \quad \ldots\ldots\ldots 1.7$$

    - More robust than variance but less mathematically tractable

Figure 1.9 shows multiple normal distributions plotted with different standard deviations to illustrate how spread changes while the mean remains constant. Wider curves represent higher variability, while narrower curves depict more tightly clustered data around the mean. Table 1.13 summarizes how standard deviation influences the shape and spread of a data distribution. It highlights that larger standard deviations produce more dispersed data, whereas smaller values indicate a more concentrated distribution.

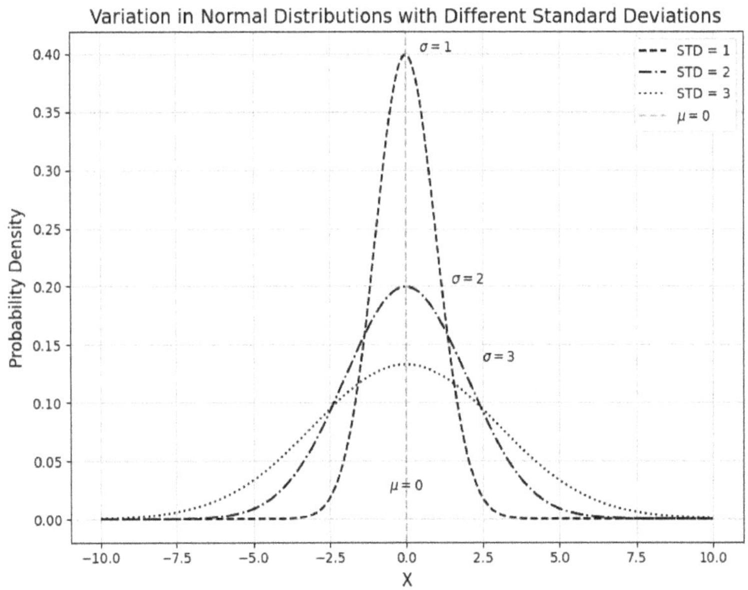

Figure 1.9 Variation in Normal Distributions with different Standard Deviations

Table 1.13: Relationship between Standard Deviation and Data Distribution

Distribution Type	Standard Deviation	Interpretation
Small σ	Narrow, peaked	Data points clustered tightly around mean
Large σ	Wide, flat	Data points spread widely from mean
Uniform	$\sigma \approx 0.29 \times$ range	Even probability across values
Normal	68-95-99.7 rule applies	68% within $\pm1\sigma$, 95% within $\pm2\sigma$, 99.7% within $\pm3\sigma$
Right-skewed	Mean > Median	Tail extends toward higher values
Left-skewed	Mean < Median	Tail extends toward lower values

1.13 Univariate Data Analysis and Visualization

Univariate data analysis involves the examination of a **single variable** at a time to understand its basic characteristics. The primary objective of univariate analysis is to describe the data, identify patterns, and summarize important features such as central tendency, spread, and distribution. It is usually the **first step in data analysis**, helping to gain an initial understanding before moving to multivariate analysis or machine learning Modelling.

In machine learning, univariate analysis helps in understanding the nature of individual features, detecting outliers, and identifying data quality issues. Visualization techniques are commonly used along with numerical measures to represent data in a clear and intuitive manner. These methods make it easier to interpret large datasets and support better decision-making.

1.13.1 Measures Used in Univariate Analysis

Univariate analysis uses statistical measures to summarize numerical data and frequency-based methods for categorical data. The most commonly used measures are shown in Table 1.14.

Table 1.14: Common Measures in Univariate Data Analysis

Category	Measure	Description
Central Tendency	Mean	Average value of the data
	Median	Middle value when data is ordered
	Mode	Most frequently occurring value
Dispersion	Range	Difference between maximum and minimum
	Variance	Measure of data spread
	Standard Deviation	Square root of variance
Shape	Skewness	Measure of asymmetry in data
	Kurtosis	Measure of peakedness of distribution

1.13.2 Univariate Data Visualisation Techniques

Visualization techniques provide a graphical representation of data and help in understanding the distribution and variation of a single variable. Some commonly used univariate visualization methods include **bar charts**, **histograms**, **pie charts**, **box plots**, and **line graphs**. These visual tools allow quick identification of trends, outliers, and dominant values in the dataset.

- **Bar charts** and **pie charts** are mainly used for categorical data.
- **Histograms** are used to represent frequency distributions of numerical data.

- **Box plots** display the median, quartiles, and outliers in the data.

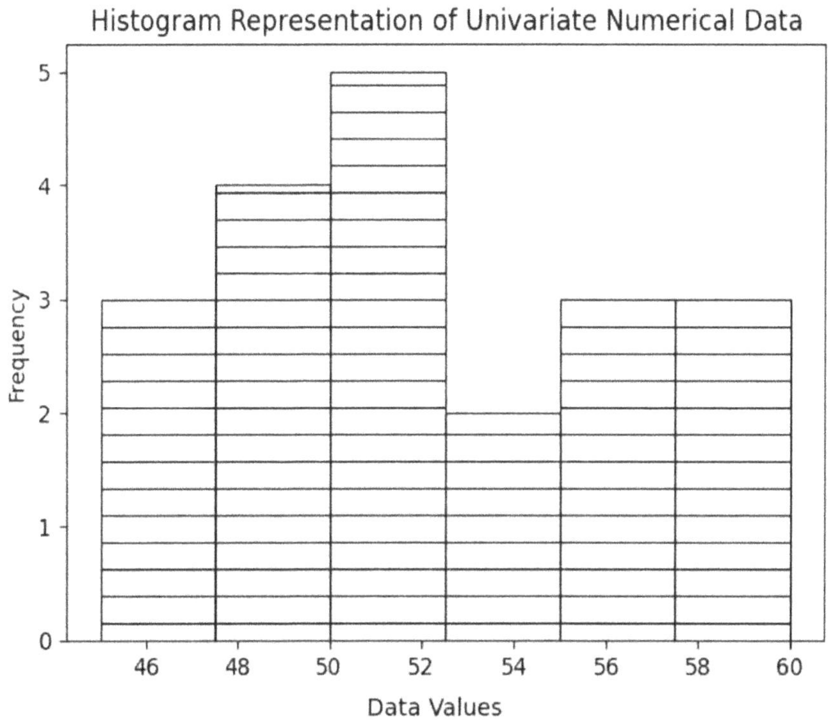

Figure 1.10 Histogram Representation of Univariate Numerical Data

The Figure 1.10 shows a histogram illustrating the frequency distribution of a single numerical variable. The horizontal axis represents the data values grouped into intervals, while the vertical axis shows the frequency of occurrence. This visualization helps in understanding data distribution, skewness, and presence of outliers.

Importance of Univariate Analysis in Machine Learning

Univariate analysis plays a vital role in feature understanding and selection. By analysing individual variables, data scientists can identify irrelevant or noisy features and improve model performance. It also helps in detecting missing values and abnormal data behaviour early in the machine learning process.

1.14 Bivariate Data and Multivariate Data

In many real-world datasets used in machine learning, more than one variable is involved. While univariate analysis focuses on a single variable, **bivariate and multivariate data analysis** examine relationships among two or more variables. These analyses help in understanding how variables interact with each other and how they influence outcomes in predictive models.

Bivariate data analysis studies the relationship between **two variables**, whereas multivariate data analysis involves **three or more variables**. Both types of analysis are important for identifying dependencies, correlations, and patterns in data, which are essential for effective feature selection and model building.

1.14.1 Bivariate and Multivariate Data

Bivariate Data

Bivariate data consists of observations on **two variables** for each data point. The main purpose of bivariate analysis is to examine the **relationship or association** between the two variables. For example, analysing the relationship between study hours and examination scores or between temperature and electricity consumption.

Common methods used in bivariate analysis include scatter plots, correlation coefficients, and cross-tabulation. Scatter plots provide a visual understanding of relationships, while correlation measures indicate the strength and direction of association between variables. Characteristics of bivariate and multivariate data nnd comparisons between them is presented in table 1.15, table 1.6 and table 1.7 respectively.

Table 1.15 Characteristics of Bivariate Data

Aspect	Description
Number of Variables	Two
Objective	Study relationship between variables

Common Examples	Height vs Weight, Price vs Demand
Analysis Methods	Scatter plot, Correlation, Cross-tabulation
Outcome	Positive, Negative, or No correlation

Multivariate Data

Multivariate data consists of **three or more variables** measured for each observation. Most machine learning problems involve multivariate datasets, where multiple input features jointly influence the output. Multivariate analysis helps in understanding complex relationships among variables.

Techniques such as *multiple linear regression, principal component analysis (PCA), classification, and clustering* are widely used for analysing multivariate data. Visualization tools such as **pair plots**, **heat maps**, and **3-D plots** assist in interpreting interactions among multiple variables.

Table 1.16 Characteristics of Multivariate Data

Aspect	Description
Number of Variables	Three or more
Objective	Analyse combined effect of variables
Common Examples	Predicting house price using area, location, and age
Analysis Methods	Regression, PCA, Clustering, Classification
Outcome	Pattern discovery and prediction

Table 1.17 Bivariate vs Multivariate Data

Feature	Bivariate Data	Multivariate Data
Number of Variables	2	3 or more
Complexity	Simple	Complex
Type of Analysis	Pairwise relationship	Multiple interactions
Visualization	Scatter plot	Pair plot, Heat map
Role in ML	Preliminary relationship analysis	Model building and prediction

Importance of Bivariate and Multivariate Data in Machine Learning

Bivariate and multivariate data analysis play a vital role in machine learning by helping to understand relationships among features, remove redundant variables, and improve model accuracy. Proper analysis ensures better feature selection, reduced dimensionality, and more reliable machine learning models.

Chapter 1: Summary

This chapter introduced the fundamentals of **Machine Learning**, emphasizing why it has become essential in today's data-driven world. The limitations of traditional programming approaches were discussed, highlighting the need for systems that can automatically learn from data and improve over time. Machine learning was explained as a key branch of Artificial Intelligence that focuses on pattern recognition, prediction, and decision-making using data.

The chapter also explored the **relationship between machine learning and other fields** such as Artificial Intelligence, Data Science, and Statistics, showing how these areas complement each other. Various **types of machine learning**—supervised, unsupervised, semi-supervised, and reinforcement learning—were introduced with simple explanations and examples. Common **challenges of machine learning**, including data quality, overfitting, underfitting, and computational complexity, were briefly discussed.

Further, the **machine learning process** was explained as a systematic pipeline involving data collection, preprocessing, model training, evaluation, and deployment. The chapter highlighted the importance of **understanding data**, including the basics of Big Data analytics and different types of analytics. Fundamental statistical concepts such as **descriptive statistics**, along with **univariate, bivariate, and multivariate data analysis**, were introduced to help students Analyse and visualize data effectively before applying machine learning algorithms.

Chapter 1: Conclusion

Machine learning forms the foundation for many modern intelligent systems used in everyday life. A strong understanding of its basic concepts, processes, and data-related aspects is essential for building effective machine learning solutions. This chapter provides the groundwork required to study advanced machine learning algorithms and applications.

By learning how data is generated, Analysed, and transformed into knowledge, students can appreciate the role of machine learning in solving real-world problems. The concepts discussed in this chapter prepare learners to move forward into more practical and algorithmic aspects of machine learning in subsequent chapters.

Chapter 1: Questions

Short Answer Questions

1. Define machine learning.
2. Why is machine learning needed in modern applications?
3. What does the term "learning" mean in machine learning?
4. List any two applications of machine learning.
5. State any two limitations of traditional programming.
6. What is Big Data?
7. List any two characteristics of Big Data.
8. What is descriptive statistics?
9. What is univariate data analysis?
10. Define bivariate data.

Medium Answer Questions

1. Explain machine learning with a suitable example.
2. Describe the need for machine learning in today's digital world.
3. Explain the different types of machine learning.
4. Discuss the basic steps involved in the machine learning process.
5. Explain Big Data analytics and its importance.
6. Describe the types of analytics used in data analysis.
7. Explain descriptive statistics and its role in data analysis.
8. Explain univariate data analysis with examples.
9. Differentiate between univariate and bivariate data analysis.
10. Explain the challenges involved in machine learning.

Application Oriented Questions

1. Explain how machine learning is used in healthcare applications.
2. Describe the role of machine learning in online shopping platforms.
3. Explain how machine learning helps in fraud detection.
4. Discuss the use of machine learning in recommendation systems.
5. Explain the importance of data understanding before applying machine learning algorithms.

Chapter - 2

Understanding Data and Basic Learning Theory

Chapter Overview

Machine learning systems rely fundamentally on data and the principles governing how learning takes place. This chapter lays a strong foundation by integrating together ideas from learning theory, data interpretation, multivariate statistics, essential mathematics, and feature engineering. The chapter begins by discussing bivariate and multivariate data, with a focus on how machine learning employs relationships between more than one variable.

Learners are introduced to key statistical and mathematical concepts that are required to work with multivariate data. These ideas help in comprehend how data is distribuions, dependencies and transformations. The chapter then discusses feature engineering and dimensionality reduction approaches, which are very important for making learning more efficient, making models less complicated, and boosting generalization performance.

The second part of the chapter talks on the basics of learning theory, such as what learning is, the many types of learning paradigms, computational learning theory, and how to make a learning system. To describe how machines learn from data, the text talks about ideas like inductive bias, concept learning, and Modelling in machine learning.

Lastly, the chapter talks about how to test and evaluate machine learning algorithms. It addresses real-world problems like overfitting, splitting up datasets, performance measures, ROC analysis, dealing with unbalanced datasets, and measuring accuracy. These topics, when put together, give you a good theoretical and practical base for understanding how to build, test, and validate data-driven learning systems.

2.1 Understanding Data

Algorithms for machine learning and artificial intelligence are built on data. Before employing any learning approach, it is important to know the nature, structure, and relationships within the data. Data involving real-life problems can be multivariate in nature, with multiple variables being evaluated at the same time. Examples include weather forecast databases including temperature, pressure, and humidity, or customer analysis datasets featuring age, income, and spending patterns.

The concept of multivariate data is presented in this section, along with the reasons why most AI and ML applications require more than just univariate or bivariate analysis. Identifying variable types, data distributions, interdependent variables, and patterns hidden across various dimensions are all part of understanding data. Feature engineering, model selection, and overall prediction accuracy are all improved by a thorough understanding of the data.

This section introduces the concept of multivariate data and explains why traditional univariate or bivariate analysis is insufficient for most AI and ML applications. Understanding data involves identifying variable types, data distributions, dependencies among variables, and patterns hidden across multiple dimensions. Proper understanding of data improves feature engineering, model selection, and overall prediction accuracy. Table 2.1 provides a comparison different types of data, structured, semi-structured and unstructured data.

Table 2.1: Comparison of different Data Types

Characteristic	Structured Data	Semi-Structured Data	Unstructured Data
Format	Fixed schema	Flexible schema	No schema
Organization	Tabular	Hierarchical/Networked	Variable
Query Ease	High	Medium	Low
Storage	RDBMS	NoSQL, XML databases	Data lakes, file systems
Processing Complexity	Low	Medium	High
ML Pre-processing Needs	Minimal	Moderate	Extensive
Scalability Challenges	Lower	Medium	Higher

2.1.1 Multivariate Statistics

Multivariate statistics deals with the analysis of data involving **two or more variables simultaneously**. Unlike univariate statistics, which focuses on a single variable, multivariate statistics captures **relationships, correlations, and interactions** among multiple variables. This approach is crucial in Machine Learning, where models often rely on several features to make predictions.

Key concepts in multivariate statistics include:

- Multivariate random variables
- Mean vector and covariance matrix
- Correlation and dependence among variables
- Dimensionality and feature space

Techniques such as **Principal Component Analysis (PCA)**, **Linear Discriminant Analysis (LDA)**, and **clustering methods** are based on multivariate statistical principles. These techniques help reduce dimensionality, remove redundancy, and uncover hidden structures in data. Multivariate statistics enables AI systems to learn complex patterns that cannot be observed by analysing variables independently.

2.1.2 Essential Mathematics for Multivariate Data

Mathematics provides the formal framework required to represent and manipulate multivariate data effectively. In AI and ML, multivariate data is often represented using **vectors and matrices**, making linear algebra a fundamental requirement. Mathematical tools help in data transformation, distance measurement, optimization, and probabilistic Modelling.

Essential mathematical concepts for multivariate data include:

- Vectors and vector spaces
- Matrices and matrix operations
- Eigenvalues and eigenvectors
- Determinants and matrix inverses
- Distance measures (Euclidean, Mahalanobis distance)

In addition, **basic multivariate calculus** concepts such as partial derivatives and gradients are used in optimization algorithms like gradient descent. Probability theory supports multivariate distributions, such as the **multivariate normal distribution**, which is widely used in statistical learning. Together, these mathematical foundations enable efficient data representation, analysis, and learning in modern AI and ML systems. ***A note to learners:*** A detailed discussion of these mathematical topics is beyond the scope and intent of this chapter and of this textbook. However, learners are strongly encouraged to familiarize themselves with these concepts independently, as they form essential prerequisites for understanding and applying multivariate data analysis and machine learning algorithms effectively Basic foundational coverage is being dwelled in the following sections.

Vectors and Matrices

In multivariate analysis, we represent data using vectors and matrices. Each observation (row) in our dataset can be viewed as a vector in p-dimensional space, where p is the number of variables.

Vector notation: For an observation with p variables, we write:

$$X = \begin{bmatrix} x_1 \\ x_2 \\ x_3 \end{bmatrix} \dots\dots \mathbf{2.1}$$

Data matrix: For n observations and p variables, our complete dataset becomes an n×p matrix:

$$X = \begin{bmatrix} x_{11} & x_{12} & \cdots & x_{1p} \\ x_{21} & x_{22} & \cdots & x_{2p} \\ \vdots & \vdots & \vdots & \vdots \\ x_{n1} & x_{n2} & \cdots & x_{np} \end{bmatrix} \dots\dots \mathbf{2.2}$$

Each row represents one observation, and each column represents one variable measured across all observations.

Mean Vectors and Centering

The mean vector summarizes the center of our multivariate data:

$$\overline{x} = \begin{bmatrix} \overline{x}_1 \\ \overline{x}_2 \\ \vdots \\ \overline{x}_n \end{bmatrix} \quad \ldots .2.3$$

Where $\overline{x}_j = \frac{1}{n}\sum_1^n x_{ij}$ s the sample mean of the jth variable.

Centered data is obtained by subtracting the mean vector from each observation, creating deviations from the mean that are crucial for understanding variability and relationships.

2.1.3 Covariance and Correlation

Correlation quantifies the strength and direction of the linear relationship between two continuous variables. The Pearson correlation coefficient (r) is the most commonly used measure, ranging from -1 (perfect negative correlation) to +1 (perfect positive correlation), with 0 indicating no linear relationship.

Bivariate analysis examines relationships between pairs of variables, quantifying how they vary together and identifying potential dependencies.

Covariance

Covariance measures the degree to which two variables change together. The formula differs for a population and a sample, as reflected in the denominator. Covariance measures how two variables change together, indicating direction but not strength of relationship. The **covariance** between two variables measures how they vary together:

$$COV\,(X_i X_j) = \frac{1}{n-1}\sum_1^n \;(X - \overline{X}_i)(X - \overline{X}_j) \ldots 2.4$$

The **covariance matrix** organizes all pairwise covariances:

$$S = \begin{bmatrix} s_{11} & s_{12} & \cdots & s_{1p} \\ s_{21} & s_{22} & \cdots & s_{2p} \\ \vdots & \vdots & \vdots & \vdots \\ s_{p1} & s_{p2} & \cdots & s_{pp} \end{bmatrix} \ldots\ldots 2.5$$

This matrix is symmetric (since cov(X_j, X_k) = cov(X_k, X_j)), and the diagonal elements are the variances of individual variables.

The **correlation coefficient** standardizes covariance to a [-1, 1] scale:

$$\mathbf{r_{ij}} = \frac{\mathbf{s_{ij}}}{\sqrt{\mathbf{s_{ii}s_{jj}}}} \ldots\ldots 2.6$$

2.2 Covariance and Correlation in Multivariate Data

Yes, covariance and correlation are absolutely fundamental to multivariate data analysis. In fact, they become even more important and informative when working with multiple variables simultaneously. Let me explain how they extend from bivariate to multivariate contexts.

2.2.1 From Bivariate to Multivariate

When you have just two variables, you calculate a single covariance or correlation value. But with p variables, you have relationships between every pair of variables, giving you p(p-1)/2 unique relationships to consider.

For example, with 5 variables, you have 10 unique pairs. With 10 variables, you have 45 pairs! This is where matrix notation becomes essential.

The Covariance Matrix

The covariance matrix (also called the variance-covariance matrix) organizes all these pairwise relationships:

Computing covariance matrix

$$\mathbf{S} = \frac{\mathbf{1}}{\mathbf{n-1}} \mathbf{X^T X} \ldots\ldots 2.7$$

This formula calculates all pairwise covariances simultaneously.

2.3 Overview of Hypothesis

The concept of hypothesis, forms a basis for learning and prediction in machine learning models. A detailed understanding is the pre-requisite for understanding machine learning model selection.

A model or function that converts input data into output predictions is represented by a hypothesis in machine learning. What the learning algorithm looks for in data is an assumed relationship between the input variables (features) and the target variable. A hypothesis is chosen from a hypothesis space, which is a collection of all potential models that the learning process may take into account, as opposed to being a fixed assertion. The goal of learning is to identify the hypothesis that, while retaining the capacity to generalize to new data, best explains the training data that has been observed.

Using a performance metric or loss function, like accuracy or mean squared error, several hypotheses are assessed during the learning process. Based on this evaluation, the algorithm adjusts model parameters to improve predictions A good hypothesis should avoid overfitting, which occurs when the model records noise rather than patterns of significance, in addition to fitting the training data well. The choice of a suitable hypothesis is intimately related to concepts like training error, generalization error, and model complexity.

There are numerous various kinds of hypotheses in real-world machine learning systems, such as neural networks, decision trees, linear functions, and rule-based models. The choice of hypothesis type depends on the nature of the problem, the available data, and computational constraints. Understanding the concept of hypothesis helps learners appreciate how machine learning models are constructed, evaluated, and refined, making it a fundamental building block for designing effective learning systems.

Linear and non-linear models represent different forms of hypotheses in machine learning. Classification and regression, on the other hand, are learning tasks in which suitable hypothesis models are selected and trained to perform prediction.

2.3.1 Feature Engineering

Feature engineering is a crucial step in the machine learning process that focuses on transforming raw data into meaningful and informative input features suitable for learning algorithms. In real-world applications, data collected from various sources is often noisy, incomplete, inconsistent, or unstructured. Machine learning models do not learn effectively from raw data; instead, their performance largely depends on how well the input features represent the underlying patterns present in the data. Feature engineering bridges this gap by improving data quality and structuring data in a form that enhances the learning capability of machine learning models.

The feature engineering process involves several key activities, including feature selection, feature transformation, and feature creation. Feature selection aims to identify and retain only the most relevant features while eliminating redundant or irrelevant ones, thereby reducing model complexity and improving interpretability. Feature transformation techniques such as normalization, standardization, and encoding of categorical variables ensure that features are represented on compatible scales and in suitable formats for learning algorithms. Feature creation, often guided by domain knowledge, derives new features from existing data—for example, generating interaction terms or extracting statistical summaries—which can significantly improve predictive performance.

Feature engineering also helps address common data-related challenges such as missing values, outliers, and imbalanced data. Techniques such as imputation, binning, log transformations, and resampling are applied to make the data more suitable for Modelling. In many applications, raw data may consist of time-series data, images, or categorical attributes. Transforming timestamps into cyclical features like "day of the week," extracting edges from images, or converting text into numerical representations are examples of domain-specific feature engineering techniques. Additionally, methods such as Recursive Feature Elimination (RFE) and mutual information are used to retain the most informative features, thereby improving computational efficiency and generalization.

Effective feature engineering requires a combination of technical skills and domain expertise and is often an iterative and experimental process.

Well-engineered features can simplify models, reduce training time, and improve robustness and interpretability. As a result, feature engineering is considered one of the most critical steps in the machine learning workflow and plays a decisive role in determining the success of a model. Figure 2.1 illustrates the key steps involved in feature engineering, including feature creation, transformation, and selection, and their impact on improving model performance.

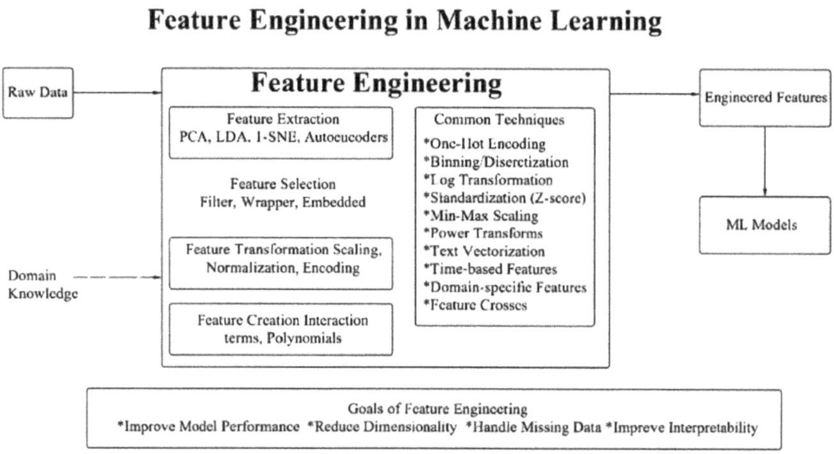

Figure 2.1: Feature Engineering in Machine Learning

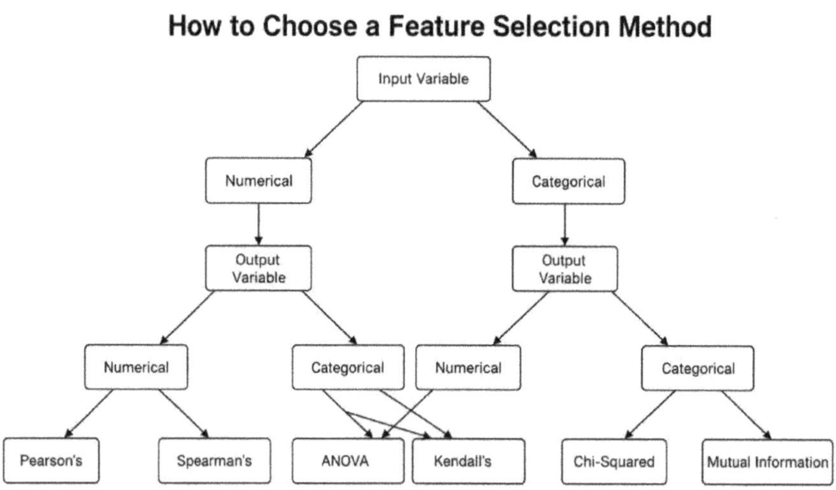

Figure 2.2: Feature Selection Methods Based on The Nature of Input and Output Variables

In parallel, figure 2.2 provides a decision tree for selecting appropriate feature selection methods based on the nature of input and output variables. It categorizes input variables as numerical or categorical and links them to the corresponding target variable type, guiding the user to methods like Pearson's correlation, ANOVA, or Chi-Squared tests. Together, these visuals demonstrate how a systematic approach to feature engineering and selection ensures that only the most relevant and impactful features are utilized, creating a strong foundation for robust machine learning models.

2.3.2 Feature Selection and Feature Extraction

Feature engineering plays an essential role in transforming raw data into forms that machine learning algorithms can process effectively. By refining and improving/optimising the input variables, this approach improves predictive model performance, efficiency, and interpretability. Feature selection is the process of determining the most relevant variables that contribute to the model's prediction power. It reduces dimensionality, reduces overfitting, and improves computational efficiency by focusing on the most important features. Statistical tests, recursive feature removal, and tree-based feature importance rankings are popular methods for determining the most important characteristics otherwise most impactful features in a dataset.

On the other hand, feature extraction involves creating new features by combining or manipulating existing variables to provide more meaningful representations. This step is especially critical when working with high-dimensional or noisy datasets. Principal Component Analysis (PCA), Singular Value Decomposition (SVD), and autoencoders are all techniques that can extract latent patterns and compress/reduce the feature space while retaining essential data. Feature extraction improves model performance by converting information into a lower-dimensional representation. It also facilitates in the visualization and interpretation of complex data. Feature selection and extraction are the foundations of effective feature engineering, bridging the gap between raw data and machine learning models.

2.3.3 Feature Selection

Feature selection identifies the most relevant subset of original features, reducing dimensionality while preserving information.

1. Filter Methods:

- Select features based on statistical measures.
- Independent of learning algorithm.
- **Examples of filter methods include:**
    - **Chi-square test:** Used for categorical features to test the independence between variables.
    - **ANOVA F-test:** Evaluates numerical features by analysing the variance between groups to identify significant features.
    - **Correlation coefficients:** Measure the linear relationship between numerical variables (e.g., Pearson or Spearman correlation).
    - **Information gain:** Measures the reduction in entropy when a feature is used to split data, commonly used in decision trees.
    - **Variance threshold:** Removes features with low variance that do not contribute significantly to the model.

2. Wrapper Methods: An Overview:

Wrapper approaches are a more advanced approach to feature selection that involves training and testing a machine learning model on subsets of the features. Unlike filter approaches, which rely on statistical metrics, wrapper methods evaluate characteristics in terms of the target learning algorithm's predictive power. These methods iteratively search for the best subset of features, using the model's performance (for example, accuracy or error rate) as an evaluation metric. While computationally expensive owing to repetitious model training, wrapper approaches are often more accurate since they account for feature relationships and interactions.

Wrapper approaches include many methods, such as Recursive Feature Elimination (RFE), forward selection, and backward elimination. RFE removes features recursively depending on their importance, keeping only the most important subset remains. Forward selection begins with an empty feature set and adds one feature at a time to optimize model performance. Backward elimination, on the other hand, starts with all features and systematically eliminates the ones that are least important. Another method, exhaustive search, assesses all possible feature subsets but is computationally impractical for high-dimensionaldata sets. Despite their computational requirements, wrapper methods are often utilized when attaining the best model performance is critical, particularly in situations where accuracy assumes prime importance pver computational time (computational complexity).

- **Examples:**
  - Recursive Feature Elimination (RFE)
  - Forward/backward selection
  - Exhaustive search
- Computationally expensive but predictions of the model are more accurate

3. Embedded Methods:

Embedded methods combine the advantages of filter and wrapper methods by performing feature selection as part of the model training process. These methods are integrated into the learning algorithm itself, which allows them to evaluate the importance of features while minimizing computational overhead. Techniques like Lasso (L1 regularization) and Ridge (L2 regularization) regression are common examples, where irrelevant or less important features are penalized and their coefficients are reduced or set to zero during training. Decision trees and ensemble methods, such as Random Forests, also inherently rank feature importance based on their contribution to reducing prediction error. Embedded methods are particularly effective in high-dimensional datasets, as they balance computational efficiency with model accuracy, making them a popular choice in practical machine learning workflows.

- Feature selection integrated into model training
- **Examples:**
    - LASSO regularization (L1)
    - Decision tree importance
    - Elastic Net
- Balance between filter and wrapper approaches

2.3.4 Feature Extraction

Feature extraction creates new features by transforming or combining original features.

1. **Dimensionality Reduction Techniques:** (please refer section 2.5 for elaboration of the concepts mentioned below)
    - Principal Component Analysis (PCA)
    - Linear Discriminant Analysis (LDA)
    - t-SNE
    - UMAP
    - Autoencoders
2. **Mathematical Transformations:**
    - Logarithmic transformation: log(x)
    - Power transformation: x^p
    - Box-Cox transformation
    - Polynomial features: x^2, x^3, xy, etc.
    - Trigonometric transformations: sin(x), cos(x)
3. **Domain-Specific Techniques:**
    - **Text:** TF-IDF, word embeddings
    - **Images:** Edge detection, HOG features
    - **Audio:** Spectral features, MFCCs
    - **Time series:** Rolling statistics, Fourier transforms

Evaluation Metrics for Feature Selection:

1. **Performance-based:**
    - Model accuracy with/without feature
    - Cross-validation score improvement
    - Information criteria (AIC, BIC)
2. **Information-based:**
    - Mutual information
    - Information gain
    - Entropy reduction
3. **Statistical:**
    - p-values from statistical tests
    - False discovery rate
    - Effect size

Table 2.2 provides a comparative analysis, helping readers appreciate the trade-offs and applications of different approaches. Combined, these resources offer a comprehensive framework for making informed decisions in feature selection.

Table 2.2 Comparison of Feature Selection Methods

Method Type	Computational Cost	Model Independence	Handles Feature Interactions	Handles Redundancy	Example Algorithms
Filter	Low	Yes	No	Partial	Variance threshold, Chi-square, Correlation
Wrapper	High	No	Yes	Yes	RFE, Sequential selection, Genetic algorithms
Embedded	Medium	No	Yes	Yes	LASSO, Decision trees, Neural network pruning

2.4 Dimensionality Reduction Techniques

Dimensionality reduction extends beyond traditional structured data represented in matrices to encompass more complex data formats such as tensors, graphs, and networks. Matrices, which are two-dimensional representations of data, often serve as the starting point for dimensionality reduction techniques like Principal Component Analysis (PCA) or Singular Value Decomposition (SVD). However, real-world datasets frequently involve higher-order relationships, which are better captured using tensors—multi-dimensional generalizations of matrices. Tensor decomposition methods, such as Canonical Polyadic Decomposition (CPD) and Tucker Decomposition, are specifically designed to reduce the dimensionality of tensor data while preserving its inherent multi-dimensional structure. These methods find applications in areas like recommendation systems, video processing, and spatiotemporal data analysis, where relationships span multiple dimensions.

For more complex data structures such as graphs and networks, dimensionality reduction focuses on preserving the relationships and topology of nodes and edges. Techniques like graph embedding map nodes in a high-dimensional graph to a lower-dimensional vector space while retaining the graph's structural information. Methods such as Node2Vec, Deep Walk, and Graph Convolutional Networks (GCNs) are instrumental in simplifying graph data for downstream tasks like clustering, classification, and link prediction. When dealing with multimodal data, where information comes from diverse sources like images, text, and audio, dimensionality reduction combines modalities into a unified lower-dimensional representation. Techniques like multimodal embeddings and autoencoders effectively integrate heterogeneous data, enabling applications in areas such as sentiment analysis, medical diagnosis, and cross-modal retrieval. These advanced approaches demonstrate the adaptability of dimensionality reduction techniques to modern, complex datasets, enhancing their relevance in cutting-edge research and practical applications. complex data types used in dimensionality reduction in running matter:(1) Graphs and Networks, (2) Multimodal Data, (3) Sparse and High-Dimensional Data, (4)

Sequential Data, (5) Hierarchical and Tree-Like Data, (6) Images and Video Data, (7) Textual Data, (8) Audio and Signal Data, (9) Spatial Data, (10) Tabular Data.

2.4.1 Dimensionality Reduction Techniques for Complex Data Types

Dimensionality reduction for tabular data—think spreadsheets with rows representing samples and columns representing features. Techniques like Principal Component Analysis (PCA) and Singular Value Decomposition (SVD) work well for this type of data. But what happens when your data isn't neatly arranged in rows and columns? Modern datasets come in many forms: social networks showing who follows whom on Twitter, videos from surveillance cameras, medical records combining X-ray images with patient notes, and sensor readings from smart cities. Each of these requires specialized approaches to find meaningful patterns in lower dimensions.

2.4.2 Beyond Matrices: Working with Tensors

While matrices are two-dimensional (rows and columns), many real-world datasets have more dimensions. Consider a color video: it has width, height, time, and color channels (red, green, blue)—that's four dimensions! These multi-dimensional arrays are called **tensors**, and you can think of them as "stacking multiple spreadsheets on top of each other."

Tensor decomposition methods break down these high-dimensional structures into simpler components while preserving important patterns. Two popular approaches are:

- **Canonical Polyadic Decomposition (CPD)**: Decomposes a tensor into a sum of simpler rank-one tensors—imagine expressing a complex 3D shape as a combination of basic building blocks.
- **Tucker Decomposition**: Similar to performing PCA along each dimension of the tensor separately, then combining the results.

Real-world example: Netflix uses tensor decomposition for its recommendation system. They organize data as (user × movie × time × context), where context might include device type or day of week. By reducing this four-dimensional tensor, they can predict what you'll want to watch next based on patterns across all these dimensions simultaneously.

Other applications include analysing brain imaging data (patients × brain regions × time points), climate Modelling (latitude × longitude × altitude× time), and quality control in manufacturing (products × sensors× production batches × time).

2.4.3 Graphs and Networks: Preserving Connections

Social networks, transportation systems, molecular structures, and the internet itself are all examples of **graph data**—collections of nodes (entities) connected by edges (relationships). Unlike tabular data where each row is independent, graphs are all about connections: who influences whom, which proteins interact, or how web pages link together.

The challenge is to represent each node as a point in a lower-dimensional space while keeping connected nodes close together and disconnected nodes far apart. This process is called **graph embedding**.

Key techniques include:

- **Node2Vec:** Treats random walks through the graph like sentences in a document, then applies natural language processing techniques to learn node representations. If you repeatedly walk through a social network starting from different people, users who appear in similar contexts get similar embeddings.
- **DeepWalk**: Similar to Node2Vec but uses simpler random walks—imagine wandering randomly through a city's street network and learning which neighborhoods are similar based on your walking paths.

- **Graph Convolutional Networks (GCNs)**: Uses neural networks that "spread" information from each node to its neighbors iteratively, similar to how rumors spread through a social network. Each node's representation becomes a summary of its neighborhood structure.

Real-world example: LinkedIn uses graph embeddings to power their "People You May Know" feature. They embed your profile and everyone else's into a lower-dimensional space where professionals in similar industries, with similar connections, and similar career paths end up close together. This makes finding relevant connections computationally efficient even with hundreds of millions of users.

Other applications include drug discovery (finding similar molecules), fraud detection (identifying suspicious transaction patterns), and traffic optimization (understanding city-wide transportation flow).

2.4.4 Multimodal Data: Combining Different Information Types

Increasingly, we work with data from multiple sources simultaneously—what we call **multimodal data**. A doctor diagnosing a patient might review X-ray images, written medical history, lab test results, and heart rate signals. An autonomous car processes camera images, LIDAR point clouds, GPS coordinates, and radar data. A social media post includes text, images, hashtags, and user engagement metrics.

The goal of **multimodal dimensionality reduction** is to create a unified representation that captures information from all these different sources in a single, lower-dimensional space.

Common approaches:

- **Multimodal embeddings**: Map different data types into a shared space where semantically similar items are close together, regardless of their original format. For instance, the image of a cat and the word "cat" should end up near each other.

- **Multimodal autoencoders**: Neural networks with a bottleneck layer that forces the model to compress information from multiple sources into a compact representation, then reconstruct the original inputs. The bottleneck representation captures the essence of all modalities combined.

Real-world example: Google's image search allows you to find photos using text descriptions like "golden retriever puppy playing in snow." Behind the scenes, they use multimodal embeddings that place images and their text descriptions in the same vector space. When you search, your text query gets embedded, and the system finds images with nearby embeddings—even if those exact words never appeared in the image metadata.

Other applications include:

- **Sentiment analysis**: Combining video (facial expressions), audio (tone of voice), and text (words spoken) to understand emotions more accurately than any single source
- **Medical Diagnosis**: Integrating patient symptoms (text), medical imaging (images), and lab results (numerical) for more accurate disease detection
- **Content recommendation**: Mixing user Behaviour (clicks, time spent), content features (text, images), and social signals (likes, shares) to suggest relevant articles or products

2.4.5 Other Complex Data Types

Beyond tensors, graphs, and multimodal data, dimensionality reduction adapts to many specialized formats:

Sequential Data (time series, text, DNA sequences): Techniques like Recurrent Autoencoders and temporal embeddings capture patterns that unfold over time. Example: Analysing stock market trends or predicting equipment failures from sensor readings.

Sparse and High-Dimensional Data (text documents, genomics): Most features are zero most of the time. Methods like Sparse PCA and feature hashing efficiently handle millions of dimensions. Example: Categorizing news articles where each unique word is a potential feature.

Hierarchical and Tree-Like Data (organizational charts, taxonomies): Hyperbolic embeddings preserve parent-child relationships better than standard Euclidean spaces. Example: Representing Wikipedia's category structure or biological family trees.

Images and Video Data: Convolutional Autoencoders and pretrained networks (like ResNet or VGG) extract visual features while dramatically reducing dimensionality. Example: Facial Recognition systems compress high-resolution photos into compact face descriptors.

Textual Data: Word embeddings (Word2Vec, GloVe) and document embeddings (Doc2Vec, BERT) convert words and documents into dense vectors. Example: Search engines understanding that "car" and "automobile" are similar.

Audio and Signal Data: Spectrogram-based methods and audio autoencoders compress sound while retaining important characteristics. Example: Music recommendation based on audio similarity, or speech recognition.

Spatial Data (maps, geographic information): Spatial autoencoders and geospatial embeddings preserve location-based relationships. Example: Urban planning tools analysing population density patterns.

Tabular Data with Mixed Types: Standard methods often assume all features are numerical, but specialized techniques handle mixtures of categorical, ordinal, and continuous variables. Example: Customer segmentation using demographics, purchase history, and preferences.

2.4.6 Key Takeaways

The fundamental principle remains the same across all these data types: **find a compact representation that preserves the most important information**. What changes is how we define "important":

- For **tensors**: Preserving multi-way interactions
- For **graphs**: Maintaining network structure and connectivity
- For **multimodal data**: Capturing relationships across different formats
- For **sequential data**: Retaining temporal or ordered patterns

As datasets grow more complex, these specialized dimensionality reduction techniques become essential tools for making sense of the modern data landscape. Whether you're analysing social networks, processing videos, or combining multiple data sources, there's likely a dimensionality reduction approach designed for your specific data structure.2.5 Basic Learning Theory:

Learning theory provides the theoretical foundation for understanding how machines learn from data, improve with experience, and generalize knowledge to unseen situations. This part of the chapter introduces fundamental ideas related to learning, types of learning, computational aspects, concept learning, inductive biases, and Modelling in machine learning. These concepts help students understand not only how learning algorithms work, but also why they work and under what conditions they are effective.

2.5 Introduction to Learning and Its Types

In machine learning, **learning** refers to the process by which a system improves its performance on a given task through experience. A widely accepted and formal definition of machine learning was given by **Tom M. Mitchell**, which states:

*"A computer program is said to learn from experience **E** with respect to some class of tasks **T** and performance measure **P**, if its performance at tasks in **T**, as measured by **P**, improves with experience **E**."*

This definition clearly identifies the three essential components of learning: the **task (T)**, the **experience (E)**, and the **performance measure (P)**. For example, in a spam email classifier, the task is classifying emails, the experience consists of labelled emails, and the performance measure may be classification accuracy.

Based on the nature of feedback available during learning, machine learning is broadly classified into different types. **Supervised learning** uses labelled data to learn input–output mappings and is commonly applied in classification and regression problems. **Unsupervised learning** deals with unlabelled data and focuses on discovering hidden patterns or structures, such as clusters or associations. **Reinforcement learning** enables an agent to learn through interaction with an environment by receiving rewards or penalties. Table 2.3 summarizes the major types of learning along with their characteristics and applications. Figure 2.3 illustrates the different learning paradigms and their interaction with data and feedback.

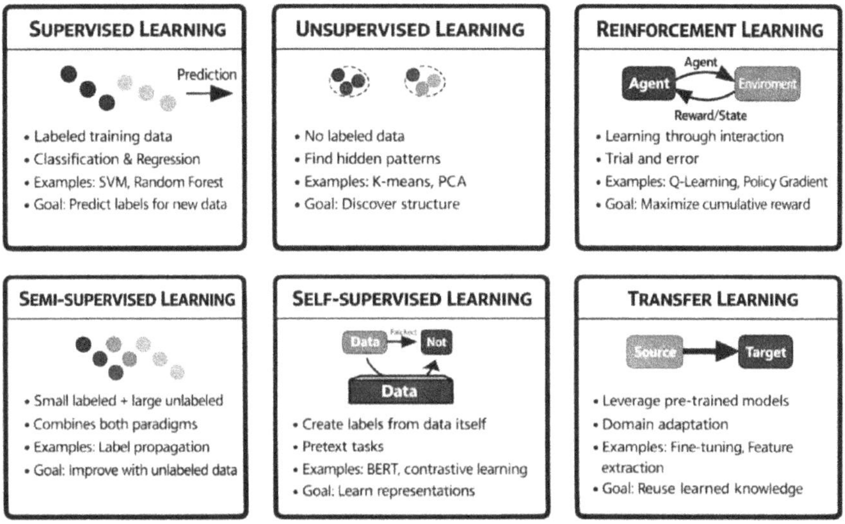

Figure 2.3 Machine Learning Paradigms Comparison.

Table 2.3 Types of Learning in Machine Learning

Type of Learning	Nature of Training Data	Learning Objective	Feedback Mechanism	Typical Algorithms	Common Applications
Supervised Learning	Labelled data (input–output pairs)	Learn a mapping from inputs to known outputs	Explicit feedback through labels	Linear Regression, Logistic Regression, Decision Trees, Support Vector Machines, k-NN	Spam detection, medical diagnosis, price prediction

Unsupervised Learning	Unlabelled data	Discover hidden patterns or structures	No explicit feedback	K-Means Clustering, Hierarchical Clustering, PCA, Association Rule Mining	Customer segmentation, anomaly detection
Semi-Supervised Learning	Small labelled set with large unlabelled set	Improve learning accuracy using limited labels	Partial feedback	Self-training, Co-training, Label Propagation	Web page classification, speech recognition
Reinforcement Learning	Interaction data from environment	Learn optimal actions to maximize reward	Reward or penalty signals	Q-Learning, SARSA, Policy Gradient Methods	Robotics, game playing, autonomous navigation
Online Learning	Streaming or sequential data	Continuously adapt to new data	Incremental feedback	Stochastic Gradient Descent, Online Perceptron	Stock market analysis, real-time recommendation syst

2.6 Introduction to Computational Learning Theory

Computational Learning Theory focuses on the **theoretical and mathematical aspects** of machine learning. It seeks to answer fundamental questions such as: *What can be learned? How much data is required? How complex should a learning model be?* This theory helps in understanding the limits and capabilities of learning algorithms.

One of the key ideas in computational learning theory is **generalization**, which refers to a model's ability to perform well on unseen data. Concepts such as **hypothesis space**, **training error**, **generalization error**, and **sample complexity** are central to this theory. Another important concept is **Probably Approximately Correct (PAC) learning**, which provides a framework for analysing whether a learning algorithm can learn a target concept within a specified accuracy and confidence.

Although the mathematical treatment of learning theory can be complex, an intuitive understanding helps students appreciate why simpler models sometimes perform better than complex ones and why overfitting must be avoided. Computational learning theory thus provides a solid theoretical foundation for practical machine learning.

2.7 Design of a Learning System

The design of a learning system involves identifying and organizing the essential components required for effective learning. A typical learning system consists of an **input representation**, a **hypothesis space**, a **learning algorithm**, and a **performance evaluation mechanism**. Each of these components plays a crucial role in determining the success of the system.

The process begins with defining the learning task and selecting appropriate data. The choice of features and hypothesis representation determines the type of patterns the system can learn. The learning algorithm searches through the hypothesis space to find the best model based on a performance measure. Finally, the system is evaluated using test data to assess its generalization capability.

Figure 2.4 shows the block diagram of a generic learning system and highlights the interaction between data, learning algorithm, and evaluation.

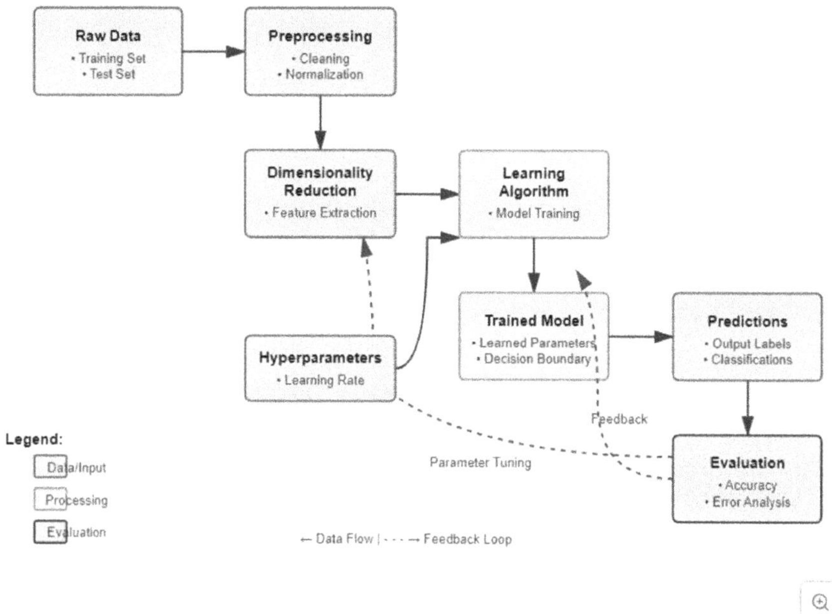

Figure 2.4 Block Diagram of a Generic Learning System and Highlights the Interaction Between Data, Learning Algorithm, And Evaluation

2.8 Introduction to Concept Learning

Concept learning is one of the earliest and most fundamental problems studied in machine learning. It involves learning a **general concept or rule** from a set of training examples. Each example is described using a set of attributes, and the goal is to determine whether an instance belongs to a particular concept or class.

Concept learning is typically illustrated using binary classification tasks, where examples are labelled as positive or negative. Algorithms such as **Find-S**, **Candidate Elimination**, and decision tree learning are classic approaches to concept learning. These methods help learners understand how hypotheses are generated, refined, and evaluated. Concept learning provides insight into how machines form generalizations from specific observations.

2.9 Inductive Biases

Inductive bias refers to the **set of assumptions** that a learning algorithm uses to generalize beyond the training data. Since multiple hypotheses may explain the observed data equally well, inductive bias guides the algorithm in choosing one hypothesis over others. Without inductive bias, learning from finite data would not be possible.

Different learning algorithms employ different types of inductive biases. For example, linear models assume linear relationships, while decision trees prefer shorter or simpler trees. Bias can be **explicit**, defined by the hypothesis space, or **implicit**, introduced by the learning algorithm itself. Understanding inductive bias helps students recognize why certain algorithms perform better for specific problems. **Table 2.4** compares inductive biases of common machine learning algorithms.

Table 2.4 Inductive Biases in Common Machine Learning Algorithms

Learning Algorithm	Hypothesis Representation	Primary Inductive Bias	Effect on Learning
Linear Regression	Linear functions	Assumes linear relationship between inputs and output	Produces simple, interpretable models
Decision Trees	Tree-structured rules	Prefers shorter and simpler trees	Enhances interpretability but may overfit
k-Nearest Neighbors (k-NN)	Instance-based	Assumes similar instances have similar outputs	Sensitive to noise and feature scaling
Naïve Bayes	Probabilistic model	Assumes feature independence	Fast learning with limited data
Support Vector Machines	Maximum-margin classifiers	Prefers maximum separation between classes	Improves generalization
Neural Networks	Layered non-linear functions	Assumes complex non-linear relationships	High expressive power but less interpretable

2.10 Modelling in Machine Learning

Modelling in machine learning refers to the process of creating a mathematical or computational representation of a real-world problem. A model defines how inputs are transformed into outputs and captures patterns present in the data. Choosing an appropriate model involves balancing **accuracy**, **complexity**, and **interpretability**.

Machine learning models can be broadly categorized into **parametric** and **non-parametric** models. Parametric models, such as linear regression, have a fixed number of parameters, while non-parametric models, such as k-nearest neighbors, adapt their complexity based on the data. The Modelling process includes selecting features, choosing a suitable algorithm, training the model, and validating its performance. Effective Modelling ensures that the learned system is robust, generalizable, and suitable for practical applications.

2.11 Machine Learning Algorithms

There are significant variations amongst machine learning algorithms in how they identify/uncover patterns, the types of data they work with, and what kinds of problems they are best at dealing with. These assumptions, which are sometimes called inductive bias, help the learning process by limiting the number of potential hypotheses and making it feasible to generalize from a limited training data. To choose the best model, one need to know about these biases as well as the pros and cons of alternative algorithms.

Linear and logistic regression are examples of algorithms that assume a linear relationship between input data and output variables. This makes them easy to understand, simple to use, and computationally efficient. But they might not work as well when they have to deal with complicated, non-linear patterns. Decision tree–based methods, on the other hand, use a hierarchical rule-based bias. This makes them easy to understand and flexible, but they can overfit if they aren't pruned or used with ensemble techniques.

Instance-based learning techniques, such as k-Nearest Neighbors, depend on similarity metrics and impose little assumptions regarding data distribution. They work well when the decision boundaries are close together, but they computationally expensive to make predictions and are sensitive to irrelevant features. Probabilistic models like Naïve Bayes make strong assumptions about independence, which makes training and inference quick. However, how accurate they are depends a lot on how well these assumptions hold good in real life.

Support vector machines and neural networks are two examples of more advanced models that can learn complex, high-dimensional representations. These algorithms are wonderful for finding patterns, recognizing images, and processing speech, but they usually need a lot of data, careful tuning of parameters, and more computing power.

Table 2.5 provides an overview of common machine learning algorithms, highlighting their characteristics, typical applications, and suitability for various types of data and tasks. This comparison serves as a quick reference for selecting appropriate algorithms based on problem requirements.

Table 2.5 Common Machine Learning Algorithms and their Characteristics

Algorithm	Inductive Bias	Strengths	Weaknesses	Typical Applications
Linear Regression	Linearity	Interpretable, stable, efficient	Limited capacity for complex patterns	Trend analysis, simple prediction, baseline Modellig
Decision Trees	Axis-parallel splits	Handles mixed data types, interpretable	High variance, prone to overfitting	Rule extraction, classification with clear decision boundaries
Random Forests	Ensemble of trees	Robust, handles high dimensionality, few parameters	Black box, computationally intensive	General-purpose supervised learning, feature importance analysis

SVM	Maximum margin	Effective in high dimensions, kernel flexibility	Sensitive to parameters and scaling	Text classification, image recognition, small-to-medium datasets
k-Means	Spherical, equal-sized clusters	Simple, scalable, intuitive	Requires k specification, sensitive to initialization	Customer segmentation, image compression, anomaly detection
Neural Networks	Hierarchical representation s	Flexible, handles complex patterns, automatic feature learning	Data hungry, black box, parameter tuning challenges	Computer vision, NLP, complex pattern recognition, deep learning applications
Naive Bayes	Conditional independence	Fast, probabilistic, works well with small data	Oversimplified independence assumption	Text classification, spam detection, real-time prediction
Gradient Boosting	Sequential error correction	High performance, handles mixed data, good with imbalanced classes	Can overfit, parameter sensitive, sequential nature limits parallelization	Competitions, tabular data problems, predictive analytics
-k-NN	Local similarity	Non-parametric, simple, adaptable	Computationall y expensive for large datasets, curse of dimensionality	Recommendatio n systems, pattern recognition, imputation

DBSCAN	Density-based clusters	Discovers arbitrary shapes, no cluster count needed	Sensitive to parameter settings, struggles with varying densities	Spatial clustering, anomaly detection, noise identification

2.12 Overfitting, Training, Testing, and Validation Sets

Once an appropriate machine learning algorithm is selected (as discussed in Section 2.11), it is essential to ensure that the learned model generalizes well to unseen data. A common challenge encountered during model development is overfitting, which occurs when a model learns noise and minor fluctuations in the training data rather than the underlying pattern.

Overfitting results in excellent performance on training data but poor performance on new or unseen samples. Conversely, **underfitting** occurs when a model is too simple to capture the data's structure. To mitigate these issues, datasets are typically divided into **training**, **validation**, and **testing** sets.

- The **training set** is used to learn model parameters.
- The **validation set** is used for hyperparameter tuning and model selection.
- The **testing set** is reserved for final, unbiased performance evaluation.

This data partitioning strategy enables systematic performance assessment and helps prevent optimistic bias in model evaluation.

May be used to illustrate common dataset splitting ratios and their purposes.

Table 2.6 presents' common dataset splitting ratios (training, testing, validation) and explains their roles in building and evaluating machine learning models.

Table 2.6 Common Dataset Splitting Ratios and Their Purposes

Dataset Split	Typical Percentage	Purpose
Training Set	60% – 70%	Used to learn model parameters and fit the machine learning algorithm
Validation Set	10% – 20%	Used for hyperparameter tuning, model selection, and preventing overfitting
Testing Set	20% – 30%	Used for final, unbiased evaluation of the trained model
Cross-Validation	k-fold (e.g., k = 5 or 10)	Provides robust performance estimation by rotating training and testing sets

2.13 The Confusion Matrix

For classification problems, performance evaluation begins with the **confusion matrix**, which provides a detailed breakdown of prediction outcomes. It compares actual class labels with predicted class labels, offering insight into different types of classification errors.

A typical confusion matrix consists of:

- **True Positives (TP)** – correctly predicted positive instances
- **True Negatives (TN)** – correctly predicted negative instances
- **False Positives (FP)** – incorrectly predicted positives
- **False Negatives (FN)** – incorrectly predicted negatives

The confusion matrix forms the foundation for most classification performance metrics.

A standard binary confusion matrix representation may be presented as Table 2.7

Table 2.7 Confusion Matrix for Binary Classification

Actual \ Predicted	Positive	Negative
Positive	True Positive (TP)	False Negative (FN)
Negative	False Positive (FP)	True Negative (TN)

2.14 Accuracy Metrics

While accuracy is the most intuitive performance measure, it alone may not adequately describe model effectiveness, especially in real-world scenarios. Accuracy is defined as the ratio of correctly classified instances to the total number of instances.

However, relying solely on accuracy can be misleading, particularly when dealing with skewed class distributions. Therefore, additional metrics derived from the confusion matrix are commonly used, including:

- **Precision**
- **Recall (Sensitivity)**
- **Specificity**
- **F1-score**

These metrics provide complementary perspectives on classification performance, especially in applications such as medical diagnosis, fraud detection, and intrusion detection.

Table 2.8 can summarize these accuracy metrics along with their mathematical expressions and interpretations.

Table 2.8 Common Accuracy Metrics Derived from the Confusion Matrix

Metric	Mathematical Expression	Interpretation
Accuracy	(TP + TN) ÷ (TP + TN + FP + FN)	Overall correctness of the model
Precision	TP ÷ (TP + FP)	Proportion of predicted positives that are truly positive
Recall (Sensitivity)	TP ÷ (TP + FN)	Ability of the model to correctly identify positive instances
Specificity	TN ÷ (TN + FP)	Ability of the model to correctly identify negative instances
F1-score	2 × (Precision × Recall) ÷ (Precision + Recall)	Harmonic mean of precision and recall

2.15 The Receiver Operating Characteristic (ROC) Curve

To evaluate classifier performance across varying decision thresholds, the **Receiver Operating Characteristic (ROC) curve** is employed. The ROC curve plots the **True Positive Rate (TPR)** against the **False Positive Rate (FPR)**.

An important scalar measure derived from the ROC curve is the **Area Under the Curve (AUC)**, which indicates the classifier's ability to distinguish between classes. A higher AUC value signifies better classification performance.

The ROC curve is especially useful when comparing multiple classifiers or when the class distribution is imbalanced.

A representative ROC curve may be illustrated in **Figure 2.5**

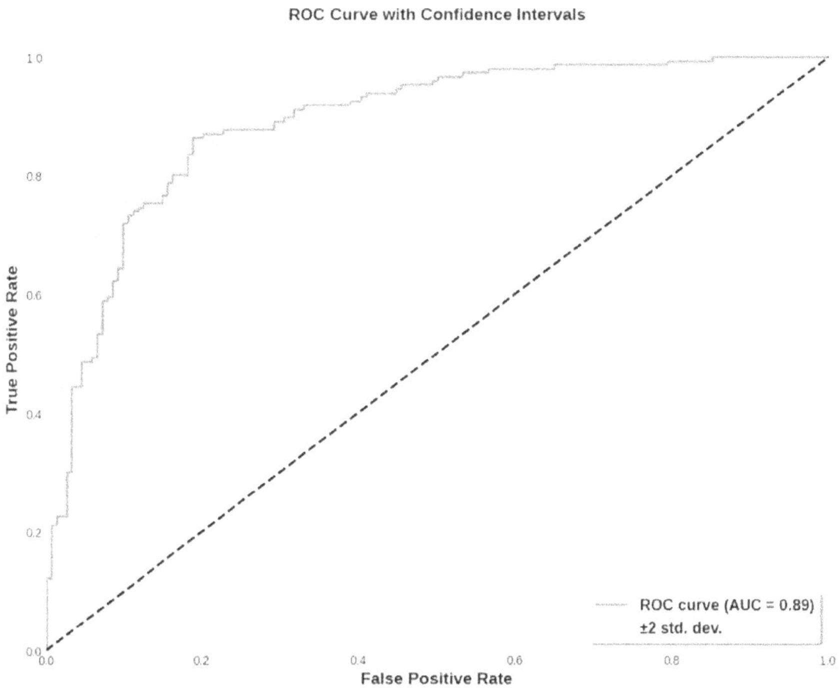

Figure 2.5 A Typical ROC Curve

2.16 Unbalanced Datasets

In many real-world machine learning applications, datasets are **unbalanced**, meaning that one class significantly outnumbers the other(s). Examples include fraud detection, rare disease diagnosis, and fault detection systems.

In such cases, high accuracy may be achieved by a trivial classifier that always predicts the majority class, while failing to identify minority class instances. Hence, performance evaluation must emphasise metrics such as recall, precision, F1-score, and AUC rather than accuracy alone.

Techniques commonly used to handle unbalanced datasets include:

- Resampling methods (oversampling and undersampling)
- Cost-sensitive learning
- Use of appropriate evaluation metrics

A conceptual illustration of class imbalance effects may be shown in **Figure 2.6**

Effect of Class Imbalance on Classification Performance

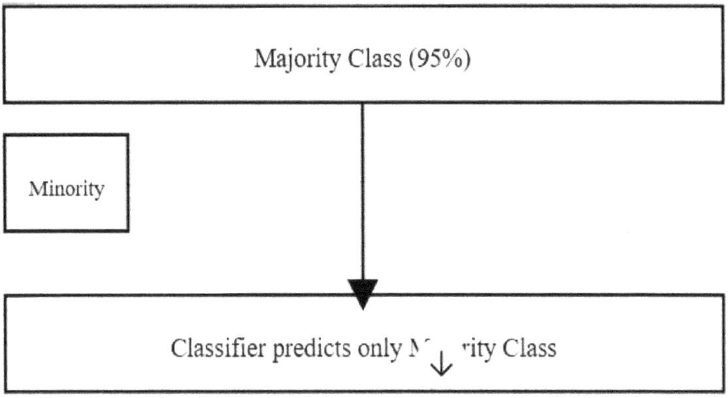

Figure 2.6 Effect of Class Imbalance on Classification Performance

2.17 Measurement Precision

Measurement precision refers to the consistency and reliability of performance estimates obtained from a machine learning model. Precision is influenced by factors such as dataset size, data variability, and evaluation methodology.

Repeated experiments using techniques like **cross-validation** help improve measurement precision by reducing variance in performance estimates. Reporting performance using confidence intervals or averaged results over multiple runs provides a more reliable assessment of model Behaviour.

Understanding measurement precision is critical when comparing algorithms or deploying models in safety-critical applications.

A summary table highlighting evaluation approaches and their impact on measurement precision may be included as Table 2.9

Table 2.9 Evaluation Approaches and Measurement Precision

Evaluation Method	Description	Impact on Measurement Precision
Hold-out Validation	Single split into training and testing sets	Simple but high variance in performance estimates
k-Fold Cross-Validation	Dataset split into k subsets, evaluated k times	Reduces variance and improves reliability
Stratified k-Fold Validation	Maintains class distribution in each fold	Especially effective for unbalanced datasets
Repeated Experiments	Multiple runs with different random seeds	Improves confidence in reported results

Section Wrap-up

Together, these concepts form the core of **machine learning model evaluation**. Proper handling of overfitting, informed dataset partitioning, robust performance metrics, and careful interpretation of results ensure that machine learning systems are both accurate and reliable in real-world applications.

Chapter 2: Summary

Chapter 2 focused on building a strong foundation for understanding data and learning mechanisms in Machine Learning. The chapter began with an introduction to **multivariate statistics**, emphasizing the importance of analysing multiple variables simultaneously to capture complex relationships in real-world datasets. This was followed by a discussion on the **essential mathematical tools for multivariate data**, highlighting the role of vectors, matrices, and related concepts as prerequisites for machine learning without delving into extensive mathematical derivations.

The chapter then introduced the **concept of hypothesis**, explaining how machine learning models represent assumptions about data and how learning algorithms search for the most suitable hypothesis within a defined hypothesis space. This understanding was extended through detailed discussions on **feature engineering**, where raw data is transformed into meaningful features, and **dimensionality reduction techniques**, which help manage high-dimensional data by preserving essential information while reducing complexity.

In the second part, the chapter presented the **basics of learning theory**, beginning with an introduction to learning and its various types, supported by Tom Mitchell's formal definition of learning. Concepts from **computational learning theory** were introduced to explain generalization, hypothesis space, and learning limitations. The chapter further explored the **design of a learning system**, **concept learning**, **inductive biases**, and **modelling in machine learning**, providing students with both theoretical and practical perspectives on how machine learning systems are constructed and evaluated.

Chapter 2: Conclusions

Understanding data and learning principles is fundamental to building effective machine learning systems. This chapter established that the success of machine learning models depends not only on algorithms but also on how data is represented, processed, and interpreted. By integrating concepts from multivariate statistics, mathematics, and learning theory, students gain a holistic view of the machine learning process.

The discussions on feature engineering and dimensionality reduction emphasised that careful data preparation often has a greater impact on model performance than algorithm selection alone. Similarly, the introduction to learning theory highlighted the importance of hypothesis selection, inductive bias, and generalization in developing reliable models. Together, these concepts prepare learners to approach advanced machine learning techniques with a solid conceptual foundation and informed decision-making skills.

End-of-Chapter Questions

A. Short Answer Questions

1. What is meant by multivariate data?
2. Define multivariate statistics.
3. What is a hypothesis in machine learning?
4. State Tom Mitchell's definition of learning.
5. Differentiate between feature selection and feature extraction.
6. What is dimensionality reduction?
7. Define inductive bias.
8. What is concept learning?
9. What is the role of a performance measure in learning?
10. Distinguish between parametric and non-parametric models.

B. Long Answer Questions

1. Explain the importance of multivariate statistics in machine learning with suitable examples.
2. Discuss the role of essential mathematical concepts in handling multivariate data.
3. Describe the concept of hypothesis and hypothesis space in machine learning.
4. Explain feature engineering and its significance in improving machine learning model performance.
5. Discuss dimensionality reduction techniques and their importance in handling high-dimensional data.
6. Explain the different types of learning in machine learning with examples.
7. Describe the basic components involved in the design of a learning system.

8. Explain concept learning and discuss any two algorithms used for it.

9. Discuss inductive bias and explain how it influences the learning process.

10. Explain the process of modelling in machine learning.

C. Application-Oriented Questions

1. Consider a dataset containing customer age, income, education level, and purchase history. How would feature engineering improve model performance?

2. Explain how dimensionality reduction can help in image classification problems.

3. Identify the task, experience, and performance measure for a movie recommendation system using Tom Mitchell's learning framework.

4. Suggest an appropriate type of learning for autonomous vehicle navigation and justify your answer.

5. Given a high-dimensional dataset with limited training samples, how would inductive bias influence model selection?

6. Design a basic learning system for predicting student academic performance and identify its key components.

Chapter - 3

Similarity Based Learning and Regression

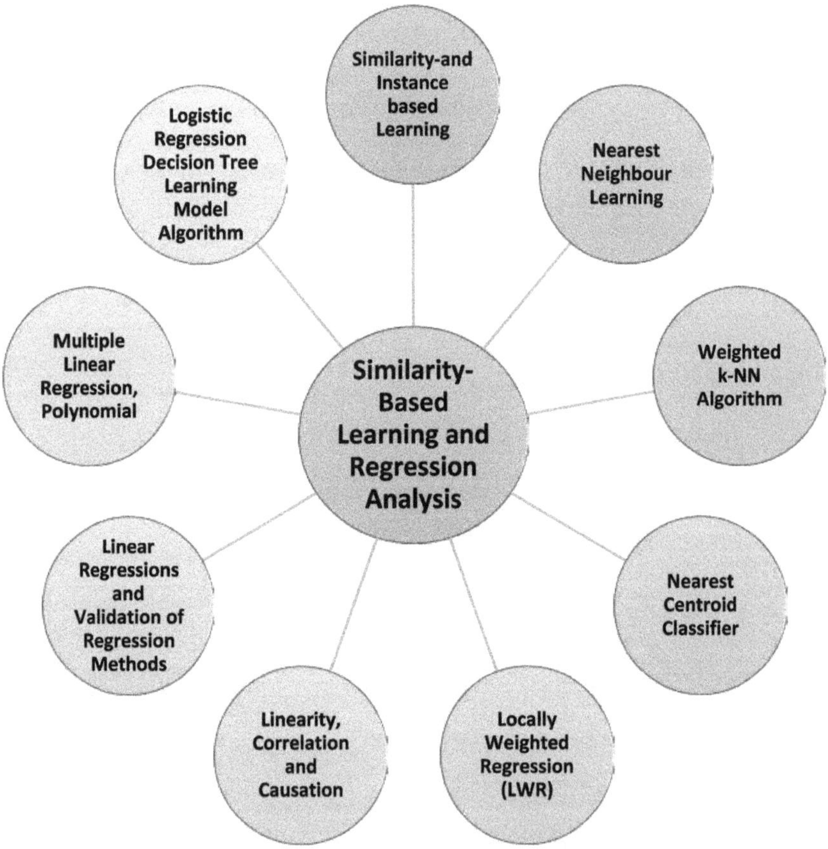

Chapter Overview

This chapter explores similarity-based learning methods and regression techniques that form essential components of the machine learning toolkit. We begin by examining how algorithms can make predictions based on the similarity between data points, focusing on k-Nearest Neighbours (k-NN) and its variants. The chapter then transitions to regression analysis, covering linear, polynomial, and logistic regression methods. Finally, we introduce decision tree learning as another powerful approach to both classification and regression tasks. Throughout the chapter, we emphasise the theoretical foundations, practical implementations, advantages, and limitations of each technique.

3.1 Introduction to Similarity-Based Learning

Similarity-based learning is an essential concept of machine learning which suggests that objects with similar features are likely to belong to the same category or produce comparable/similar results. An intuitive method mimics the way humans categorize and perceive things around them-the world. For instance, we could classify an unknown fruit as an apple because it shares attributes such as color, size, and form with previous apples we've seen. This concept is formalized in machine learning by comparing data points with a similarity measure like Euclidean distance, cosine similarity, or other domain-specific metrics.

The k-Nearest Neighbours (k-NN) method exemplifies/epitomizes similarity-based learning. It classifies a given data point by examining its k nearest neighbours in the feature space and assigns it to the majority class among those neighbours. This algorithm is simple yet powerful, as it makes predictions directly from stored data without the need for explicit training. In addition to classification, similarity-based algorithms are employed in regression, recommendation systems, and clustering tasks, showing their versatility. These methods' strength lies in their ability to adapt to complex patterns and relationships in data while staying interpretable and simple to implement.

While similarity-based learning is apparent/intuitive it does have disadvantages/challenges. When a dataset has noise, irrelevant features, or uneven distributions, the performance of such algorithms suffers. In addition, they frequently necessitate careful parameter tuning/adjustments, such as the number of neighbours (k), to prevent underfitting or overfitting. Notwithstanding these challenges, similarity-based learning has become an important concept in machine learning, providing as a foundation for more complex models and methodologies.

3.1.1 Nearest Neighbour Learning

Nearest Neighbour (NN) learning is one of the most intuitive machine learning algorithms, using a similarity principle to develop predictions. When presented with a new instance, the algorithm finds the closest comparable example in the training dataset and assigns it a label to new instance. This strategy is based on the assumption that similar data points are likely to have the same label or output. Its simplicity, lack of a formal training phase, and flexibility to adapt to different types of data input make NN learning a fundamental idea in machine learning.

Three important factors determine Nearest Neighbour Learning's performance. First, a distance metric is used to measure the similarity of data points, with prominent choices being Euclidean distance, Manhattan distance, and cosine similarity. Second, a set of labelled training examples is necessary to compare to the new instance. These instances describe the knowledge basis from which predictions are arrived at. Finally, a decision rule is employed to assign a label, usually by selecting the label from the nearest training example. This simple strategy can be expanded to include multiple neighbours, as demonstrated in k-Nearest Neighbour (k-NN), to improve robustness and noise reduction. While NN learning is computationally expensive for big datasets, its simplicity and effectiveness have made it a key component of instance-based learning systems.

1. **A distance metric:** A method to quantify similarity between data points
2. **Training examples:** A collection of labelled instances

3. **A decision rule:** How to assign a label based on nearest neighbours

The most common distance metrics include: Euclidean and Manhattan distance.

Euclidean Distance: The Euclidean distance is the straight-line distance between two points in a multidimensional space. It is defined as:

Euclidean Distance

$$\sqrt{\sum_{i=1}^{n} \quad (x_i - y_i)^2} \ldots\ldots \mathbf{3.1}$$

Manhattan Distance: The Manhattan distance, also known as the **L1 norm** or **taxicab distance**, measures the total absolute difference between the coordinates of two points in a multi-dimensional space. This distance metric is particularly useful when measuring distances in grid-like paths, such as city blocks or pixels in images.

Manhattan Distance = $\sum_{i=1}^{n} \quad |x_i - y_i| \ldots\ldots \mathbf{3.2}$

Minkowski Distance: Minkowski Distance Minkowski distance is a generalized metric for measuring the distance between two points in a multi-dimensional space. **Minkowski distance** of order p is defined as:

Minkowski Distance= $\mathbf{D_p(x, y)} = (\sum_{i=1}^{n} \quad |x_i - y_i|^p)^{1/P} \ldots \ldots \mathbf{3.3}$ where:

- n = number of dimensions (features)
- p≥1= order of the distance metric
- x_i,y_i = feature values of the two data points

Cosine similarity: Cosine similarity measures the similarity between two vectors by calculating the cosine of the angle between them. It evaluates how aligned two vectors are, regardless of their magnitude, making it especially useful in text analysis and high-dimensional data.

$$Cosinesimilarity = \frac{A \cdot B}{\| A \| \| B \|} \quad ....3.4$$

Where:

- A·B is the dot product of vectors A and B,
- ||A|| and ||B|| are the magnitudes of A and B respectively.

The choice of distance metric significantly influences the performance of nearest neighbour algorithms and should be selected based on the specific characteristics of the data.

Advantages of Nearest Neighbour methods:

- Simple to understand and implement
- No explicit training phase required
- Can model complex decision boundaries
- Adapts easily as new training data becomes available

Disadvantages:

- Computationally expensive during prediction
- Sensitive to irrelevant features
- Requires careful feature scaling
- Memory-intensive (must store entire training set

Illustration of Nearest Neighbour classification in a 2D feature space is presented in figure 3.1

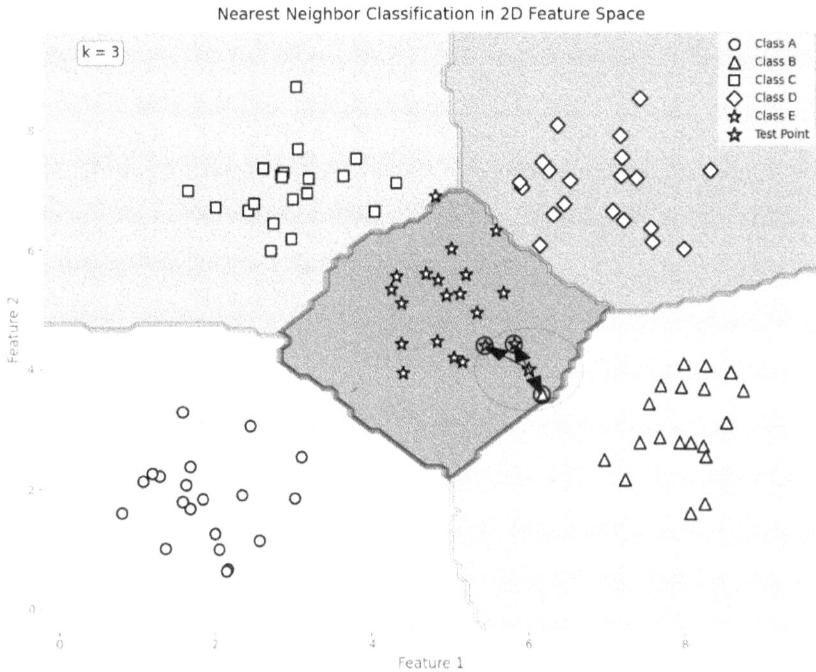

Figure 3.1 Illustration of Nearest Neighbour Classification in A 2D Feature Space

3.1.2 k-Nearest Neighbour (k-NN) Algorithm

The k-Nearest Neighbour (k-NN) approach is a non-parametric, instance-based learning to classify a data point based on the labels of its k nearest neighbours in the feature space. Unlike single-nearest neighbour techniques, which rely exclusively on the closest data point for prediction, k-NN uses information from multiple neighbours to make a decision. This aggregation is resistant to noise and outliers, as consensus from numerous points frequently leads to better predictions. The hyperparameter k has a substantial impact on model performance. A little k could lead to overfitting, whereas a large $k$can smooth out crucial information.

The algorithm operates in three stages. The distance between the query point and all data points in the training set is first calculated using a distance metric, such as the Euclidean, Manhattan, or Minkowski Distance. The query point's neighbourhood is formed by identifying the k nearby points. Finally, for classification tasks, the query point is assigned the class label that appears the most frequently among its neighbours, and for regression tasks, the algorithm predicts the average or weighted average of the neighbours' results. This simplicity and versatility make k-NN a crucial building component for machine learning applications ranging from image categorization to anomaly detection.

While k-NN is easy to implement and interpret, it is computationally intensive, particularly for large datasets. Its reliance on distance metrics makes it sensitive to feature scale and distribution, necessitating normalization or standardization. In addition, irrelevant or highly correlated features might skew/distort distance forecasts, necessitating feature selection or dimensionality reduction as pre-processing steps. Despite these challenges, k-NN is still commonly used due to its versatility, ease of implementation, and ability to handle classification and regression problems.

Algorithm steps:

1. Choose a value for k and a distance metric
2. For a new instance x: a. Calculate distance between x and all training examples b. Select the k training examples closest to x c. Assign the most common class among these k neighbours (for classification) d. Calculate the average of the k neighbours' target values (for regression)

Selecting k:

- **Small k values:** More sensitive to noise but can capture fine-grained patterns
- **Large k values:** Smoother decision boundaries but may miss important patterns
- **Common practice:** Use odd values of k (to avoid ties in binary classification)
- k can be optimized using cross-validation

Algorithmic complexity:

Time complexity= O(nd+ nlogn)..........3.5

Sace complexity =o(nd)..................3.6

Pseudocode for k-NN classification:

```
function k_NN_Classify(training_set, x_new, k):
  distances = []
  for each example (x_i, y_i) in training_set:
    d = distance(x_new, x_i)
    distances.append((d, y_i))
  sort distances in ascending order
  neighbours = first k elements of distances
  return most_frequent_class(neighbours)
```

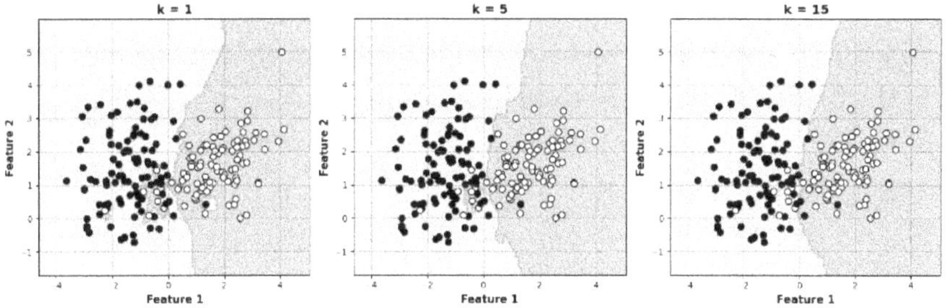

Figure 3.2 Effect of Different K Values on Decision Boundaries

Figure 3.2 show that the choice of **K in k-NN** significantly affects the shape of the decision boundary. Smaller K values create complex, irregular boundaries (overfitting), while larger K values produce smoother, more generalized boundaries (underfitting).

3.2 Extensions to k-NN

While the basic k-NN algorithm is powerful, several extensions have been developed to address its limitations and enhance its performance across different scenarios.

3.2.1 Weighted k-NN

In standard k-Nearest Neighbour (k-NN), all neighbours contribute equally to the classification or regression decision, regardless of distance from the query position. This equal weighting can often result in inadequate/suboptimal predictions, particularly when closer neighbours better match the query point's true class or value. Weighted k-NN overcomes this limitation by weighting neighbours according to their distance from the query point. Closer neighbours are typically given higher weights, indicating that they are more relevant to the prediction. This adjustment can increase the model's sensitivity to local trends while reducing the impact of outliers or less important distant points.

In weighted k-NN, the inverse of the distance is commonly used as a weighting system. For example, $\boldsymbol{w_i = 1 / d_i}$. The distance between the query point and the i-th neighbour is denoted by di Other versions, such as Gaussian or exponential decay functions, are also employed to highlight proximity while smoothing out the effect of weight discrepancies. By incorporating these weights, weighted k-NN enhances its ability to handle datasets with varying density or noise levels, resulting in more robust and accurate predictions. This flexibility makes weighted k-NN an important expansion of the traditional k-NN algorithm, especially in complex real-world situations where local context is vital for decision-making.

Common weighting schemes:

1. **Inverse distance weighting:** The weight decreases inversely with the distance between the query point x and its neighbour x_i

$$x_i = \frac{1}{d(x, x_i)} \dots\dots\dots\dots 3.7$$

Exponential weighting: Exponential weighting assigns weights to neighbours based on an exponential decay function, where closer neighbours receive higher weights.

$$w_i = e^{-d(x,x_i)} \dots\dots 3.8$$

Where:

- W_i is the weight assigned to the ith neighbour,
- $d(x,x_i)$ is the distance between the query point x and the ith neighbour.

2. **Kernel weighting:** Kernel weighting, particularly using the Gaussian kernel, assigns weights based on the squared distance between the query point and its neighbours, scaled by a parameter σ which controls the spread of the weights.

$$w_i = e\frac{-d(x,x_i)^2}{2\sigma^2} \quad ....3.9$$

- W_i is the weight assigned to the ith neighbour,
- $d(x,x_i)$ is the distance between the query point x and the ith neighbour.
- σ i s the bandwidth parameter that influences the smoothness of the weights.

Algorithm modification:

- For classification: Instead of counting votes equally, sum the weights associated with each class
- **For regression:** Calculate a weighted average of target values

Advantages:

- Reduces the influence of distant neighbours
- Smoother transition between decision regions
- Often better performance than standard k-NN

Implementation considerations:

- Weight normalization: o normalize the weights so they sum to 1, the following equation is used. This normalization ensures that the weights are proportional and their total contribution is uniformly scaled.

$$w' = \frac{w'}{\sum_{i=1}^{n} \quad w_j} \ldots\ldots\ldots \mathbf{3.10}$$

Where:

- w_i' is the normalized weight for the i-th neighbour,
- W_i is the original weight assigned to the i-th neighbour,
- $\sum_{j=1}^{k} \quad W_j$ is the sum of the weights of all k neighbours.
- Kernel bandwidth selection (for kernel weighting)
- Computational overhead slightly higher than standard k-NN

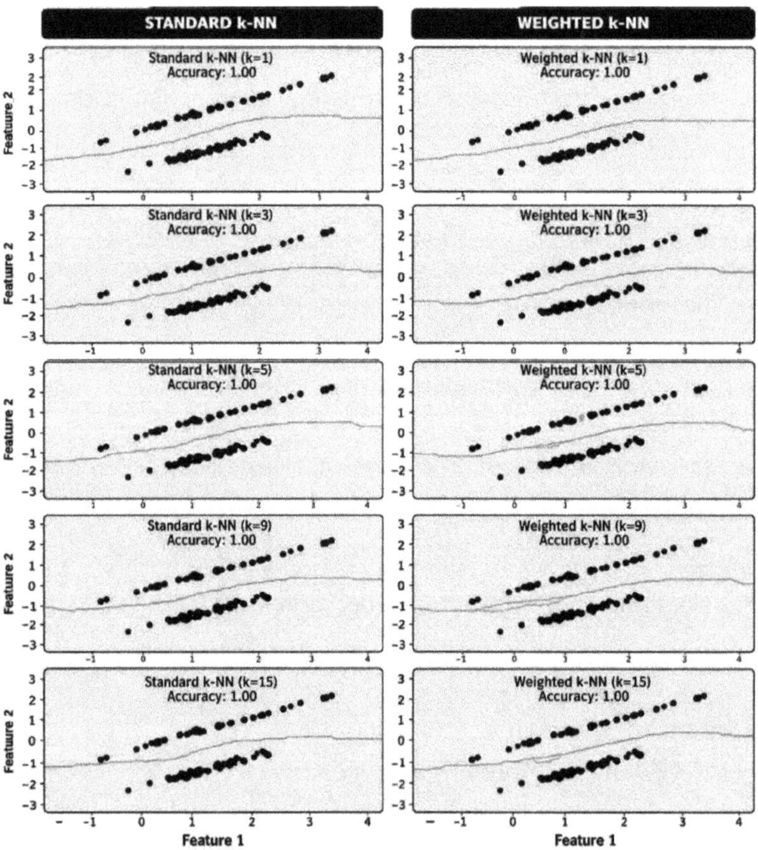

Figure 3.3 Comparison of Standard k-NN and Weighted k-NN Decision Boundaries

Figure 3.3 illustrates the impact of varying k-values on the decision boundaries of **standard k-NN** and **weighted k-NN** classifiers. The left column shows decision boundaries for standard k-NN, where all neighbours contribute equally, while the right column demonstrates weighted k-NN, which assigns higher importance to closer neighbours using distance-based weights. As k increases (from k=1 to k=15k), the decision boundaries become smoother. Smaller k values lead to more detailed and jagged boundaries, making the model highly sensitive to noise and prone to overfitting. On the other hand, larger k values result in smoother boundaries, reducing noise sensitivity but risking underfitting by oversimplifying the decision regions.

The comparison highlights the strengths of weighted k-NN, where closer neighbours influence the decision more than distant ones, leading to refined decision boundaries. Weighted k-NN performs better in scenarios with imbalanced or noisy data by reducing the impact of less-relevant points. Standard k-NN relies solely on the majority vote among k neighbours, making it more susceptible to outliers and distant points. Figure 3.3 emphasises the importance of selecting an appropriate k-value and showcases how weighted k-NN can provide more reliable classifications in complex or unevenly distributed datasets.

3.2.2 Nearest Centroid Classifier

The Nearest Centroid Classifier is a lightweight alternative to k-NN that lessens computational complexity while retaining good classification performance. Instead of saving all training examples, this algorithm computes the centroid (or mean vector) of each class during training. A centroid is the geometric center of all data points from that class in the feature space. During prediction, a new instance is classified by calculating its nearest centroid using a distance metric, such as Euclidean or Manhattan distance. The Nearest Centroid Classifier uses significantly fewer memory and computing resources than k-NN since it summarizes each class with a single representative point.

This strategy is more effective when classes are linearly separable or the data points in each class are distributed symmetrically around a central mean. It may struggle with non-linear boundaries or datasets with overlapping classes, though, because the centroid does not capture complex distributions or intra-class shifts/variations. Despite its simplicity, the Nearest Centroid Classifier is widely employed in applications such as text classification, which frequently have sparse and high-dimensional information. Its interpretability, efficiency, and ease of implementation make it a useful tool for situations requiring quick and approximate classifications.

Algorithm steps:

1. **Training phase:**
    - Calculate the centroid for each class
    - Store only these centroids
2. **Prediction phase:**
    - Assign the new instance to the class with the closest centroid

Key characteristics:

- Significantly faster prediction time than k-NN
- Much lower memory requirements
- Less sensitive to individual noisy examples
- Unable to model complex decision boundaries
- Works best when classes are well-separated and roughly spherical

Variations:

The Regularized Nearest Centroid classifier modifies the traditional technique by reducing the class centroids to the global centroid of all training data points. This regularization reduces the effects of noisy or sparsely distributed data, particularly when individual class centroids are affected / skewed by outliers. In moving the centroids closer to the global center, the model becomes more robust / resilient to minor variations in the data and achieves higher generalization. This approach is especially useful when dealing with small datasets or datasets with highly skewed class distributions, as class-specific centroids may not properly represent the underlying data structure.

- **Regularized Nearest Centroid:** Shrinks class centroids toward the global centroid

The Soft Nearest Centroid classifier utilizes a probabilistic methodology, assigning new examples to classes based on their relative distances from all centroids. Instead of making a hard decision-making based merely on the nearest centroid, the algorithm considers/computes probabilities for each class, frequently employing a softmax function. These probabilities represent the likelihood that a new instance will belong to each class. This soft decision-making approach yields more nuanced predictions and is especially beneficial in cases involving high uncertainty or large data point overlap between classes. Both of these enhancements will increase the Nearest Centroid Classifier's versatility and applicability, allowing it to handle a greater range of real-world datasets effectively.

- **Soft Nearest Centroid:** Uses probabilistic assignments based on distances

Table 3.1 provides a comprehensive comparison of three k-NN variants—Standard k-NN, Weighted k-NN, and Nearest Centroid—across critical metrics including computational efficiency, performance characteristics, and practical implementation considerations. This comparative analysis highlights the trade-offs between these algorithms, illustrating how Standard k-NN offers complex decision boundaries but poor scalability, Weighted k-NN improves handling of imbalanced data while maintaining flexibility, and Nearest Centroid dramatically reduces computational requirements at the expense of modelling capability.

Table 3.1 Comparison of k-NN Variants Across Different Metrics

Feature	Standard k-NN	Weighted k-NN	Nearest Centroid
Training time	O(1) - No explicit training	O(1) - No explicit training	O(n) - Computing centroids
Prediction time	O(nd + n log k)	O(nd + n log k)	O(cd) - c = number of classes

Memory requirements	High - Entire training set	High - Entire training set	Low - Only centroids
Decision boundary complexity	Complex, non-linear	Complex, non-linear	Linear
Sensitivity to noise	High with small k	Moderate	Low
Sensitivity to irrelevant features	High	High	Moderate
Handling of imbalanced classes	Poor with standard k	Better with distance weighting	Poor without adjustments
Interpretability	High - Based on similar examples	High - Based on similar examples	High - Based on class prototypes
Hyperparameter tuning	k value	k value and weighting function	Few or none
Scalability to large datasets	Poor	Poor	Good
Handling of missing values	Requires imputation	Can incorporate in distance metric	Robust if few missing values
Adaptability to new data	Excellent - Just add examples	Excellent - Just add examples	Requires recomputing centroids
Optimal application scenarios	Small to medium datasets with clear local patterns	Problems where distance is meaningful for similarity	Well-separated classes with roughly spherical distributions

3.3 Locally Weighted Regression (LWR)

Locally Weighted Regression (LWR) is a versatile extension of similarity-based learning created to solve regression problems. Unlike global regression models, which apply a single function to an entire dataset, LWR creates localized models that are tailored to a specific region of the feature space near the query point. This is accomplished by giving higher weights to nearby data points while decreasing the influence of ones farther away. weighing is usually carried out using a kernel function, such as a Gaussian kernel, with weights determined by the distance between the query and data points. This approach enables LWR to adapt its predictions to local patterns and variations, making it especially useful in situations involving non-linear relationships or heterogeneous data distributions.

The procedure involves using a simple model, typically a linear regression, on a weighted subset of data points around the query point. The model is recalculated for each query point, focusing on local data while ignoring distant portions of the feature space. This localized method makes LWR extremely adaptable, capturing complicated patterns without assuming a set global structure. In contrast to traditional linear regression, LWR is capable of modelling deviations in relationships between features and output across regions.

However, the benefits of LWR are offset by higher computational costs. Since the model must recompute weights and train a local regression for each query point, it can be computationally expensive for big/large datasets or high-dimensional feature spaces. Choosing the appropriate kernel function and bandwidth parameter (σ) is essential for optimal performance. Despite these problems, LWR remains a powerful tool for regression tasks demanding great flexibility and adaptation, particularly in domains like as robotics, economics, and medical diagnostics, where localized patterns are prevalent.

Figure 3.4 illustrates the difference between Global Linear Regression [see section 3.4] (top) and Locally Weighted Regression (LWR) with different bandwidth parameters (bottom). The top plot shows a single linear model trying to fit non-linear data, resulting in higher error (MSE: 6.7814). Tau (τ) is the bandwidth parameter in LWR that controls the "locality" of the regression - smaller values (τ=0.5) create very local models that fit the data more closely, while larger values (τ=2.0) result in smoother but less accurate fits. As shown in the bottom plots, the smallest τ value produces the lowest error (MSE: 0.1979) because it most precisely follows the non-linear pattern in the data.

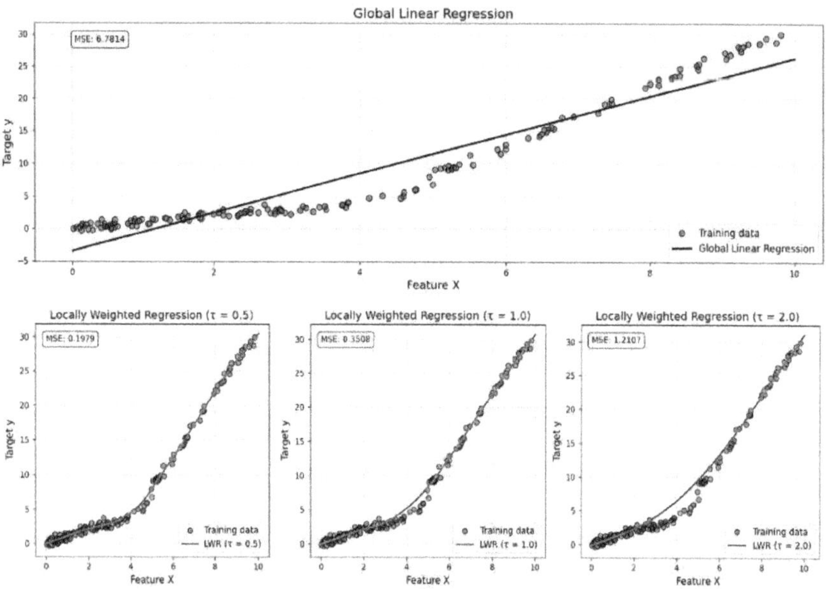

Figure 3.4 Comparison of Global Linear Regression and Locally Weighted Regression

3.3.1 Applications and Limitations

Locally Weighted Regression (LWR) is a versatile technique that has found applications in a number of domains. In time series prediction, LWR can adapt to changing trends and local patterns, making it useful for forecasting instances/problems where variable relationships change over time. In computer vision, it is used for tasks such as image smoothing and augmentation by approximating pixel intensities based on their surroundings. LWR enhances adaptability in control systems and robotics by allowing robots to make decisions based on localized data patterns, such as altering motor control or trajectory planning. Additionally, recommender systems benefit from LWR's ability to model user preferences locally, providing individualized recommendations depending on user Behaviour. Spatial data analysis also use LWR for tasks such as mapping and geographic modelling, which require localized interactions.

3.3.2 Limitations of LWR

Despite its usefulness, LWR has some significant limits. The computational cost of LWR is considerable for large datasets since the model must recomputed weights and solve a local regression problem for each query point. This renders it less suitable for real-time applications involving vast amounts of data. LWR performance is highly dependent on the kernel function and bandwidth parameter (τ), which must be carefully tuned to avoid overfitting or underfitting. LWR also fails in high-dimensional spaces because to the curse of dimensionality, in which data points become sparse and the concept of "locality" loses significance. Finally, it is vulnerable to noisy data, as outliers might disproportionately affect local models unless robust weighting mechanisms /schemes are used. Despite these problems, LWR is nevertheless an effective tool for applications that rely heavily on localized, non-linear associations/relations.

Computational complexity: Must perform a new regression for each prediction

1. **Curse of dimensionality:** Performance degrades in high-dimensional spaces
2. **Bandwidth selection:** Critical parameter that affects bias-variance tradeoff
3. **Boundary effects:** May perform poorly near the edges of the feature space
4. **Data sparsity issues:** Requires sufficient local data density

3.3.3 Implementation considerations

- Fast neighbour lookup structures (KD-trees, ball trees)
- Approximate methods for large datasets
- Adaptive bandwidth selection techniques
- Feature selection or dimensionality reduction as pre-processing

3.4 Introduction to Regression

Regression analysis represents a fundamental approach to modelling relationships between variables, focusing on predicting continuous outputs rather than discrete categories.

- **Regressor:** Refers to the independent variable(s) (also called predictors, explanatory variables, or features) in regression analysis. these are the variables machine learning expert use to explain or predict the outcome.
- **Dependent variable** (target outcome)**:** The variable you are trying to predict or explain.

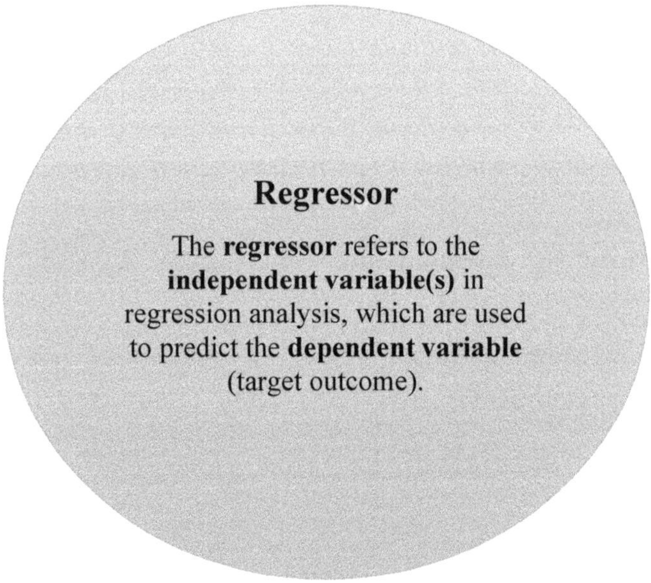

Regressor Examples:

- **In predicting house prices:**
  - **Regressors:** Number of bedrooms, square footage, location
  - **Dependent variable:** House price

- **In predicting stock prices:**
    - **Regressors:** Historical stock prices, trading volume, economic indicators
    - **Dependent variable:** Future stock price
- **In estimating student performance:**
    - **Regressors:** Study hours, attendance, previous test scores
    - **Dependent variable:** Final exam score

Key concepts in regression:

- **Dependent variable:** The target value we want to predict
- **Independent variables:** Features used to make predictions
- **Residuals:** Differences between predicted and actual values
- **Fitted values:** The model's predictions on the training data
- **Regression coefficients:** Parameters that quantify relationships between variables.

Types of Regression Problems

Regression problems can be categorized based on several dimensions:

By relationship type:

- **Simple regression:** Single independent variable
- **Multiple regression:** Multiple independent variables
- **Linear regression:** Linear relationship between variables
- **Nonlinear regression:** Nonlinear relationships modeled

By regression task:

- **Univariate regression:** Predicting a single output variable
- **Multivariate regression:** Predicting multiple output variables simultaneously
- **Ordinal regression:** Predicting ordered categorical variables

- **Count regression:** Predicting count data (e.g., Poisson regression)

By statistical approach:

- **Parametric regression:** Fixed form with finite parameters
- **Non-parametric regression:** Flexible form with unlimited parameters
- **Bayesian regression:** Incorporating prior distributions on parameters
- **Frequentist regression:** Maximum likelihood estimation approach

3.4.1 Introduction to Linearity, Correlation and Causation

Understanding the nature of relationships between variables is essential in regression analysis and machine learning. Before building predictive models, it is important to distinguish between linearity, **correlation**, and **causation**, as these concepts guide how models are designed, interpreted, and validated.

3.4.1.1 Introduction to Linearity

Linearity refers to a relationship between variables in which the change in the dependent variable is proportional to the change in one or more independent variables. In a linear relationship, the effect of an input variable on the output remains constant across its range.

In machine learning and statistics, linearity is a fundamental assumption in many regression models, especially **linear regression**. A simple linear relationship between an independent variable x and a dependent variable y is expressed as:

$y = mx + c$.....3.11

where:

- y = dependent (output) variable
- x = independent (input) variable

- m = slope of the line
- c = intercept

Importance of Linearity in Machine Learning

- Simplifies model interpretation
- Reduces computational complexity
- Acts as a baseline for complex models
- Allows easy visualization and diagnostics

When linearity does not hold, techniques such as **polynomial regression** or **feature transformation** are used.

3.4.2 Introduction to Correlation and Causation

Correlation:

Correlation measures the **strength and direction** of association between two variables. The most common measure is the **Pearson correlation coefficient** (r).

Mathematical Formula is

$$r = \frac{\sum(x_i - \overline{x_\iota})(y_i - \overline{y_\iota})}{\sqrt{\sum(x_i - \overline{x_\iota})^2 (y_i - \overline{y_\iota})^2}} \ldots\ldots. \mathbf{3.11}(\boldsymbol{a})$$

Where:

- $r \in [-1, +1]$
- $r = +1$: Perfect positive correlation
- $r = -1$ Perfect negative correlation
- $r = 0$ No correlation

3.5 Introduction to Linear Regression

Linear Regression is one of the most fundamental and widely used techniques in regression analysis and machine learning for Modelling the relationship between a dependent variable and one or more independent variables. It assumes that this relationship can be approximated by a straight line, making the model simple, interpretable, and computationally efficient. By estimating the best-fit line through observed data, linear regression enables prediction of continuous outcomes and provides insights into how changes in input variables influence the output. Because of its clarity and strong mathematical foundation, linear regression serves as a baseline model and a building block for more advanced regression and learning algorithms.

3.5.1 Simple Linear Regression

Simple Linear Regression

Simple linear regression establishes a relationship between one independent variable (X) and one dependent variable (Y) using a linear equation.

The Model:

$$Y = \beta_0 + \beta_1 X + \varepsilon \text{..............} \mathbf{3.12}$$

Where

- Y: Dependent variable
- X: Independent variable (Known as Regressor
- β_0: Y-intercept (value of Y when X=0)
- β_1: Slope (change in Y for a unit change in X)
- ε: Error term (random variation not explained by the model)

Assumptions:

1. Linearity: The relationship between X and Y is linear
2. **Independence:** Observations are independent of each other
3. **Homoscedasticity:** Variance of residuals is constant across all X values
4. **Normality:** Residuals follow a normal distribution

Linear regression provides the foundation for many regression techniques, while polynomial regression extends this approach to capture non-linear relationships. **Figure 3.5** illustrates the relationship between a regressor (independent variable) and the dependent variable using a simple regression model. The data points represent observed values, while the dashed red line shows the fitted regression line. The text box highlights that the **regressor (X)** serves as the input feature used to predict the **dependent variable (y)**.

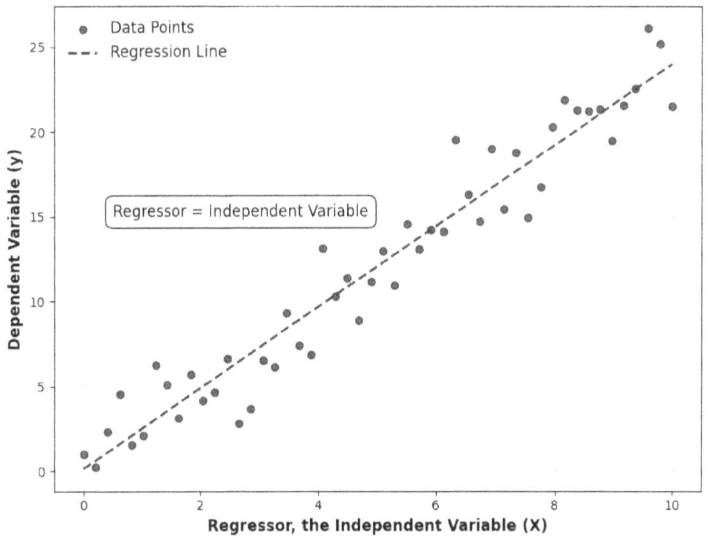

Figure 3.5 Illustrating the Relationship between Regressor and Dependent Variable

3.5.2 Linear Regression: Assumptions and Implementation

Linear regression models the relationship between a dependent variable y and one or more independent variables X using a linear combination:

$$y=\beta_0+\beta_1x_1+\beta_2x_2+\cdots+\beta_nx_n+\epsilon \ldots\ 3.13$$

Where:

- β_0 = Intercept (constant term)
- $\beta_1,\beta_2,\ldots,\beta_n$ = Regression coefficients (weights of predictors)

- $x_1, x_2, \ldots, x_n$ = Independent variables (predictors/features)
- ϵ = Random error (residual term)

Key assumptions:

1. **Linearity:** The relationship between X and y is linear
2. **Independence:** Observations are independent of each other
3. **Homoscedasticity**[a]**:** Constant variance of errors [see Heteroscedasticity footnote [b]]
4. **Normality:** Errors are normally distributed
5. **No multicollinearity:** Independent variables are not highly correlated

a. **Homoscedasticity:** Refers to the condition where the variance of residuals is constant across all levels of the independent variable.2Heteroscedasticity: **heteroscedasticity** refers to **varying variance** of residuals, not necessarily always increasing. The variance could increase, decrease, or fluctuate irregularly across the independent variable.

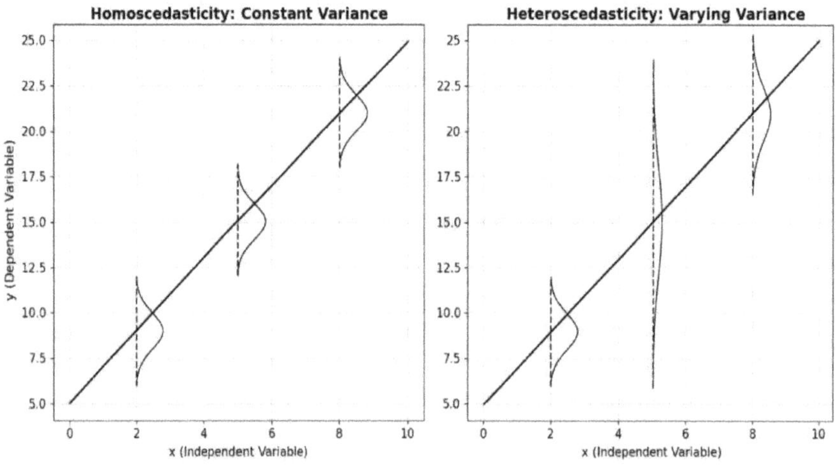

Figure 3.6 Illustration of The Concepts of Homoscedasticity and Heteroscedasticity

Figure 3.6 contrasts the difference between homoscedasticity and heteroscedasticity in regression. In the first plot, residuals exhibit constant variance (homoscedasticity), fulfilling a key regression assumption. In contrast, the second plot shows increasing variance in residuals (heteroscedasticity), which violates this assumption and may impact the reliability of regression inferences.

Ordinary Least Squares (OLS) estimation: The coefficients are estimated by minimizing the sum of squared residuals:

Objective Function (Least Squares)

$$\textbf{\textit{minimize}}\sum_{i=1}^{n}\left(y_i-\left(\beta_0+\beta_1x_1+.....+\beta_px_p\right)\right)^2 \text{.....}\mathbf{3.13}$$

Matrix formulation is $y = \boldsymbol{X\beta} + \varepsilon$.........**3.14**

Where:

- $\mathbf{y} = \begin{bmatrix} y_1 \\ y_2 \\ \vdots \\ y_n \end{bmatrix}$ (response vector)
- $\mathbf{X} = \begin{bmatrix} 1 & x_{11} & x_{12} & \cdots & x_{1p} \\ 1 & x_{21} & x_{22} & \cdots & x_{2p} \\ \vdots & \vdots & \vdots & \ddots & \vdots \\ 1 & x_{n1} & x_{n2} & \cdots & x_{np} \end{bmatrix}$ (design matrix)
- $\boldsymbol{\beta} = \begin{bmatrix} \beta_0 \\ \beta_1 \\ \vdots \\ \beta_p \end{bmatrix}$ (parameter vector)

Implementations:

1. **Closed-form solution:** Direct computation using matrix operations
2. **Gradient descent:** Iterative optimization for large datasets

3. **Stochastic gradient descent:** Processing one example at a time
4. **Ridge and Lasso regularization:** Adding penalty terms to prevent overfitting

3.6 Validation of Regression Methods

Validation of regression methods is the process of assessing how well a regression model performs on unseen data and how accurately it predicts continuous outcomes. Since a model may fit training data well but perform poorly on new data, validation is essential to detect problems such as **overfitting** and **underfitting**. Common validation approaches include splitting data into training and testing sets, cross-validation, and analysing prediction errors using evaluation metrics. In this section, regression models are evaluated using widely used error measures such as **Mean Squared Error (MSE)**, **Root Mean Squared Error (RMSE)**, and **Mean Absolute Error (MAE)**. MSE penalizes larger errors more heavily by squaring them, RMSE provides error values in the same units as the target variable, and MAE measures the average magnitude of errors without considering their direction. Together, these metrics provide a quantitative basis for comparing regression models and selecting the most appropriate one for a given problem.

Evaluation metrics:

- **Mean Squared Error (MSE):**

$$\mathbf{MSE} = \sum_{i=1}^{n} (y_i - \hat{y}_i)^2 \, \mathbf{.....3.15}$$

- **Root Mean Squared Error (RMSE):**

$$\mathbf{RMSE} = \sqrt{\mathbf{MSE}} = \sqrt{\sum_{i=1}^{n} (y_i - \hat{y}_i)^2} \, \mathbf{......3.16}$$

- **Mean Absolute Error (MAE):**

$$\mathbf{MAE} = \frac{\mathbf{1}}{\mathbf{n}} |y_i - \hat{y}_i| \, \mathbf{........3.17}$$

- **Coefficient of Determination (R^2):** Proportion of variance explained by the model

$$\left(\mathbf{R}^2\right) = 1 - \frac{\sum_{i=1}^{n}\left(y_i - \hat{y}_i\right)^2}{\sum_{i=1}^{n}\left(y_i - \bar{y}\right)^2} \quad \text{.......}3.18$$

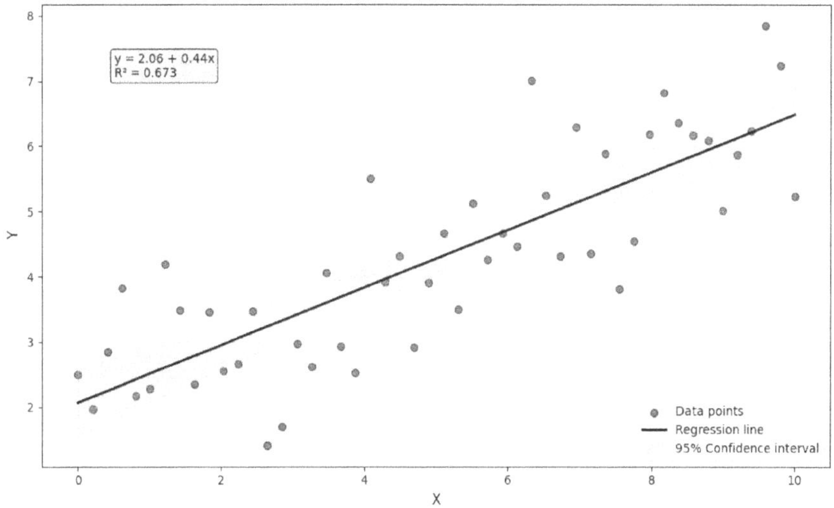

Figure 3.7 Linear Regression with Confidence Intervals.

Figure 3.7 depicts linear regression analysis, with the line representing the best-fit linear relationship among X and Y variables and the shaded grey region indicating the 95% confidence interval around the regression line. The confidence interval reflects the range of uncertainty in the predictions; it is broader at the extremes of the data range and narrower toward the canter, signifying greater uncertainty when extrapolating beyond the observed data points.

3.6.1 Multiple Linear Regression

Multiple Linear Regression (MLR) is an extension of simple linear regression that models the relationship between **one dependent variable** and **two or more independent variables**. In many real-world problems, an output variable is influenced by several factors rather than a single input. Multiple linear regression captures this combined influence by fitting a linear equation that includes multiple predictors. It is widely used in areas such as economics, engineering, business analytics, and machine learning to predict continuous outcomes and to understand the relative importance of different input variables.

3.6.2 Mathematical Model

The general form of a multiple linear regression model is:

$$y = \beta_0 + \beta_1 x_1 + \beta_2 x_2 + \dots + \beta_n x_n \dots\dots 3.19$$

where:

- y = dependent (output) variable
- β_0 =intercept
- $w_1, w_2 \dots w_n$ = independent (input) variables
- $\beta_1, \beta_2, \dots\beta_n$ =regression coefficients

The constant term β_0 has the following meanings:

1. **Baseline Value of the Output**
   β_0 represents the expected value of the dependent variable y **when all independent variables are zero.**
2. **Intercept of the Regression Plane**
   In geometric terms, it is the point where the regression line (or plane) intersects the y-axis.
3. **Adjustment for Systematic Bias**
   It captures the effect of factors influencing y that are **not** explicitly included as independent variables in the model.
4. **Improves Accuracy of Predictions**
   Including the constant allows the model to fit data more realistically. Without it, predictions are often biased because the model is forced to pass through the origin.

3.6.3 Applications

- House price prediction

- Sales and demand forecasting
- Performance analysis in education
- Cost estimation in engineering projects

In figure 3.8 house price predations using linear regression with area of the house (area/square foot) as one of the variables is presented.

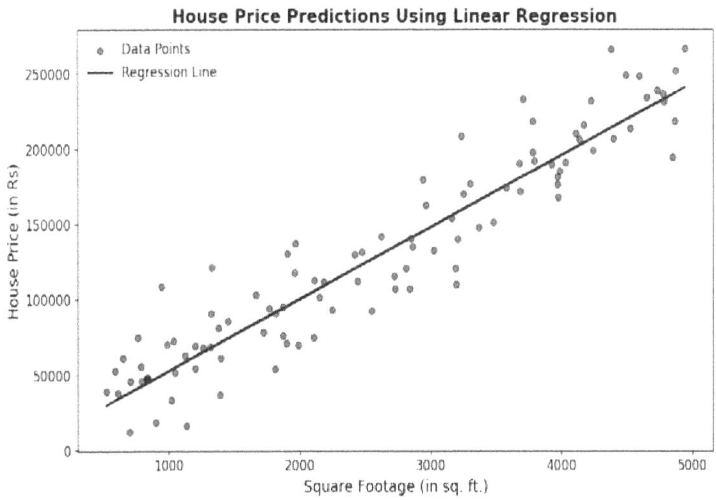

Figure 3.8 House Price Predations Using Linear Regression with Area of the House (Area/Square Foot) as One of the Variables

3.7 Polynomial Regression

Polynomial regression is a powerful extension of linear regression that enables modelling of non-linear relationships between variables. While linear regression assumes a straight-line relationship between the independent variable (X) and dependent variable (Y), many real-world phenomena exhibit curved patterns that cannot be adequately captured by a linear model.

3.7.1 Key Characteristics:

- Extends linear regression by incorporating polynomial terms of independent variables
- Captures non-linear relationships while maintaining computational efficiency
- Remains linear in coefficients despite non-linear relationships in variables
- Particularly valuable when data exhibits peaks, troughs, inflection points, or other non-linear patterns

Polynomial regression extends linear regression by adding polynomial terms of the independent variables to capture non-linear relationships. Polynomial regression analyses the relationship between an independent variable (x) and a dependent variable (y) using an n-degree polynomial. Unlike linear regression, which assumes a straight-line relationship, polynomial regression may represent curved patterns in data, making it suited for capturing non-linear relationships. This flexibility is especially valuable in cases where data points depart from a linear trend and exhibit peaks, troughs, or other deviations.

3.7.2 Mathematical Foundation

The general polynomial regression model of degree p is expressed as:

Equation 3.19:

The model equation for polynomial regression is given as in equation 3.19.

$$Y = \beta_0 + \beta_1 X + \beta_2 X^2 + \beta_3 X^3 + \ldots.\beta_p X^p + \varepsilon \ldots\ldots 3.20$$

The Model:

- Y= Dependent variable
- X:=Independent variable
- X^2, X^3, ..., X^p= Polynomial terms
- β_0, β_1, ..., β_p=Regression coefficients
- ε = Error term

For example, a quadratic regression (n=2) models a parabolic curve, while a cubic regression (n=3) can capture inflection points. Polynomial regression involves transforming the original independent variable into additional features that indicate its powers (e.g., x^2, x^3 , ...). These features are subsequently used as inputs into a linear regression model. Despite the non-linear relationship between $x$and y, the transformed regression problem stays linear in the model coefficients, making it computationally efficient to solve.

However, care must be used while selecting the degree of the polynomial. Higher-degree polynomials can fit the training data extremely well, resulting in over fitting and poor generalization for new data. Conversely, an insufficient degree may fail to capture the underlying patterns. Cross-validation techniques can help determine the polynomial's appropriate degree in order to strike a balance between underfitting and overfitting.

3.7.3 Common Polynomial Forms

Polynomial regression models are classified based on their degree, which determines the highest power of the independent variable in the equation and fundamentally influences the model's capacity to capture complex patterns in data. The degree of a polynomial directly corresponds to the flexibility and expressiveness of the model, with each incremental increase introducing additional curvature and turning points that enable the representation of increasingly sophisticated relationships. Lower-degree polynomials, such as linear (p=1) and quadratic (p=2) models, provide simpler, more interpretable relationships and are less prone to overfitting, making them suitable for data with straightforward trends or single-peaked patterns. Higher-degree polynomials, including cubic (p=3), quartic (p=4), and beyond, offer greater modelling flexibility and can capture multi-modal distributions, inflection points, and complex oscillatory Behaviour, though they carry increased risk of fitting noise rather than signal. The selection of an appropriate polynomial degree is a critical modelling decision that must balance the need for adequate representation of the underlying data structure against the dangers of model complexity, computational cost, and overfitting. In practice, polynomial forms ranging from degree 1 to 5 are most commonly employed in applied settings, as higher degrees often lead to numerical instability, poor interpretability, and unreliable extrapolation beyond the observed data range. The following subsections examine the most frequently used polynomial forms, detailing their mathematical properties, geometric interpretations, and practical applications in statistical modelling and machine learning.

3.7.4 Quadratic Regression

A **quadratic regression** is a type of **polynomial regression** where the relationship between the independent variable x and the dependent variable y is modeled using a **second-degree polynomial**. It can capture simple curvature in data that a straight line cannot.

Quadratic Model (p = 2):

The quadratic model, also known as second-degree polynomial regression, represents one of the most commonly used non-linear regression forms in statistical modelling. The equation 3.20 represents the quadratic model

$$\mathbf{Y = \beta_0 + \beta_1 X + \beta_2 X^2 + \varepsilon ....3.21}$$

This model produces a parabolic curve characterized by a single turning point (either a maximum or minimum), making it ideal for capturing U-shaped or inverted U-shaped relationships in data. The sign of the coefficient β_2 determines the curvature direction: when $\beta_2 > 0$, the parabola opens upward (convex, U-shaped), indicating that the rate of change in Y accelerates as X increases; conversely, when $\beta_2 < 0$, the parabola opens downward (concave, inverted U-shaped), suggesting diminishing returns or saturation effects. The vertex of the parabola occurs at $X = -\beta_1/(2\beta_2)$, which represents the optimal or critical point in the relationship. Quadratic models are particularly interpretable because they maintain mathematical simplicity while capturing non-linearity, and they can be easily differentiated to find maximum or minimum points, making them valuable for optimization problems.

Machine Learning Applications:

Quadratic models find extensive applications across various machine learning domains. In **cost function optimization**, many learning algorithms utilize quadratic approximations in their objective functions, particularly in Newton's method and quasi-Newton optimization techniques where the Hessian matrix characterizes the local quadratic Behaviour of the loss landscape. In **economics and business analytics**, quadratic models are employed to represent the law of diminishing returns, pricing strategies, and profit maximization problems—for instance, modelling how advertising expenditure initially increases sales but eventually plateaus or decreases due to market saturation. In **environmental science and climate modelling**, quadratic relationships capture phenomena such as the relationship between temperature and plant growth, where moderate temperatures promote growth (upward parabola portion) but extreme temperatures inhibit it. In **computer vision**, quadratic models are used in image processing for edge detection and feature enhancement through second-order derivatives (Laplacian operators). Additionally, in **recommender systems**, quadratic models can represent user preference curves where moderate levels of certain features are preferred over extreme values, such as movie length or music tempo preferences.

3.7.5 Cubic Regression

A **cubic regression** is a form of **polynomial regression** that models the relationship between x and y using a **third-degree polynomial**. It can represent more complex, S-shaped trends and multiple bends in the data.

Cubic Model (p = 3)

The cubic model, also known as third-degree polynomial regression, represents a significant advancement in modelling capability over quadratic forms, enabling the representation of more complex non-linear relationships in statistical analysis. The equation 3.21 represents the cubic model:

$$Y = \beta_0 + \beta_1X + \beta_2X^2 + \beta_3X^3 + \varepsilon \ldots\ldots\ldots\ldots\ldots 3.22$$

Detailed Description:

The cubic model, or third-degree polynomial regression, introduces an Q(sigmoid-like) curves and one inflection point where the curve changes from concave to convex or vice versa. The inflection point occurs at $X = -\beta_2/(3\beta_3)$, which represents a critical transition point in the relationship's Behaviour. This model is particularly powerful because it can represent both increasing and decreasing rates of change within the same function, making it suitable for phenomena that exhibit initial acceleration followed by deceleration (or vice versa). The coefficient β_3 determines the overall shape: positive values create an increasing function with varying curvature, while negative values produce a decreasing pattern. Cubic polynomials can exhibit two turning points (one local maximum and one local minimum), allowing them to model complex real-world processes that have multiple phases or regimes. The first derivative ($3\beta_3X^2 + 2\beta_2X + \beta_1$) reveals the rate of change at any point, while the second derivative ($6\beta_3X + 2\beta_2$) indicates the concavity and identifies the inflection point.

Machine Learning Applications:

Cubic models are extensively utilized in machine learning for modelling complex temporal and spatial patterns. In **growth modelling and population dynamics**, cubic functions effectively represent three-phase growth patterns: slow initial growth (lag phase), rapid exponential growth (log phase), and eventual saturation (stationary phase)—commonly seen in bacterial growth, viral spread models (including epidemic modelling), and technology adoption curves. In **neural network activation functions**, cubic approximations have been explored as alternatives to standard activations, particularly in polynomial neural networks where they can capture more complex decision boundaries than quadratic functions while maintaining computational tractability. In **time series forecasting**, cubic trends are used to model economic indicators, stock prices, and seasonal patterns that exhibit changing growth rates, such as GDP growth that accelerates during economic booms and decelerates during recessions. In **robotics and control systems**, cubic splines (piecewise cubic polynomials) are fundamental for trajectory planning and smooth path generation, ensuring continuous position, velocity, and acceleration profiles for robot movement. In **natural language processing**, cubic models have been applied to model word frequency distributions and sentiment intensity curves that show non-monotonic relationships. Additionally, in **drug response modelling** (pharmacokinetics), cubic functions describe concentration-time curves showing absorption, distribution, and elimination phases of medications in the body.

3.7.6 Quartic Regression

A **quartic regression** is a type of **polynomial regression** where the relationship between the independent variable x and the dependent variable y is modelled using a **fourth-degree polynomial**. It can fit highly nonlinear relationships and capture multiple inflection points.**Quartic Model (p = 4)**

$$Y = \beta_0 + \beta_1 X + \beta_2 X^2 + \beta_3 X^3 + \beta_4 X^4 + \varepsilon \ldots\ldots\ldots\ldots\ldots 3.23$$

Detailed Description:

The quartic model, or fourth-degree polynomial regression, represents a highly flexible modelling approach capable of capturing complex multi-modal relationships with up to three turning points (local maxima and minima) and up to two inflection points. This increased flexibility allows the model to represent W-shaped or M-shaped patterns, multiple peaks and valleys, and other intricate non-linear Behaviours that simpler polynomials cannot accommodate. The coefficient β_4 plays a crucial role in determining the end Behaviour: when $\beta_4 > 0$, both tails of the function extend toward positive infinity (creating a U-shape overall with possible intermediate fluctuations); when $\beta_4 < 0$, both tails extend toward negative infinity (inverted U-shape overall). Finding the critical points requires solving a cubic equation ($4\beta_4X^3 + 3\beta_3X^2 + 2\beta_2X + \beta_1 = 0$), which may yield one or three real solutions, corresponding to potential local extrema. However, this flexibility comes with increased risk of overfitting, particularly with limited data, as the model may fit noise rather than underlying patterns. The quartic model's ability to oscillate makes it suitable for phenomena with multiple regimes or phases, but practitioners must carefully validate that the additional complexity is justified by the data and domain knowledge.

Machine Learning Applications:

Quartic models find specialized applications in machine learning scenarios requiring multi-modal pattern recognition and complex relationship modelling. In **computer vision and image processing**, quartic functions are employed in advanced edge detection algorithms and surface reconstruction techniques, where they can model complex intensity variations and texture patterns that exhibit multiple peaks and valleys—such as in medical imaging for detecting tissue boundaries or in satellite imagery for terrain analysis. In **financial modelling and quantitative finance**, quartic polynomials are used to model volatility smiles and skews in options pricing, where implied volatility exhibits complex non-monotonic relationships with strike prices, creating distinctive multi-peaked patterns that simpler models cannot capture. In **anomaly detection systems**, quartic models can establish baseline patterns for normal Behaviour in network traffic, system performance, or sensor data that naturally exhibits multiple operational modes or states, making it easier to identify deviations that signal potential security threats or equipment failures. In **materials science and engineering**, quartic energy potentials are fundamental in molecular dynamics simulations and crystal structure modelling, where they represent complex force fields and potential energy surfaces governing atomic interactions. In **acoustic signal processing and speech recognition**, quartic functions model formant frequencies and resonance patterns that exhibit multiple peaks in spectral analysis. Additionally, in **hyper parameter optimization** for machine learning models, quartic functions can approximate complex loss landscapes with multiple local minima, helping algorithms like Bayesian optimization navigate intricate search spaces more effectively. In **bioinformatics**, quartic models are applied to protein folding energy landscapes and gene expression patterns that show complex regulatory Behaviour with multiple activation and repression states.

3.8 Implementation Approach

Having dealt with common polynomial forms of polynomial regression, it is imperative to dwell on the following:

1. Create polynomial features by raising X to different powers
2. Generate polynomial features (x^2, x^3, etc.)
3. Treat these as additional independent variables
4. Apply standard linear regression techniques
5. Use these polynomial features as independent variables in a standard linear regression model
6. OLS can still be used for parameter estimation

3.8.1 Choosing the Polynomial Degree

- Higher degrees offer more flexibility but risk overfitting
- Lower degrees may not capture the true relationship (underfitting)
- Cross-validation can help determine the optimal degree

3.8.2 Implementation approach

Degree selection: Choosing the right degree for a polynomial regression model is essential for striking a fair balance between model complexity and generalizability. The degree determines the model's flexibility, with higher degrees capturing more detailed patterns but increasing the risk of overfitting. Lower degrees, on the other hand, may result in underfitting, which occurs when the model fails to capture the underlying trends in the data. The following bulleted points reveals the mechanism of choosing.

- Higher degree → More flexible model → Risk of over fitting
- Lower degree → Less flexible model → Risk of under fitting
- Cross-validation typically used to select optimal degree

Advantages:

- Simple extension of linear regression
- Can capture non-linear relationships
- Well-understood statistical properties
- Standard software implementations available

Limitations:

- Sensitive to outliers
- May oscillate between data points (high variance)
- Poor extrapolation beyond the range of training data
- Curse of dimensionality with interaction terms

Table 3.2 provides examples of polynomial regression models with varying degrees and their respective equations, R^2, and RMSE values. It demonstrates how increasing the degree of the polynomial improves model fit (higher R^2 and lower RMSE), but with diminishing returns beyond a certain degree.

Table 3.2 Example of Polynomial Regression Models

Model	Equation	R^2	RMSE
Linear (p=1)	$Y = 10 + 5X$	0.75	12.5
Quadratic (p=2)	$Y = 8 + 3X + 2X^2$	0.89	8.2
Cubic (p=3)	$Y = 7 + 2X + 1.5X^2 + 0.5X^3$	0.94	6.1
Quartic (p=4)	$Y = 7 + 2X + 1.5X^2 + 0.5X^3 + 0.1X^4$	0.95	5.8

3.8.3 Best Practices and Recommendations

Data Pre-processing

1. **Feature Scaling:** Always standardize features before regularization
2. **Outlier Detection:** Identify and handle outliers appropriately

3. **Missing Values:** Address missing data before modelling
4. **Train-Test Split:** Reserve data for unbiased evaluation

Model Selection

1. **Start Simple:** Begin with low-degree polynomials
2. **Visualize:** Plot fitted curves against data
3. **Cross-Validate:** Use systematic validation procedures
4. **Compare Metrics:** Evaluate multiple performance measures
5. **Check Assumptions:** Verify residual diagnostics

Avoiding Common Pitfalls

1. **Over-Parameterization:** Resist using unnecessarily high polynomial degrees
2. **Extrapolation:** Be cautious when predicting beyond training data range
3. **Ignoring Regularization:** Consider regularization even for moderate complexity
4. **Single Metric Focus:** Evaluate models using multiple criteria
5. **Data Leakage:** Ensure proper separation of training and validation data

3.9 Logistic Regression

What is Logistic Regression?

Logistic Regression is an algorithm for supervised machine learning that is frequently used to model the likelihood of a given class or occurrence. It is most effective when the data is linearly separable, and the output variable is binary or dichotomous. This makes logistic regression suitable for binary classification problems which require predicting an output variable with two distinctive classes.

Binary classification involves foreseeing distinct outcomes such as Yes/No, Pass/Fail, Win/Loss, and Cancerous/Non-cancerous. Logistic regression is widely used in a variety of fields, including health, economics, and social sciences, for purposes such as disease diagnosis, credit risk assessment, and user behaviour modelling.

Despite its name, logistic regression is essentially a classification procedure, not a regression approach. It is used to predict whether an observation belongs to one of two classes (binary classification). Logistic regression produces probabilities on a continuous scale between 0 to 1, which can be threshold to provide a certain class label. This makes it ideal for applications such as spam identification, medical diagnosis, and binary decision-making tasks.

3.9.1 Classification Using Logistic Regression

The logistic regression model is expressed as: 3.24

$$P(y = {}^{1}/_{x}) = \frac{1}{1 + e^{-(\beta_0+\beta_1 x_1+\beta_2 x_2+\dots+\beta_n x_n)}} \dots . 3.24$$

Here:

- $P\left(y = {}^{1}/_{X}\right)$ Represents the probability of the target variable y being 1 given the input features X.
- β_0 Is the intercept term, and $\beta_1, \beta_2, \beta_p$, are the coefficients for the features.
- $X_1, X_2, \dots$, are the independent variables (features).
- e is the base of the natural logarithm.

The decision boundary is determined by a threshold, typically 0.5. For example, if $P\left(y = {}^{1}/_{X}\right) > 0.5$, the observation is classified as belonging to class 1: otherwise it is classified as belonging to class 0.

The logistic regression model is trained by maximizing the likelihood of the observed data. This involves finding the coefficients (β) that maximize the likelihood function: eqn 3.25

$$L(B) = \prod_{1}^{n} \quad P(y|\, {}^{1}/_{x})^{y_i} (P(y|\, {}^{1}/_{x}))^{1-y_i} \dots .. 3.25$$

Likelihood is often used to simplify computation 3.26

$$\boldsymbol{LogL(B)} = \sum_{1}^{n} \left|\mathbf{ylogP}(y_i| \,^1/_x) + 1 - \mathbf{ylogP}(y_i| \,^1/_x)\right| \ldots \mathbf{3,26}$$

The coefficients are typically estimated using optimization techniques like gradient descent. Logistic regression's simplicity, interpretability, and probabilistic framework make it a popular choice for binary classification tasks.

Decision Boundary:

- Classify as positive if $P\left(y_i \mid {}^1\!/_X\right)$ > threshold (typically 0.5)
- This creates a linear decision boundary in the feature space

3.9.2 Types of Logistic Regressions

There are two types of logistic regression. They are (1) **Simple Logistic Regression** utilizes a single independent variable to predict a binary result, and (2) **Multiple Logistic Regression:** Utilizes multiple independent variables to predict a binary outcome, allowing for more complex relationships between predictors and target variables.

Multiple Logistic Regression

- Refers to logistic regression with **multiple independent variables (features/predictors)**
- Still predicts a **binary outcome** (two classes: 0/1, yes/no, etc.)
- **Example:** Predicting disease (yes/no) based on age, weight, blood pressure, and cholesterol
- It's "multiple" because of multiple input features, not multiple output classes

Multiclass Logistic Regression

- Refers to logistic regression that predicts **more than two classes** (3 or more categories)

- Can have one or multiple independent variables
- **Example:** Classifying an image as cat, dog, or bird
- Common techniques include:
    - **One-vs-Rest (OvR)** / One-vs-All
    - **Multinomial Logistic Regression** (Softmax Regression)

Key Difference

- **Multiple** = multiple **inputs** (features)
- **Multiclass** = multiple **outputs** (classes/categories)

You can also have both:

- **Multiple Multiclass Logistic Regression** = Multiple input features AND multiple output classes

So, they are different concepts! The term "multiple" refers to the number of predictors, while "multiclass" refers to the number of outcome categories.

Logistic regression is an extension of linear regression tailored for classification problems. It applies the sigmoid (logistic) function to linearly predicted values, transforming them into probabilities within the range of 0 and 1. A threshold value, typically 0.5, is then used to classify the predictions into binary outcomes. Figure 3.8 contrasts the key difference between linear and logistic regression for binary classification. While linear regression can produce predictions beyond the range of 0 and 1, logistic regression uses the sigmoid function to constrain predictions within this range, making it more suitable for classifying binary outcomes with a threshold, typically set at 0.5.

Logistic regression models the relationship between independent variables (X) and the probability of an outcome (P) using the logistic (or sigmoid) function. The logistic function converts any real-valued input into a value between 0 and 1, guaranteeing that expected probability are correct.

Figure 3.9 depicts the sigmoid function used in logistic regression, showing how it maps input values to probabilities between 0 and 1. The decision boundary at x=0 and the classification threshold at P=0.5 highlight the separation of binary classes.

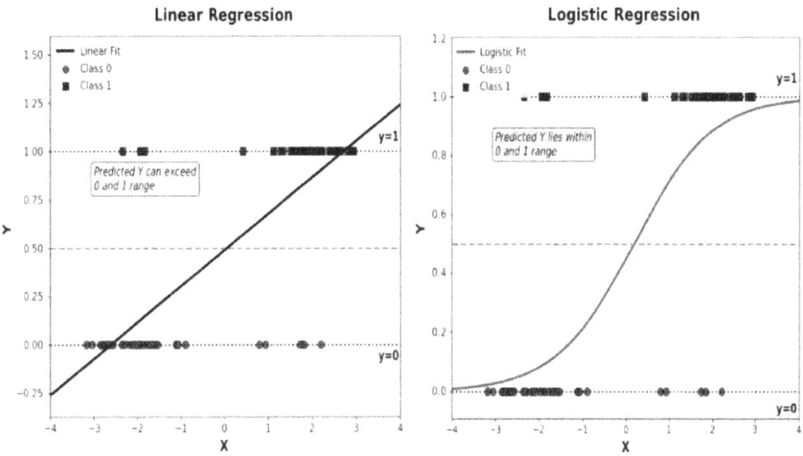

Figure 3.9 Comparison of Linear Regression and Logistic Regression for Binary Classification

Figure 3.10 illustrates how the logistic (sigmoid) function maps input values into probabilities between 0 and 1. The decision boundary is shown where the probability equals 0.5, separating data into two classes.

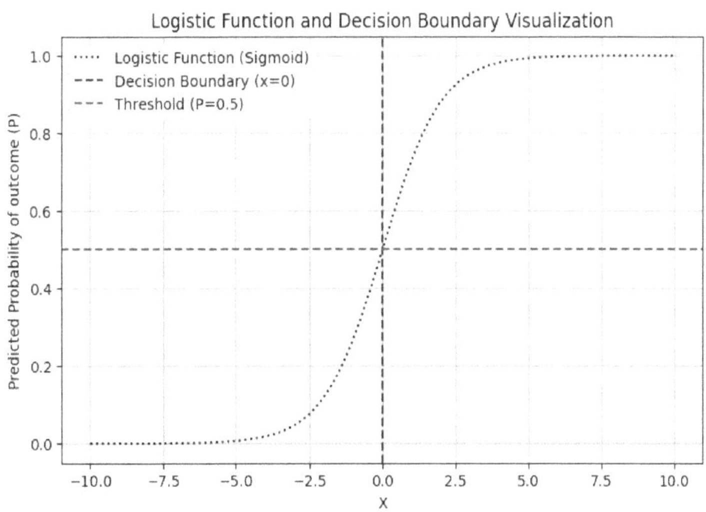

Figure 3.10 Logistic Function and Decision Boundary Visualization

3.9.3 Performance Evaluation Metrics

Proper evaluation of logistic regression models requires metrics that provide deeper insights into the model's performance beyond simple accuracy. These metrics assess the balance between true positives, false positives, and false negatives, helping to evaluate the model's effectiveness in various classification scenarios. The following are commonly used evaluation metrics in logistic regression:

3.10 Common Evaluation Metrics

1. **Accuracy:**

$$Accurac = \mathbf{TP \div FP + TN + FP + FN \ldots .3.27}$$

2. **Precision:**

$$Precision = \mathbf{TP \div TP + FP \ldots .3.28}$$

3. **Recall (Sensitivity):**

$$Recall = \mathbf{TP \div TP + FN \ldots .3.29}$$

4. **F1-Score:**

$$F1\ score = \mathbf{2XPrecision \div Precision + Recall \ldots .3.30}$$

AUC-ROC: Area under the Receiver Operating Characteristic curve

5. **Log loss (Binary Entropy:** Log loss measures the uncertainty of probability predictions, while AUC–ROC evaluates the model's discriminative ability independent of classification threshold.

$$\mathbf{LogLoss} = -\frac{\mathbf{1}}{\mathbf{n}}\sum_{1}^{n} |y_i\mathbf{log(p_1)} + (1 - y_i)\mathbf{log((1 - (p_1)} | \ldots .3.31$$

These metrics collectively provide a comprehensive assessment of logistic regression model performance, guiding improvements and comparisons across models.

Threshold Selection:

- Different thresholds prioritize precision vs. recall
- ROC curve and precision-recall curve help visualize tradeoffs
- Domain-specific considerations guide threshold selection

Table 3.3 outlines the strengths, limitations, and ideal use cases of various evaluation metrics for logistic regression. It provides guidance on selecting the most appropriate metric based on the problem context and data characteristics.

Table 3.3 Advantages and Disadvantages of Different Evaluation Metrics

Metric	Advantages	Disadvantages	Best Used When
Accuracy	Simple, intuitive	Misleading with imbalanced data	Classes are balanced
Precision	Focuses on false positive rate	Ignores false negatives	False positives are costly
Recall	Focuses on false negative rate	Ignores false positives	False negatives are costly
F1-Score	Balances precision and recall	Still affected by class distribution	Need balance between precision/recall
AUC-ROC	Threshold-independent	Less intuitive	Need probability estimates
Log Loss	Sensitive to probability calibration	Hard to interpret directly	Well-calibrated probabilities matter
MAE	Less sensitive to outliers	May underestimate error impact	Outliers should have less weight
RMSE	Penalizes large errors	Sensitive to outliers	Large errors should be penalized more

Regression predicts numerical outcomes, like prices or yields, while classification assigns inputs to predefined categories, such as spam or not-spam. Their differences are evident in output type, evaluation metrics, and the loss functions used during training. Table 3.4 Illustrates the key aspects of regression and classification

Table 3.4 Aspects of Regression and Classification

Aspect	Regression	Classification
Output Type	Continuous values	Discrete categories
Loss Function	Typically squared error	Log loss, 0-1 loss, etc.
Evaluation Metrics	RMSE, MAE, R^2	Accuracy, F1-score, AUC
Example Applications	Price prediction, yield forecasting	Spam detection, disease diagnosis

Table 3.5 compares different regression techniques based on their computational requirements, highlighting variations in complexity and resource usage.

Table 3.5 Comparison of Computational Requirements Between Regression Techniques

Technique	Training Complexity	Prediction Complexity	Memory Requirements	Scalability to Large Datasets	Real-time Applicability
Linear Regression	$O(nd^2)$	O(d)	O(d)	Good	Excellent
Polynomial Regression	$O(nd^2)$	O(d)	O(d)	Good	Excellent
k-NN Regression	O(1)*	O(nd + n log n)	O(nd)	Poor	Poor
Locally Weighted Regression	O(1)*	$O(nd^2 + nd)$	O(nd)	Poor	Poor
Decision Tree Regression	O(nd log n)	O(log n)	O(nodes)	Moderate	Good

3.10.1 Confusion Matrix Components

- **True Positives (TP):** Correctly predicted positive cases
- **True Negatives (TN):** Correctly predicted negative cases
- **False Positives (FP):** Incorrectly predicted positive cases
- **False Negatives (FN):** Incorrectly predicted negative cases

3.11 Decision Tree Learning

Decision tree learning is a powerful yet straightforward and intuitive machine learning technique that can be applied to both classification and regression tasks. This works by recursively partitioning the feature space into regions based on feature values, leading to a tree-like structure in which each internal node represents a feature-based decision, each branch represents the outcome of that decision, and each leaf node corresponds to a final output (such as a class label for classification or a numerical value for regression). The procedure starts at the root node, where the algorithm chooses a feature and a threshold to separate/splits the data into subsets, with the goal of maximizing the homogeneity of the groups. This homogeneity is frequently quantified in classification using metrics such as Gini impurity or entropy, whereas in regression, variance reduction is commonly utilized. The recursive splitting process continues until a stopping requirement is satisfied, such as a maximum tree depth or a minimum number of samples per node, resulting in an easy-to-understand and visualize model.

A decision tree is built by picking the optimum feature and threshold at each node in order to optimize a specific criterion. For instance, in classification, the algorithm may use the Gini impurity, which assesses the likelihood of incorrectly classifying a randomly selected element in a node and prioritize splits that lower this impurity. In regression, the goal is to minimize the variance in the target variable within each node. CART (Classification and Regression Trees) algorithms are frequently employed to construct decision trees by greedily selecting the split that maximizes the improvement in the specified metric. However, this greediness can result in overfitting, in which the tree grows excessively complex and gathering noise in the training data. To address this, approaches such as pruning (removing branches with minimal predictive significance/power) and constraint setting (for example, minimum samples per leaf) are used to balance model complexity with generalization.

Decision trees have various advantages, including interpretability and the ability to handle both numerical and categorical data with minimal pre-processing. They are capable of modelling nonlinear interactions and are robust to irrelevant features because the algorithm automatically selects the most informative ones. However, they are sensitive to slight changes in the data, which can result in completely different trees, and they may struggle with imbalanced datasets or tasks that need smooth predictions, such as regression over continuous surfaces. Ensemble approaches, such as Random Forests or Gradient Boosting, frequently use decision trees to improve robustness and accuracy by integrating several trees and reducing variance or bias. These attributes make decision trees an essential tool in machine learning, with applications ranging from medical diagnosis to forecasting finances.

Despite its advantages, decision trees have limitations that must be overcome in reality. Their tendency to overfit is accentuated with high-dimensional datasets, where the tree can grow overly complex in order to catch false patterns. Furthermore, decision trees may be biased toward features with multiple categories, which generate more potential splits. Methods such as feature significance analysis, which is based on the decrease of impurity or variation across splits, aid in determining which features drive the model's decisions. By recognizing these trade-offs and combining decision trees with ensemble approaches or careful tuning, practitioners can take utilize of their intuitive structure to achieve robust and effective predictive modelling.

3.11.1 Introduction to Decision Tree Models

A decision tree is a hierarchical model that makes decisions by following conditions from the root to the leaves:

Key Components:

- **Root node:** The starting point of the tree
- **Internal nodes:** Represent tests on attributes

- **Branches:** Outcomes of the tests
- **Leaf nodes:** Final predictions (class labels or values)

Advantages of Decision Trees:

- Easy to understand and interpret
- Require minimal data pre-processing
- Handle both numerical and categorical features
- Implicitly perform feature selection
- Model non-linear relationships
- No assumptions about data distribution

Limitations:

- Prone to overfitting, especially with deep trees
- Can be unstable (small data changes may result in different trees)
- May create biased trees if classes are imbalanced

Limited in expressing certain relationships (e.g., XOR problems) Figure 3.11 illustrates how the maximum depth parameter affects decision tree complexity and performance. It shows that as depth increases, trees grow more complex with more nodes and leaves, leading to higher training accuracy but potentially worse test accuracy due to overfitting.

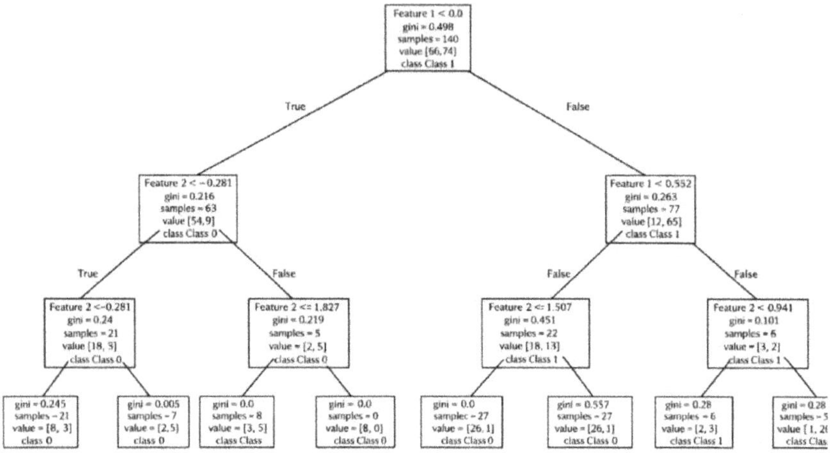

Figure 3.11 Example Decision Tree for a Classification Problem

3.11.2 Decision Tree Induction Algorithms

Several algorithms exist for constructing decision trees from data:

CART (Classification and Regression Trees):

- Binary splits at each node
- Gini impurity or MSE as splitting criteria
- Supports both classification and regression

ID3 (Iterative Dichotomiser 3):

- Information gain as splitting criterion
- Handles categorical features naturally
- Only for classification problems

C4.5 (Successor to ID3):

- Uses information gain ratio to address bias toward features with many values
- Handles both continuous and discrete attributes
- Pruning to reduce overfitting

Common Splitting Criteria:

1. **Gini Impurity:**

$$\boldsymbol{Gini\ Impurity} = \mathbf{1} - \ \textstyle\sum_{-=1}^{nc} \boldsymbol{p_i^2})\ldots\ldots\ldots\mathbf{3.31}(\boldsymbol{a})$$

Where C is the number of classes and p is the proportion of elements belonging to class i

2. **Information Gain:**

$$\boldsymbol{Information\ gain} =$$
$$\boldsymbol{H}(\boldsymbol{Parent}) \textstyle\sum_{i=1}^{m} \frac{\boldsymbol{nj}}{\boldsymbol{n}}\ \boldsymbol{H}(\boldsymbol{Child_j})\ldots\ldots\ldots\mathbf{3.31(b)}$$

- **H(parent):** Entropy of the parent node.
- **H(child$_j$):** Entropy of the j-th child node.
- **n:** Total number of samples in the parent node.
- **n$_j$:** Number of samples in the jth child node.
- **m:** Total number of child nodes.

3. **Variance Reduction:**

$$\boldsymbol{Variance\ reduction}$$
$$= \boldsymbol{var}(\boldsymbol{parent})$$
$$- \sum_{i=1}^{m} \frac{\boldsymbol{nj}}{\boldsymbol{n}}\ \boldsymbol{variance}(\boldsymbol{Child_j})\ldots\ldots\ldots\mathbf{3.31}(\boldsymbol{c})$$

Where

- **var(parent):** variance of the parent node.
- **var(child$_j$):** variance of the j-th child node.
- **n:** Total number of samples in the parent node.
- **n$_j$:** Number of samples in the jth child node.
- **m:** Total number of child nodes.

Pruning techniques:

- **Pre-pruning:** Early stopping during tree construction
- **Post-pruning:** Building the full tree then removing nodes
- **Cost-complexity pruning:** Trading off tree size and accuracy

Pseudocode for basic decision tree induction:

```
function BuildTree(data, features):
  if stopping_condition(data) is True:
    return create_leaf_node(data)
  best_feature = find_best_split(data, features)
  tree = create_node(best_feature)
  for each value v of best_feature:
    subset = data where best_feature = v
    subtree = BuildTree(subset, features - {best_feature})
    add subtree as child of tree with branch v
  return tree
```

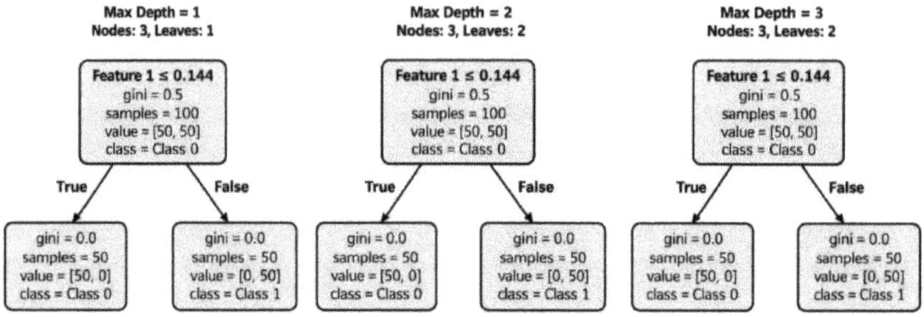

(a)

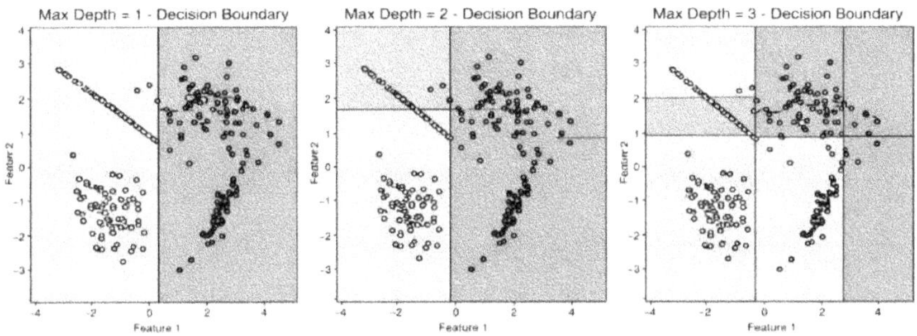
Max Depth = 1 - Decision Boundary
Max Depth = 2 - Decision Boundary
Max Depth = 3 - Decision Boundary
Feature 1
Feature 2

(b)

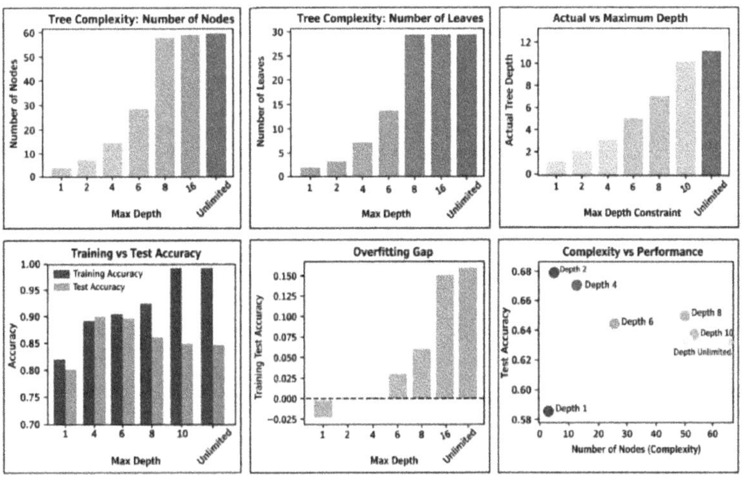
Tree Complexity: Number of Nodes
Number of Nodes
Max Depth
Tree Complexity: Number of Leaves
Number of Leaves
Max Depth
Actual vs Maximum Depth
Actual Tree Depth
Max Depth Constraint
Training vs Test Accuracy
Training Accuracy
Test Accuracy
Accuracy
Max Depth
Overfitting Gap
Training Test Accuracy
Max Depth
Complexity vs Performance
Depth 1
Depth 2
Depth 4
Depth 6
Depth 8
Depth 10
Depth Unlimited
Test Accuracy
Number of Nodes (Complexity)

(c)

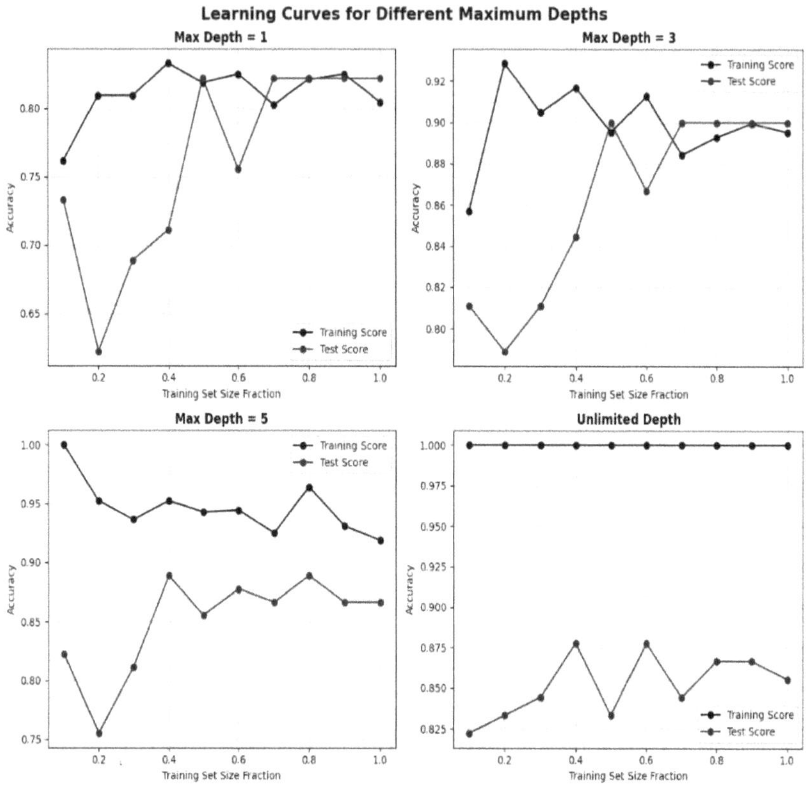

(d)

Figure 3.12 Effect of Maximum Depth Constraint on Decision Tree Complexity

Key Observations from Figure 3.12

Complexity Growth: As maximum depth increases, the number of nodes and leaves increases exponentially, indicating greater model complexity, as shown in the tree structures and decision boundaries, figure 3.12 (a). Optimal Depth: The optimal maximum depth balances complexity and generalization, typically around 2–5 for this dataset, where test accuracy is high and overfitting is minimal.

Training Accuracy: Deeper trees provide higher training accuracy, often reaching 100% for unlimited depth, since they fit the training data more precisely, including noise. Figure 3.12 (b).

Test Accuracy and Overfitting: Test accuracy peaks at moderate depths (e.g., 2 or 3, with 0.900 accuracy) and decreases for deeper trees (e.g., 0.856 at unlimited), indicating overfitting, as measured by the growing overfitting gap (e.g., 0.144 at unlimited) figure 3.12 (c).

Learning Curves: The separate learning curves illustration indicates that shallower trees (e.g., depth 1) perform consistently with less data, whereas deeper trees require more data to avoid overfitting, emphasizing the importance of having enough data with complicated models. figure 3.12 (d)

Chapter 3: Summary

Chapter 3 introduces two important families of machine learning techniques: **Similarity-based learning** and **Regression analysis**. These approaches form the foundation for many predictive models used in real-world applications such as recommendation systems, pattern recognition, forecasting, and classification.

The first part of the chapter focuses on **Similarity-based (Instance-based) Learning**, where learning is performed by comparing new data points with stored training examples. Unlike model-based learning, these methods do not build an explicit global model; instead, they rely on distance or similarity measures. Techniques such as **Nearest-Neighbour Learning** and **K-Nearest-Neighbour (K-NN)** classify or predict outcomes based on the closest examples in the feature space. The **Weighted K-Nearest-Neighbour algorithm** improves basic K-NN by assigning higher influence to nearer neighbours, enhancing prediction accuracy. The **Nearest Centroid Classifier** simplifies classification by representing each class through its centroid, making it computationally efficient. **Locally Weighted Regression (LWR)** extends the idea of locality to regression problems by fitting local models around query points, allowing flexible approximation of complex functions.

The second part of the chapter introduces **Regression Analysis**, which is used to model relationships between dependent and independent variables. The chapter begins by explaining the concepts of **linearity**, **correlation**, and **causation**, emphasizing that correlation does not necessarily imply causation. **Linear Regression** is presented as the simplest and most widely used regression technique for continuous output prediction. The importance of **validation of regression methods** is discussed using techniques such as residual analysis and error metrics. The chapter further explores **Multiple Linear Regression**, which handles multiple input variables, and **Polynomial Regression**, which models non-linear relationships. Finally, **Logistic Regression** is introduced as a classification method that predicts probabilities and is widely used in binary classification problems.

Overall, the chapter highlights how similarity-based methods rely on data proximity, while regression methods focus on learning mathematical relationships from data.

Chapter 3: Conclusion

This chapter establishes essential learning paradigms that bridge intuitive reasoning and mathematical Modelling. **Similarity-based learning methods** demonstrate how intelligent systems can make predictions by recalling and comparing past experiences, making them simple yet powerful tools for many applications. Their performance, however, depends heavily on distance measures, feature scaling, and data quality.

Regression techniques, on the other hand, provide a structured approach to understanding and predicting relationships between variables. Linear and multiple regression models offer interpretability, while polynomial regression adds flexibility for non-linear patterns. Logistic regression plays a critical role in classification tasks by combining statistical rigor with probabilistic interpretation.

Together, these methods form a strong foundation for advanced machine learning topics. Understanding their assumptions, strengths, and limitations enables students to select appropriate techniques for real-world problems and prepares them for more complex models introduced in later chapters.

Chapter 3: Review Questions

Short Answer Questions

1. What is similarity-based or instance-based learning?
2. How does Nearest-Neighbour Learning differ from model-based learning?
3. Why is feature scaling important in K-Nearest-Neighbour algorithms?
4. What is the purpose of assigning weights in Weighted K-NN?
5. Define a centroid in the context of the Nearest Centroid Classifier.
6. What is Locally Weighted Regression (LWR)?
7. What is the difference between correlation and causation?
8. Define linear regression.
9. What is meant by validation of regression models?
10. What type of problems is logistic regression used for?

Descriptive Questions

1. Explain the working of the K-Nearest-Neighbour algorithm with an example.
2. Discuss the advantages and limitations of similarity-based learning methods.
3. Describe the Nearest Centroid Classifier and its applications.
4. Explain Locally Weighted Regression and how it differs from global regression models.
5. Discuss the assumptions of linear regression.
6. Explain Multiple Linear Regression with a suitable example.

7. Describe Polynomial Regression and justify when it should be used.
8. Explain Logistic Regression and its role in classification problems.

Application-Oriented Questions

1. Compare K-NN and Linear Regression in terms of learning approach and computational cost.
2. How does Weighted K-NN improve prediction accuracy over basic K-NN?
3. Explain how regression models can be validated using error metrics.
4. Identify real-world applications of similarity-based learning.
5. Discuss scenarios where logistic regression is preferred over linear regression.

Chapter - 4

Probabilistic Models and Neural Networks

Chapter Overview

This chapter introduces two fundamental and widely used machine learning paradigms: **Decision Tree–based models** and **Bayesian learning approaches**. These models are valued for their interpretability, solid mathematical foundations, and effectiveness in solving real-world **classification and regression** problems across domains such as healthcare, finance, and text analytics.

The chapter begins with **Decision Trees**, explaining their structure and working principle for classification tasks. Decision trees represent decision-making using a hierarchical tree structure in which **internal nodes denote attribute tests, branches denote outcomes of tests, and leaf nodes denote final predictions or class labels**. Their transparency and visual clarity make them especially useful in domains that demand explainable AI and human-understandable logic.

Next, the chapter discusses **impurity measures** used in decision tree construction, including **Entropy, Information Gain, Gini Index, and Misclassification Error**. These measures guide optimal feature selection at each split, enabling effective data partitioning and improved predictive accuracy. The **properties of Decision Tree Classifiers (DTC)** are examined, highlighting advantages such as interpretability, minimal preprocessing, and flexibility, along with limitations like **overfitting and sensitivity to noisy data**.

The practical relevance of decision trees is demonstrated through an **application in breast cancer data analysis**, where models assist in distinguishing benign and malignant tumors based on clinical features. The chapter further extends tree-based learning to **regression problems**, introducing **Decision Tree Regression**, where outputs are continuous values and splits are chosen to minimize prediction error or variance.

In the latter part, **Bayesian Learning** is introduced as a **probability-driven framework** for reasoning under uncertainty. The fundamentals of **Bayes' Theorem** are explained, illustrating how prior knowledge is updated with observed evidence to compute posterior probabilities. The discussion then moves to **classification using Bayesian models**, focusing on the **Naïve Bayes classifier**. In addition, the chapter covers **Naïve Bayes for Continuous Attributes**, where numerical features are modeled using the **Gaussian (Normal) Probability Distribution**, enabling efficient handling of real-valued datasets such as medical measurements and financial indicators.

Overall, this chapter equips learners with essential knowledge of **tree-based and probabilistic learning techniques**, forming a strong conceptual foundation for advanced ensemble methods and probabilistic inference models in machine learning.

4.1 Introduction to Decision Tree

A **Decision Tree** is a supervised learning model that represents decision-making logic in the form of a hierarchical tree structure. It is used for both **classification** and **regression** tasks and works by recursively partitioning the input data based on selected features. Each partition aims to increase the homogeneity of the resulting subsets with respect to the target variable.

A decision tree mimics human decision-making by asking a sequence of questions. Starting from the root node, the data is split into branches based on attribute tests, and this process continues until a terminal condition is reached. The final outcome is represented at the leaf nodes.

Structure of a Decision Tree

A typical decision tree consists of the following elements:

- **Root Node**: Represents the entire dataset and the first splitting criterion
- **Decision (Internal) Nodes**: Represent tests on attributes
- **Branches**: Represent outcomes of the tests
- **Leaf Nodes**: Represent final predictions (class labels or values)

Figure 4.1 presents a general structure of a decision

Advantages of decision trees:

- Easy to understand and interpret
- Require minimal data pre-processing
- Handle both numerical and categorical features

- Implicitly perform feature selection
- Model non-linear relationships
- No assumptions about data distribution

Limitations:

- Prone to overfitting, especially with deep trees
- Can be unstable (small data changes may result in different trees)
- May create biased trees if classes are imbalanced
- Limited in expressing certain relationships (e.g., XOR problems)

Figure 4.1 illustrates the hierarchical structure of a decision tree, showing how decisions flow from the root node to leaf nodes through internal decision nodes.

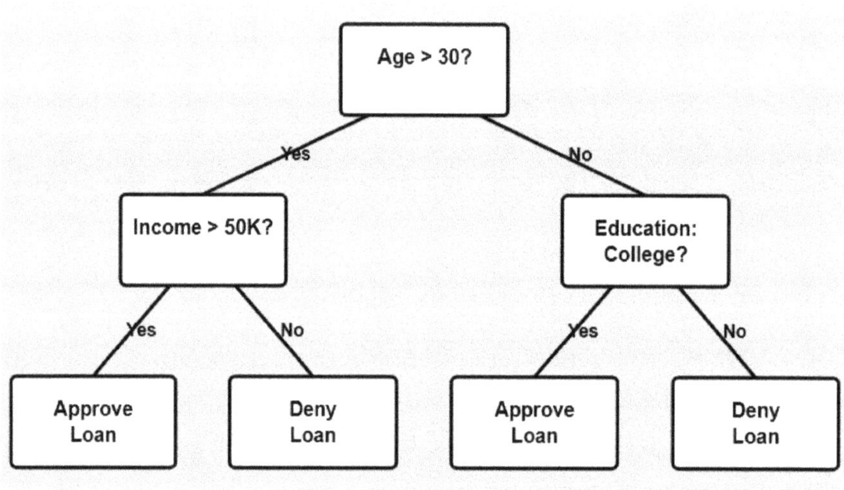

Figure 4.1 Decision Tree Structure for Binary Classification

Decision trees select the best attribute for splitting using **impurity measures** such as entropy, information gain, or Gini index. The process continues recursively until all data points belong to the same class or a predefined stopping condition is met.

Decision trees are widely preferred due to their **simplicity**, **interpretability**, and **ability to handle mixed data types**. However, unrestricted tree growth may lead to **overfitting**, which can be controlled using pruning techniques or depth limitations. Table 4.1 lists the major components of a decision tree along with their descriptions.

Table 4.1 Components of a Decision Tree

Component	Description
Root Node	Represents the complete dataset and initial decision
Internal Node	Performs a test on an attribute
Branch	Outcome of a decision or test
Leaf Node	Final output (class label or value)
Tree Depth	Length of the longest path from root to leaf

4.1.1 Decision Tree for Classification

A Decision Tree for Classification is used when the target variable is categorical. The primary objective is to classify input instances into one of the predefined classes by following a series of attribute-based decisions.

At each internal node, the algorithm selects the attribute that best separates the data into different classes. This selection is guided by **impurity measures**, which quantify the degree of class mixing at a node. The attribute that produces the highest reduction in impurity is chosen for splitting. Figure 4.2: Decision Tree for Classification (Example)**.** Binary decision tree for tumor classification using tumor size and texture attributes to predict benign or malignant outcomes.

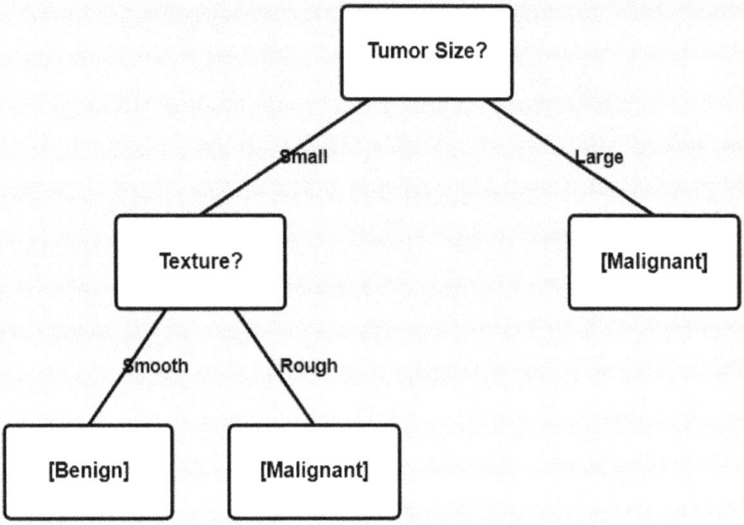

Figure 4.2 Decision Tree for Classification (Example)

Classification Process

1. Training data with known class labels is provided.
2. The best splitting attribute is selected using an impurity measure.
3. The dataset is split into subsets based on attribute values.
4. Steps 2 and 3 are repeated recursively.
5. Leaf nodes assign a final class label.

During prediction, a new instance traverses the tree from the root to a leaf node, following the outcomes of attribute tests, and the class label at the leaf node is assigned. Table 4.2 summarizes commonly used decision tree classification algorithms and their key characteristics.

Table 4.2 Common Decision Tree Classification Algorithms

Algorithm	Splitting Criterion	Handles Continuous Data	Pruning
ID3	Information Gain	No	No
C4.5	Gain Ratio	Yes	Yes
CART	Gini Index	Yes	Yes

Decision tree classifiers are extensively used in medical diagnosis, credit scoring, fault detection, and customer behaviour analysis because they provide transparent decision rules that are easy to interpret. However, they may become unstable when trained on noisy or small datasets.

4.2 Impurity Measures for Decision Tree Construction

In decision tree learning, the quality of a split at any node is evaluated using **impurity measures**. An impurity measure quantifies how mixed or heterogeneous the class labels are within a node. The objective of decision tree construction is to **reduce impurity** at each split, thereby increasing the homogeneity of the resulting child nodes.

At each internal node, the algorithm evaluates all possible splits using a chosen impurity measure and selects the attribute that produces the **maximum reduction in impurity**. This reduction is commonly referred to as **information gain** or **impurity reduction**, depending on the measure used.

The most commonly used impurity measures are:

- **Entropy**
- **Information Gain**
- **Gini Index**
- **Misclassification Error**

4.2.1 Entropy

Entropy is a measure of randomness or uncertainty in a dataset. It originates from information theory and is widely used in decision tree algorithms such as **ID3**.

For a dataset containing nnn classes, entropy is defined as:

$$\boldsymbol{Entropy}\ (\boldsymbol{S}) = -\sum_{1}^{n} \ \boldsymbol{p_i Log_2 p_i} \ldots\ldots\ldots \mathbf{4.1}$$

Where p_i is the probability of class i in dataset S.

- Entropy is **0** when all instances belong to a single class (pure node).
- Entropy is **maximum** when instances are evenly distributed across classes

Figure 4.3 illustrates how entropy varies with class distribution. Entropy is minimum when a node is completely pure and maximum when classes are equally mixed.

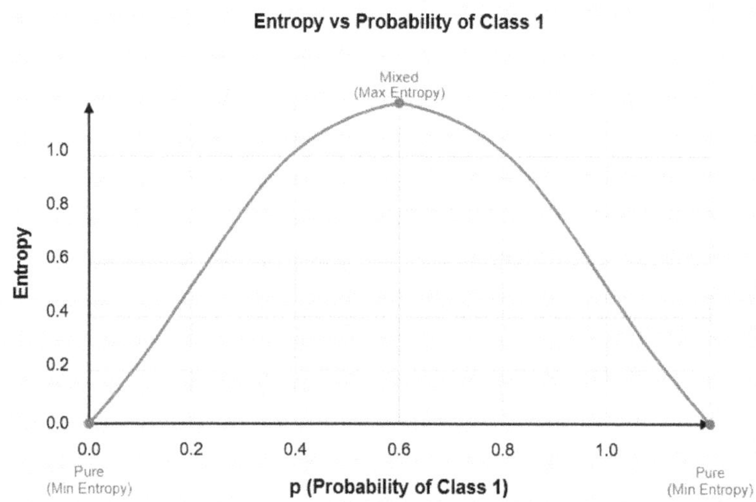

Figure 4.3 Illustrates How Entropy Varies with Class Distribution

4.2.2 Information Gain

Information Gain (IG) measures the reduction in entropy achieved after splitting a dataset on an attribute. It determines how well an attribute separates the training examples according to their target classification.

$$\boldsymbol{InformationGain(S, A) = Entropy(S) - \sum_{v \in values(A)} \frac{|s_v|}{|S|} Entropy\,(S_v) \ldots\ldots 4.2}$$

where:

- A is the attribute used for splitting
- S_v is the subset of S for which attribute A has value v

The attribute with the **highest information gain** is selected for splitting.

4.2.3 Gini Index

The **Gini Index** measures the probability of incorrectly classifying a randomly chosen instance if it were labelled according to the class distribution of the node. It is used primarily in the **CART** algorithm.

$$Gini(S) = 1 - \sum_{1}^{n} p_2^i \ldots\ldots\ldots\ldots 4.3$$

- A Gini Index of **0** indicates a pure node.
- Higher values indicate greater impurity.

Compared to entropy, the Gini Index is computationally simpler and often preferred in practice.

4.2.4 Misclassification Error

Misclassification Error measures the fraction of instances that do not belong to the majority class in a node.

Misclassification Error(S) =1-maxp_i 4.4

Although simple to compute, misclassification error is **less sensitive to changes in class distribution** and is therefore less commonly used for decision tree construction.

Although simple to compute, misclassification error is **less sensitive to changes in class distribution** and is therefore less commonly used for decision tree construction. Table 4.3 presents the impurity measures used in Decision Tree construction.

Table 4.3: Impurity Measures Used in Decision Tree Construction

Impurity Measure	Formula	Range	Interpretation
Entropy	Refer to equation 4,1	0 to 1	Measures uncertainty
Gini Index	Refer to equation 4,2	0 to 0.5 (binary)	Measures class mixing
Misclassification Error	Refer to equation 4,3	0 to 0.5 (binary)	Measures incorrect classification

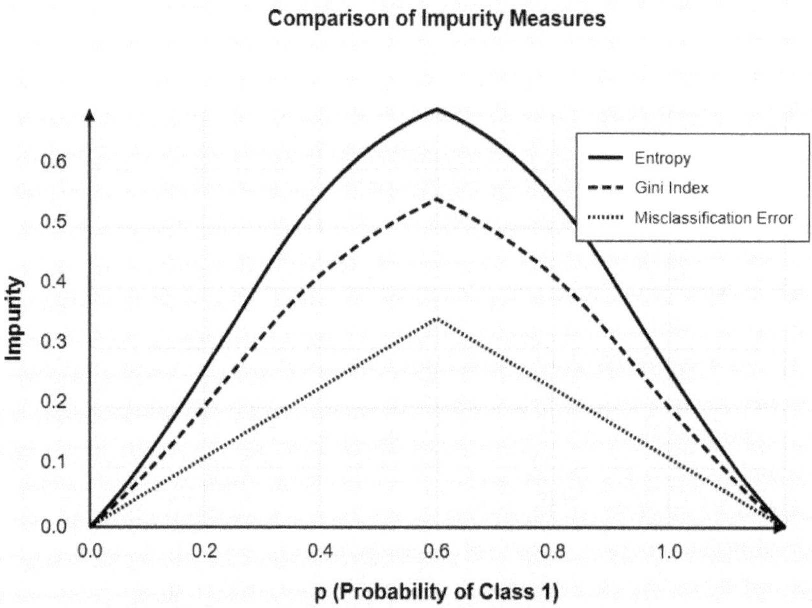

Figure 4.4 Comparison of Impurity Measures

Figure 4.4 compares entropy, Gini index, and misclassification error for different class distributions. Entropy and Gini index are more sensitive to changes in class proportions than misclassification error. Table 4.4 compares the impurity measures.

Table 4.4 Comparison of Impurity Measures

Criterion	Entropy	Gini Index	Misclassification Error
Sensitivity	High	High	Low
Computational Cost	High	Medium	Low
Used in Algorithm	ID3, C4.5	CART	Rarely used
Practical Effectiveness	Very High	High	Moderate

4.2.4 Selection of Impurity Measures

The choice of impurity measure affects the structure and performance of the decision tree. While entropy and information gain provide a strong theoretical foundation, the Gini index is often preferred due to its computational efficiency. In practice, entropy and Gini index usually produce similar trees. The role of impurity measures in tree selection is presented in figure 4,5.

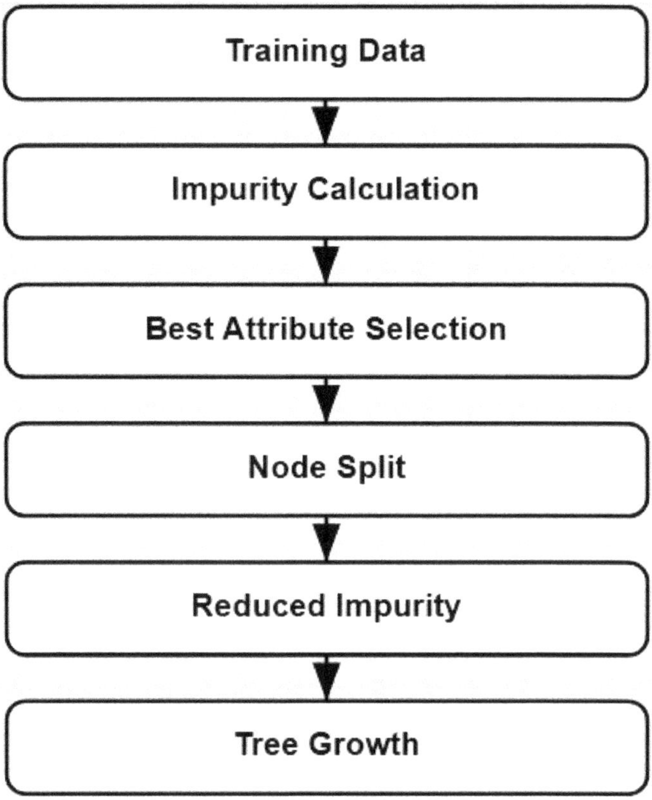

Figure 4.5 Role of Impurity Measures in Tree Construction

4.3 Properties of Decision Tree Classifier (DTC)

A **Decision Tree Classifier (DTC)** is a supervised learning model that predicts categorical class labels by recursively partitioning the feature space. Due to its rule-based structure, the DTC is widely used in domains where **model interpretability** is as important as predictive accuracy.

4.3.1 Key Properties of DTC

1. **Interpretability and Transparency**

   Decision trees provide explicit decision rules in the form of if–then conditions, making them easy to understand and explain.

2. **Non-parametric Nature**

   DTCs do not assume any prior distribution of the data, making them flexible for complex, non-linear relationships.

3. **Handling of Mixed Data Types**

   Decision trees can work with both **categorical** and **numerical** attributes without extensive preprocessing.

4. **Minimal Data Preparation**

   Scaling and normalization of data are generally not required.

5. **Recursive Partitioning**

   The model is built using a top-down, greedy approach, selecting the best split at each node.

6. **Sensitivity to Overfitting**

   Deep trees may overfit training data; pruning is often required to improve generalization.

In table 4.5 properties of decision tree classifier are presented. Figure 4.6 illustrates how a decision tree classifier processes input features through successive decision nodes to arrive at a final class label.

Table 4.5 Properties of Decision Tree Classifier

Property	Description
Interpretability	Easy to understand decision rules
Model Type	Non-parametric
Data Handling	Supports numerical and categorical features
Preprocessing	Minimal
Overfitting Risk	High for deep trees
Stability	Sensitive to small data changes

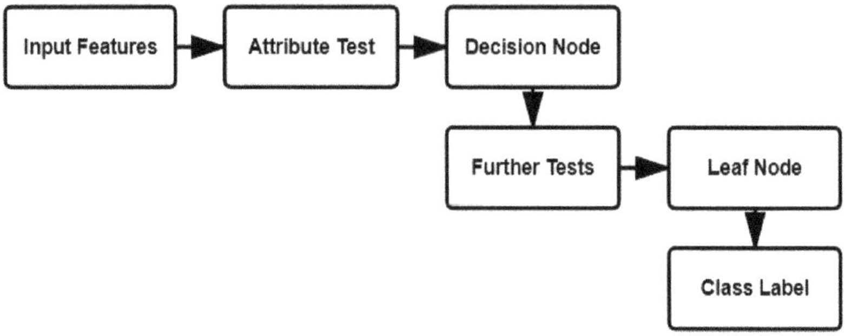

Figure 4.6 General Decision-Making Process of a Decision Tree Classifier

4.3.2 Applications in Breast Cancer Data

Decision Tree Classifiers are widely used in medical diagnosis, particularly in **breast cancer detection**, where interpretability is crucial for clinical decision-making.

Problem Description

The objective is to classify tumours as **benign** or **malignant** based on clinical attributes such as:

- Tumour radius
- Texture
- Smoothness
- Compactness
- Concavity

Using these features, a decision tree learns classification rules that can assist doctors in diagnosis.

Example: Breast Cancer Classification

A simplified decision rule learned by a decision tree may be:

- If **tumour radius ≤ threshold** and **texture is smooth**, then Benign
- Else if **tumour radius > threshold**, then **Malignant**

Table 4.6 Sample Features Used in Breast Cancer Classification

Feature	**Description**
Radius	Mean distance from center to tumor boundary
Texture	Variation in gray-scale values
Smoothness	Local variation in radius lengths
Compactness	Measure of tumor density
Diagnosis	Benign / Malignant

Figure 4.7 presents a decision tree that classifies breast cancer cases into categories (e.g., benign or malignant) based on input features. Each node represents a feature-based decision, and the final leaf nodes indicate the predicted class outcome.

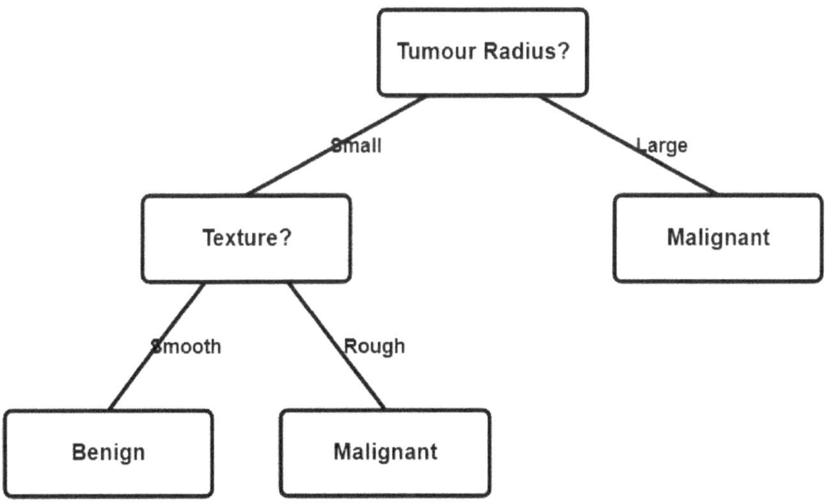

Figure 4.7 Decision Tree for Breast Cancer Classification (Conceptual)

4.4 Regression Based on Decision Tree

While decision trees are commonly associated with classification, they can also be used for **regression problems**, where the target variable is **continuous**. Such models are known as **Decision Tree Regressors**.

In decision tree regression, each leaf node represents a numerical value, typically the **mean of target values** of the training samples reaching that node.

4.4.1 Working Principle of Decision Tree Regression

- The dataset is recursively split based on feature values.
- The splitting criterion minimizes **variance**, **mean squared error (MSE)**, or **mean absolute error (MAE)**.
- Predictions are continuous values instead of class labels.

Figure 4.8 shows how a decision tree regression model splits the data into regions based on feature values. Each leaf node represents a predicted continuous value, typically the average of the target values in that region.Table 4.7 compares Classification and Regression Decision Trees.

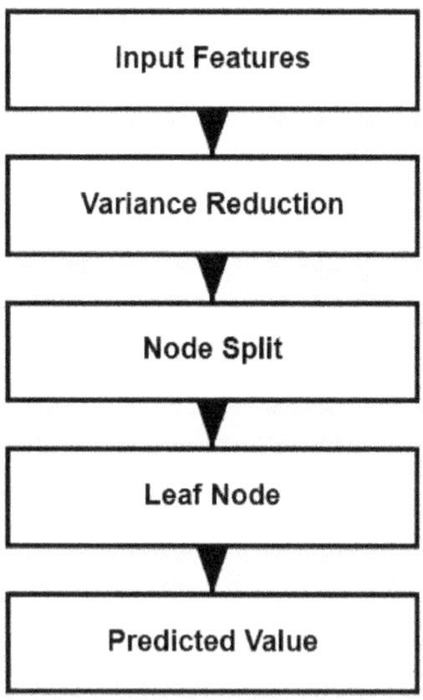

Figure 4.8 Decision Tree Regression Model Structure

Table 4.7 Comparison of Classification and Regression Decision Trees

Aspect	Classification Tree	Regression Tree
Output	Discrete class labels	Continuous values
Splitting Criterion	Entropy, Gini Index	Variance, MSE
Leaf Node	Class label	Numerical value
Typical Applications	Disease diagnosis	Price prediction

4.4.2 Advantages and Limitations of Decision Tree Regression

Decision Tree Regression offers several advantages, including easy interpretability, the ability to model non-linear relationships, and minimal data preprocessing requirements such as feature scaling or normalization. It can naturally handle interactions between variables and is robust to outliers in the input space. However, decision tree regressors suffer from notable limitations, most importantly their tendency to overfit the training data, especially when the tree grows deep. Small variations in the data can lead to significantly different tree structures, making the model unstable. Additionally, decision trees often provide piecewise constant predictions, which may result in poor generalization and reduced predictive smoothness compared to ensemble-based regression methods.Table 4.8 list the advantages and disadvantages.

Table 4.8 Advantages and Limitations of Decision Tree Regression

Advantages	Limitations
Handles non-linear data	Prone to overfitting
No data scaling required	High variance
Interpretable model	Poor extrapolation
Flexible feature selection	Sensitive to noise

4.4.3 Summary of Properties of Decision Tree Classifier (DTC) and Regression Based Decision Tree

Decision Tree Classifiers offer transparent and intuitive decision-making capabilities, making them suitable for sensitive domains such as medical diagnosis. Their application to breast cancer data demonstrates how interpretable machine learning models can support healthcare decisions. Decision Tree Regression extends tree-based learning to continuous prediction tasks, offering flexibility and interpretability, though care must be taken to control overfitting.

4.5 Bayesian Learning

Bayesian Learning is a probabilistic approach to machine learning in which uncertainty is explicitly represented and managed using the principles of probability theory. Instead of making decisions based solely on observed data, Bayesian methods combine prior knowledge with evidence from data to update beliefs about model parameters or class memberships. This learning paradigm is especially useful in situations involving noisy data, limited training samples, or incomplete information. By relying on Bayes' theorem, Bayesian learning provides a mathematically sound framework for reasoning under uncertainty and forms the basis for several widely used classification algorithms such as the Naïve Bayes classifier.

4.5.1 Introduction to Probability-based Learning

Probability-based learning refers to a class of learning methods in which predictions are made by estimating the likelihood of outcomes based on probabilistic models. In this approach, both input features and target outcomes are treated as random variables, and learning involves estimating probability distributions from data. A key idea is that uncertainty is unavoidable in real-world problems, and therefore models should express confidence in their predictions rather than making absolute decisions.

In probability-based learning, the learning process typically begins with a prior probability distribution that represents existing knowledge or assumptions about the problem. As new training data becomes available, this prior knowledge is updated to form a posterior probability distribution using Bayes' theorem. The final decision is then made by selecting the class or outcome with the highest posterior probability. This framework enables models to adapt incrementally as new evidence is observed and supports robust decision-making in uncertain environments. Table 4.9 elaborates key components of probability-based learning.

Table 4.9 Key Components of Probability-Based Learning

Component	Description
Random Variable	Represents uncertain features or outcomes in the learning problem
Prior Probability	Initial belief about a hypothesis before observing data
Likelihood	Probability of observing the data given a hypothesis
Posterior Probability	Updated belief after incorporating observed data
Decision Rule	Selection of the most probable class or outcome

4.5.2 Fundamentals of Bayes' Theorem

Bayes' Theorem provides a mathematical rule for updating the probability of a hypothesis when new evidence becomes available. It forms the foundation of Bayesian learning by enabling models to revise prior beliefs in the light of observed data. In classification problems, the hypothesis usually represents a class label, while the evidence corresponds to the observed feature values. Bayes' Theorem combines prior knowledge with data-driven likelihood to compute posterior probabilities, thereby supporting rational decision-making under uncertainty.

Mathematically, Bayes' Theorem is expressed as:

$$\boldsymbol{p(A|B) = p(B|A)P(A) \div P(B)},,,,,,,,,\mathbf{4.5}$$

Where:

- **P(A|B)** - the posterior probability (what we want to find after observing evidence B)
- **P(B|A)** - the likelihood (how probable the evidence B is given hypothesis A)
- **P(A)** - the prior probability (our initial belief about A before seeing evidence)
- **P(B)** - the marginal probability (the total probability of observing evidence B)

Table 4.10 give a clear understanding of terminology usage of Bayes's theorem in machine learning context.

Table 4.10 Terms Used in Bayes' Theorem

Term	Symbol	Description
Hypothesis / Class	A	Possible class or outcome being predicted
Evidence / Data	B	Observed feature values
Prior Probability	P(A)	Initial probability of class A
Likelihood	P(B|A)	Probability of observing BBB given class A
Posterior Probability	P(A|B)	Updated probability of class A after observing B
Normalization Constant	P(B)	Ensures posterior probabilities sum to one

Figure 4.9 provides a geometric interpretation of Bayes' theorem. The shaded regions represent the intersection of events A and B, showing that the joint probability $P(A \cap B)$ can be expressed as both $P(A)P(B|A)$ and $P(B)P(A|B)$.

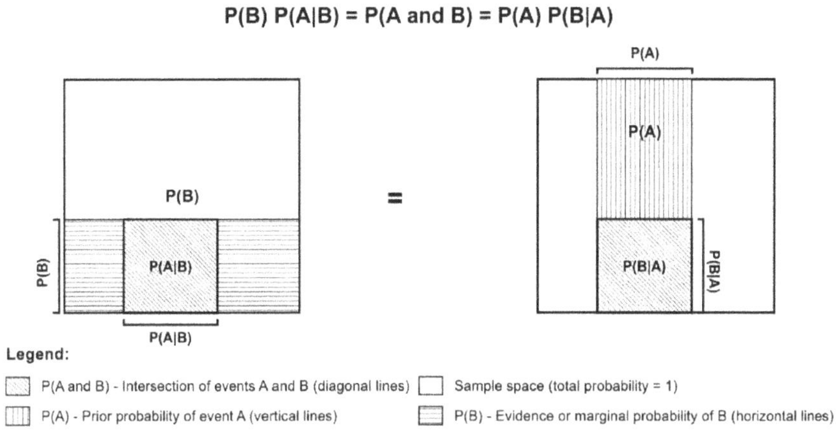

Figure 4.9 Geometric Interpretation of Bayes' Theorem

4.5.3 Classification Using Bayes Model

Classification using the Bayes model is a probabilistic approach in which class labels are assigned to input data based on the computation of posterior probabilities. Given an input instance described by a set of features, the Bayes classifier evaluates the probability of each possible class using Bayes' theorem and assigns the class with the highest posterior probability. This approach allows the classifier to explicitly handle uncertainty and make decisions based on likelihood rather than fixed rules.

In a typical Bayes classification framework, each class is treated as a hypothesis A_i, and the observed feature set is considered as evidence B. The posterior probability $P(A_i|B)$ is computed for all classes, and the class with the maximum value is selected. In practical implementations, the computation is simplified by comparing the products $P(B|A_i)$, since the normalization term P(B) remains constant across classes. This makes Bayes-based classifiers computationally efficient and suitable for large datasets.

One of the most widely used Bayes classifiers is the **Naïve Bayes classifier**, which assumes conditional independence among features given the class label. Despite this simplifying assumption, Naïve Bayes performs remarkably well in many real-world applications such as text classification, spam detection, medical diagnosis, and sentiment analysis.

Its simplicity, scalability, and ability to work well with limited training data make it a popular choice in practical machine learning systems.

In summary section 4.5, Bayesian learning provides a powerful and mathematically grounded framework for reasoning under uncertainty. By combining prior knowledge with observed data through Bayes' theorem, Bayesian models offer a flexible approach to classification and decision-making. The concepts of prior probability, likelihood, and posterior probability form the foundation of probability-based learning and enable adaptive learning as new data becomes available. Bayesian classifiers, particularly Naïve Bayes, strike an effective balance between simplicity and performance, making them an important class of models in machine learning and data-driven decision systems.

4.5.4 Naïve Bayes Algorithm for Continuous Attributes

The basic Naïve Bayes classifier is naturally suited for **categorical (discrete) attributes**, where probabilities are estimated using frequency counts. However, in many real-world machine learning problems—such as height, weight, temperature, income, or sensor measurements—attributes are **continuous (numerical)** rather than discrete. To handle such cases, the Naïve Bayes algorithm is extended by **assuming a probability distribution** for each continuous feature, most commonly the **Gaussian (Normal) distribution**. This variant is often called **Gaussian Naïve Bayes**.

Concept

For a continuous feature x, instead of counting occurrences, we estimate:

- **Mean (μ)** of the feature for each class
- **Standard Deviation (σ)** of the feature for each class

The likelihood

P(x|Ck) is then computed using the **Gaussian Probability Density Function (PDF):**

$$P(x \mid Ck) = \frac{1}{\sqrt{2\pi\sigma_k^2}} exp\left(-\frac{(x-\mu_k)^2}{2\sigma_k^2}\right) \quad 4.6$$

Where:

- x = observed feature value
- μ_k = mean of feature in class C_k
- σ_k = standard deviation of feature in class C_k
- C_k = class label

The classifier still follows Bayes' theorem and the only difference is that $P(x \mid Ck)$ is obtained from a **continuous probability distribution** rather than frequency counts.

Steps in Naïve Bayes for Continuous Attributes

1. **Separate training data by class.**
2. **Compute mean (μ) and standard deviation (σ)** for each continuous attribute within each class.
3. **Calculate prior probability** P(Ck) for each class.
4. **For a new instance:**
    - Use Gaussian PDF to compute $P(x_i|C_k)$ for each feature.
    - Multiply all likelihoods with prior probability.
5. **Assign the class** with the highest posterior probability.

Advantages

- Works well with **high-dimensional numerical data**.
- **Fast training and prediction**.
- Requires relatively **small training data**.
- Performs surprisingly well even with independence assumptions.

Limitations

- Assumes **feature independence**, which may not hold in practice.
- Assumes **normal distribution**, which may not fit all datasets.
- Sensitive to **incorrect distribution assumptions**.

Thus, to sum-up: **Naïve Bayes** for continuous attributes extends the traditional classifier by replacing frequency-based likelihood estimation with **probability density estimation**, typically Gaussian. This adaptation allows the algorithm to be applied effectively to numerical datasets such as medical measurements, financial indicators, and sensor data, while preserving the simplicity and computational efficiency that make Naïve Bayes a popular baseline classifier in machine learning.

Chapter Summary

Chapter 4 presented two major machine learning approaches: **Decision Tree models** and **Bayesian learning methods**, both widely used for their interpretability, efficiency, and theoretical strength in classification and regression tasks.

The chapter opened with **Decision Trees**, supervised learning models that represent decisions through a structured hierarchy of nodes and branches. Decision trees are easy to interpret and visualize, making them suitable for both technical and non-technical stakeholders.

The process of constructing decision trees was explained using **impurity measures** such as **Entropy, Information Gain, Gini Index, and Misclassification Error**, which help select the most informative attributes for splitting data. The **properties of Decision Tree Classifiers** were Analysed, emphasizing their strengths—simplicity, minimal preprocessing, and capability to handle mixed data types—alongside limitations such as **overfitting and instability** with small data variations.

A practical case study on **breast cancer classification** illustrated the real-world application of decision trees in healthcare decision support systems. The chapter then introduced **Decision Tree Regression**, extending tree logic to predict **continuous numerical outputs** using criteria such as variance reduction and mean squared error minimization.

The second half of the chapter focused on **Bayesian Learning**, presenting **Bayes' Theorem** as the mathematical foundation for probabilistic reasoning. It explained how prior probabilities are updated with evidence to obtain posterior probabilities. The **Naïve Bayes classifier** was discussed as a fast and scalable classification technique based on the assumption of conditional independence among features. The extension to **continuous attributes using Gaussian distribution** was also covered, enabling Naïve Bayes to effectively work with numerical datasets.

Chapter Conclusions

- **Decision Trees** offer a simple, intuitive, and powerful framework for both classification and regression tasks.
- **Impurity measures** are essential for constructing accurate and efficient decision trees.
- **Decision Tree Classifiers** are highly interpretable and suitable for applications requiring transparency.
- **Decision Tree Regression** enables prediction of continuous values using tree-based logic.
- **Bayesian Learning** provides a mathematically sound mechanism for reasoning under uncertainty.
- **Bayes' Theorem** integrates prior knowledge with new evidence to improve prediction accuracy.
- **Naïve Bayes classifiers** are computationally efficient and perform well in high-dimensional data.
- **Gaussian Naïve Bayes** effectively handles **continuous attributes** using probability density estimation.
- Decision Tree and Bayesian approaches form the **foundation for advanced ensemble and probabilistic models** in machine learning.

A. Short Answer Questions

1. What is a Decision Tree?
2. Define Entropy in Decision Tree learning.
3. What is Information Gain?
4. Name any two impurity measures used in Decision Trees.
5. What is a leaf node in a decision tree?
6. What is Decision Tree Regression?
7. State Bayes' Theorem.
8. Define Prior Probability.
9. What is Posterior Probability?
10. What assumption does the Naïve Bayes classifier make?
11. Which distribution is commonly used for continuous attributes in Naïve Bayes?
12. Mention one real-world application of Bayesian learning.

B. Medium Answer Questions

1. Explain the structure and components of a Decision Tree with a diagram.
2. Describe Entropy and Information Gain in decision tree construction.
3. Discuss the Gini Index and Misclassification Error.
4. Explain the advantages and limitations of Decision Tree Classifiers.
5. How are Decision Trees used for classification tasks?
6. Describe Decision Tree Regression and its splitting criteria.
7. Explain Bayes' Theorem with a suitable example.
8. How does Bayesian learning manage uncertainty in predictions?
9. Explain the working of the Naïve Bayes classifier.
10. Describe Naïve Bayes for **continuous attributes** using Gaussian distribution.
11. Compare Decision Tree Classification and Regression.
12. Differentiate Decision Tree and Naïve Bayes approaches.

C. Application-Oriented / Analytical Questions

1. Explain how Decision Trees can be applied to **breast cancer diagnosis** using relevant medical features.
2. Design a Decision Tree model to classify emails as **spam or non-spam**.
3. Analyse how impurity measures influence the final structure of a Decision Tree.
4. Discuss the suitability of Decision Trees in **medical decision-making systems**.
5. Apply Bayes' Theorem to compute the probability of disease given test results.
6. Explain how Bayesian classifiers are used in **text classification** problems.
7. Compare Decision Tree and Naïve Bayes classifiers for a **medical diagnosis dataset**.
8. Design a Decision Tree Regression model to **predict house prices**.
9. Demonstrate how **Gaussian Naïve Bayes** can classify a dataset with continuous attributes such as height and weight.
10. Discuss the importance of **probabilistic models** in uncertain real-world environments such as weather prediction or risk analysis.

Chapter - 5

Clustering and Reinforcement Learning Artificial Neural Networks

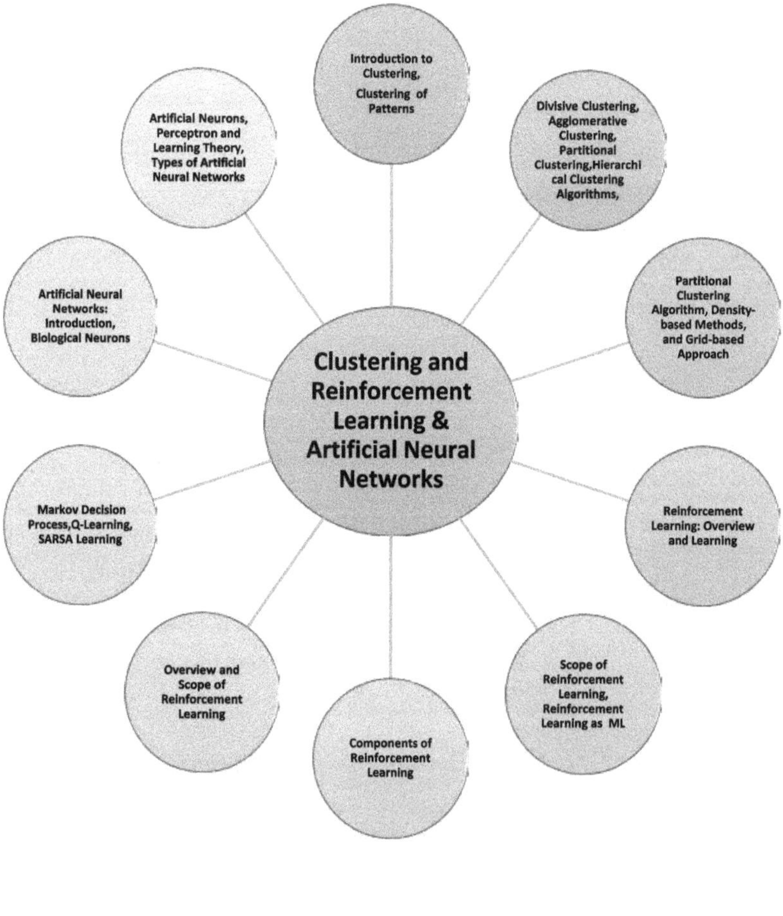

Chapter Overview

This chapter discusses two important kinds of machine learning that do not require labelled data or set outcomes: clustering and reinforcement learning. Clustering is the process of finding hidden patterns and structures in data by grouping things that are connected together. Reinforcement Learning, on the other hand, is the process of learning the most effective/optimal way to perform tasks by interacting with an environment that offers rewards and punishments.

The first part of the chapter addresses clustering methods. It starts with an overview of clustering and pattern clustering, then goes into further detail into hierarchical clustering methods, including divisive and agglomerative clustering, and partitional clustering approaches.

The second section of the chapter dwells on Reinforcement Learning (RL) in more detail, focusing on the main concepts, areas of study, and significant components, like agents, environments, states, actions, and rewards. The chapter concludes with an introduction to Q-Learning, that is one of the most basic and extensively used model-free reinforcement learning algorithms. These subjects give learners a strong base in making decisions and learning unsupervised learning and decision making under uncertainty.

5.1 Introduction to Clustering

Clustering is a fundamental technique used in unsupervised learning for organizing a group/collection of data objects into meaningful groups, or clusters. Objects in the same cluster are very similar to each other, while objects in different clusters are very different. Clustering does not depend on labelled data like supervised learning does. Instead, it finds hidden patterns and structures directly from the data.

The primary objective of clustering is to show how data is naturally organized and to transform large datasets into simpler ones. Clustering is widely used in areas like market segmentation, social network analysis, image processing, bioinformatics, pattern recognition, and data mining. Clustering can help with knowledge discovery, decision support, and exploratory data analysis through bringing related data points together.

There are many various kinds of techniques for clustering, and they all depend on how the clusters formed. These are hierarchical clustering, partitional clustering, density-based clustering, and model-based clustering. The type of clustering method chosen depends on factors such as such as the nature of data, similarity measures, scalability, and application requirements.

A typical clustering process consists of data preprocessing, the selection of similarity or distance metrics, the implementation of a clustering algorithm, and the validation of the resultant clusters. Because clustering is an exploratory endeavour, the quality of the results can frequently be evaluated by whether they are internally or externally, rather than exact correctness. Figure 5.1 illustrates the conceptual representation of clustering by grouping similar data points into distinct clusters.

Table 5.1 Characteristics of Clustering

Aspect	Description
Type of Learning	Unsupervised learning
Input Data	Unlabelled data
Output	Groups (clusters) of similar objects
Objective	Maximize intra-cluster similarity and minimize inter-cluster similarity
Common Similarity Measures	Euclidean distance, Manhattan distance, Cosine similarity
Applications	Customer segmentation, image analysis, document clustering, bioinformatics

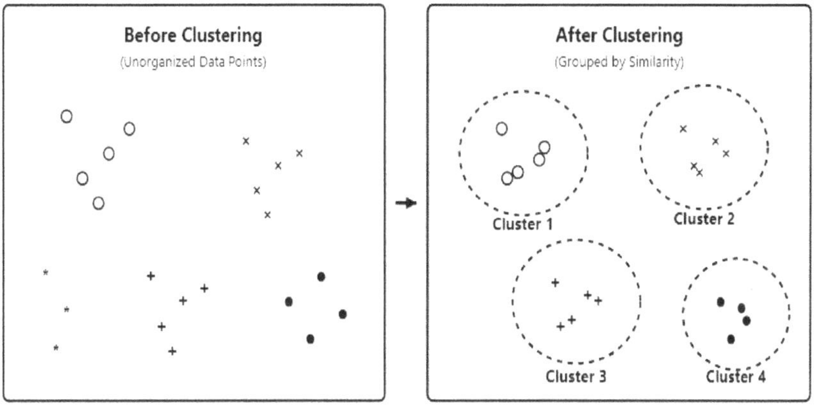

Figure 5.1 Conceptual Representation of Clustering

5.1.1 Clustering of Patterns

Clustering of patterns involves/refers to grouping data patterns or feature vectors together in a multidimensional feature space based on the degree of their similarity t. A pattern represents an object described by a set of attributes or features. For example, pixels in an image, words in a document, or numbers in a dataset. The aim of pattern clustering is to identify fundamental groupings within these patterns without any prior knowledge of class names.

In pattern clustering, each item is represented as a feature vector. To find out how similar two patterns a distance or similarity metrics is used. Patterns that exhibit similar characteristics are assigned to the same cluster. This approach is particularly useful in applications where manual labelling is difficult, expensive, or impractical.

Pattern clustering is frequently utilized in applications like images, segmentation, speech, recognition, handwriting, and in biological data analysis. In image processing, for example, pixels with similar colors or textures can be grouped together to separate objects in an image. In the same way, documents with similar word distributions can be grouped together in document analysis.

The success of pattern clustering relies on factors such as feature selection, data normalization, choice of similarity measure, and the clustering algorithm. Even using an advanced algorithm, poor feature selection could result to wrong clusters. Therefore, preprocessing and feature engineering are very important steps in grouping patterns. **Table 5.2** summarizes representative application domains of pattern clustering along with their corresponding pattern representations and clustering objectives.

Table 5.2 Examples of Pattern Clustering Applications

Domain	Pattern Representation	Clustering Objective
Image Processing	Pixel intensity, color, texture	Image segmentation
Text Mining	Word frequency vectors	Document grouping
Bioinformatics	Gene expression levels	Functional gene grouping
Marketing	Customer attributes	Market segmentation
Speech Recognition	Acoustic features	Speaker or sound clustering

Having understood clustering of patterns, let us now understand clustering methods such as divisive clustering, agglomerative clustering, and partitional clustering.

5.2 Divisive Clustering

In divisive clustering, all data objects initially belong to the same cluster. This is a top-down hierarchical clustering method. The algorithm keeps breaking clusters down into smaller sub-clusters until each object has its own cluster or a particular/specified stopping condition is met. The approach focuses on identifying disparities within a cluster and dividing it into more uniform/homogeneous subsets.

The divisive clustering procedure starts by treating the whole dataset as one cluster. At each stage/step, the cluster that is most different from the others is picked and split into two or more clusters based on an identified/chosen criterion. This process keeps on in a loop, creating-recursively, a hierarchy of clusters that can be perceived with a dendrogram.

Divisive clustering is helpful when the overall structure of the data is important. However, it is computationally expensive, especially for large datasets, and is less commonly used than agglomerative clustering in practical applications. Figure 5.2 illustrates the top-down approach of divisive clustering, wherein a singular extensive cluster is progressively split into smaller clusters.

Divisive (Top-Down) Clustering

- Starts with all data points in one cluster
- Recursively splits clusters into smaller sub-clusters
- Continues until each point is in its own cluster or stopping criterion is met.

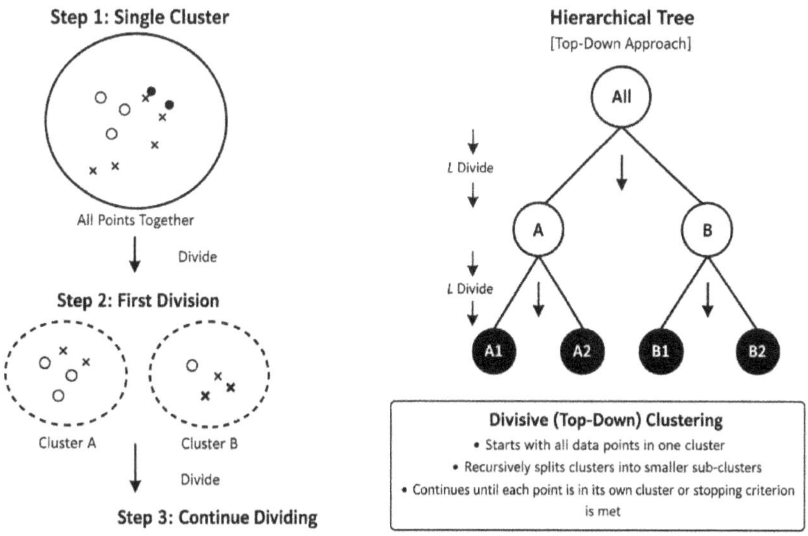

Figure 5.2 Divisive Clustering Process

Table 5.3 Key Features of Divisive Clustering

Feature	Description
Clustering Approach	Top-down
Initial State	All objects in one cluster
Splitting Strategy	Based on dissimilarity
Output Structure	Hierarchical (dendrogram)
Computational Cost	High
Typical Use	Small datasets, conceptual analysis

5.3 Agglomerative Clustering

Agglomerative clustering is a bottom-up hierarchical clustering method that starts with each data object making its own cluster. The algorithm iteratively merges the most related/similar clusters until all of the objects are in one cluster or a set number of clusters is reached.

Linkage criteria like single linkage, complete linkage, or average linkage are used to find the distance between clusters at each iteration. The two clusters that are closest together are combined, which gradually creates a hierarchy of clusters. A dendrogram that shows how the merging process works typically serves to demonstrate the result.

Agglomerative clustering is widely used because it is easy to understand, can employ several distance measurements, and is simple to use. However it doesn't work well with extremely large datasets, because once clusters are combined, the procedure can't be undone/reversed The steps are:

Agglomerative (Bottom-Up) Clustering

- Starts with each data point as an individual cluster
- Iteratively merges the closest pair of clusters

- Continues until all points merge into one cluster or stopping criterion is met.

Figure 5.3 illustrates the bottom-up merging of individual data points into larger clusters in agglomerative clustering.

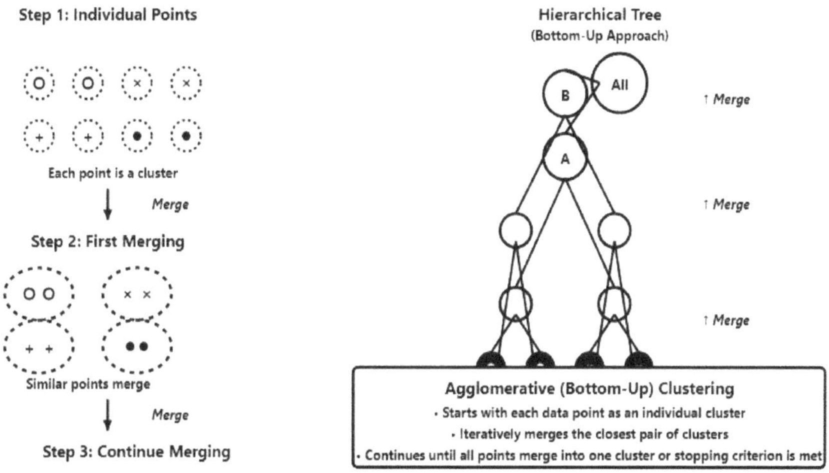

Figure 5.3 Agglomerative Clustering Process

Table 5.4 Linkage Methods in Agglomerative Clustering

Linkage Method	Description
Single Linkage	Minimum distance between cluster members
Complete Linkage	Maximum distance between cluster members
Average Linkage	Average distance between all pairs
Centroid Linkage	Distance between cluster centroids

5.4 Partitional Clustering

Partitional clustering is a way to group data that isn't hierarchical, namely it is non-hierarchical clustering. It splits the data directly into a fixed number of groups, which is commonly called k. Partitional clustering does not create a dendrogram like hierarchical algorithms do. Instead, it tries to find the best clustering objective function.

The K-Means algorithm is the most popular example of partitional clustering. It groups data points by minimizing the sum of the squared distances between them and their cluster centroids. The algorithm keeps assigning data points to the closest centroid and updating the centroids until they all converge.

Partitional clustering methods are computationally efficient and scalable, making them suitable for large datasets. However they need to know how many clusters there are ahead of time, and they are sensitive

Steps in the k means algorithm are:

Figure 5.4 shows partitional clustering where data points are grouped around cluster centroids.

to how the first cluster is chosen and noise in the data.

K-Means Clustering Algorithm

1. **Initialize:** Randomly select K centroids (C1, C2, ..., Ck)
2. **Assignment:** Assign each data point to the nearest centroid based on distance
3. **Update:** Recalculate centroids as the mean of all points in each cluster
4. **Iterate:** Repeat steps 2-3 until centroids no longer move significantly (convergence)

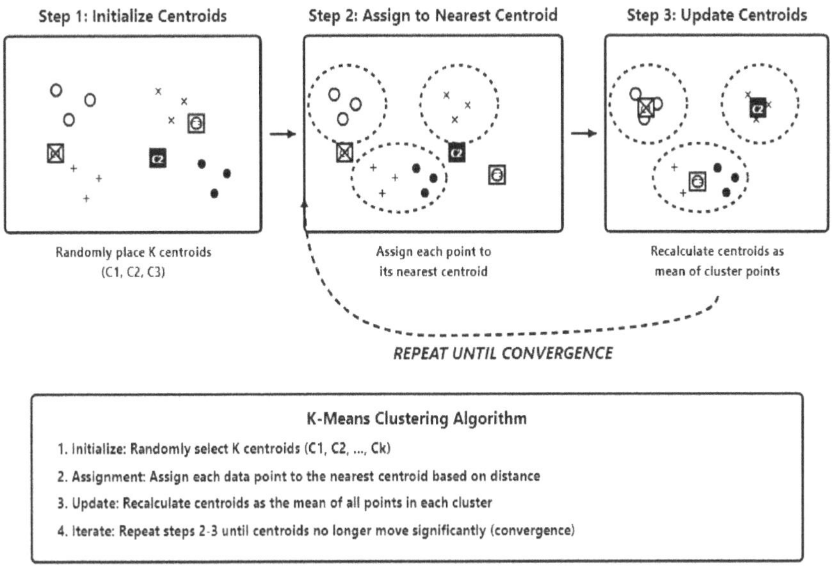

Figure 5.4 Partitional Clustering Using Centroids

Table 5.5 Characteristics of Partitional Clustering

Aspect	Description
Clustering Type	Non-hierarchical
Number of Clusters	Predefined
Common Algorithm	K-Means
Scalability	High
Output	Flat cluster structure
Limitation	Sensitive to initialization

5.5 Clustering Algorithms: Introduction to Clustering Approaches

Clustering Algorithms

5.5.1 Introduction to Clustering Algorithms

Clustering is an **unsupervised machine learning technique** used to group similar data points into clusters based on inherent patterns or similarities in the data. Unlike supervised learning, clustering does not rely on labelled outputs. Instead, it discovers hidden structures within datasets by analysing relationships among variables.

In real-world scenarios, clustering helps in **data exploration, pattern recognition, and knowledge discovery** where predefined classes are unavailable. The goal is to ensure that **objects within the same cluster are highly similar**, while **objects in different clusters are significantly dissimilar**.

Key Characteristics of Clustering

1. **Unsupervised Nature** – No prior labels or target variables are provided.
2. **Similarity Measurement** – Distance or similarity metrics such as Euclidean distance, Manhattan distance, or Cosine similarity are commonly used.
3. **Data Structure Discovery** – Identifies natural groupings and hidden relationships.
4. **Scalability Considerations** – Efficient algorithms are required for large datasets.
5. **Interpretability** – The resulting clusters should be meaningful and understandable.

General Clustering Approaches

Clustering techniques can broadly be categorized into several major approaches:

1. Partitioning Methods

These methods divide the dataset into a predefined number of clusters (**k clusters**). Each data point belongs to exactly one cluster.

Examples:

- K-Means Clustering
- K-Medoids (PAM)

Characteristics:

- Efficient for large datasets
- Sensitive to initial centroid selection
- Works well with spherical or convex cluster shapes

2. Hierarchical Methods

Hierarchical clustering builds a **tree-like structure (dendrogram)** representing nested groupings of data points.

Two Strategies Exist:

- **Agglomerative (Bottom-Up):** Starts with individual data points and merges them step by step.
- **Divisive (Top-Down):** Starts with one cluster and splits it recursively.

Characteristics:

- No need to specify the number of clusters initially
- Computationally expensive for large datasets
- Produces interpretable visual structures

3. Density-Based Methods

These methods form clusters based on **data density**. Regions with higher density of points are treated as clusters, while sparse regions are considered noise or outliers.

Examples:

- DBSCAN
- OPTICS

Characteristics:

- Effective for arbitrary shaped clusters
- Handles noise well
- Requires careful parameter tuning

4. Grid Based Methods

Grid-based clustering divides the data space into a finite number of cells (grids) and performs clustering on these grids rather than individual data points.

Examples:

- STING
- CLIQUE

Characteristics:

- Fast processing time
- Suitable for large datasets
- Dependent on grid resolution

5. Model-Based Methods

These approaches assume that data is generated from a mixture of underlying probability distributions and attempt to estimate model parameters.

Examples:

- Gaussian Mixture Models (GMM)
- Expectation–Maximization (EM)

Characteristics:

- Statistically grounded
- Flexible cluster shapes
- Computationally intensive

Applications of Clustering

- **Customer Segmentation** in marketing
- **Image Segmentation** in computer vision
- **Document Classification** and topic Modelling
- **Anomaly Detection** in cybersecurity

- **Biological Data Analysis** such as gene expression studies

Figure 5.5 illustrates the major types of clustering approaches, such as partition-based, hierarchical, density-based, and model-based clustering.

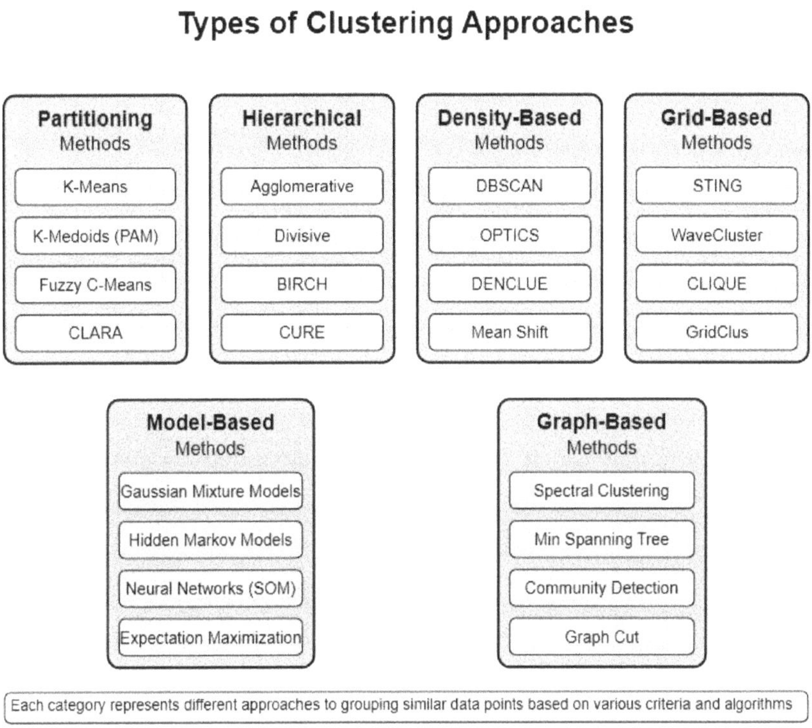

Figure 5.5 Types of Clustering Approaches

5.6 Proximity Measures

Proximity measures quantify the degree of similarity or dissimilarity between data points and form the mathematical foundation of all clustering algorithms. The effectiveness of clustering largely depends on selecting an appropriate proximity measure, as different measures capture different notions of "closeness" in data. Proximity can be expressed either as **distance (dissimilarity)** or **similarity**.

5.6.1 Distance Measures

1. Euclidean Distance

Euclidean distance is the most widely used metric for **continuous numerical attributes**. It calculates the straight-line distance between two points in multidimensional space. It works well for compact, spherical clusters but is sensitive to differences in scale and outliers.

$$d(x,y) = \sqrt{\sum_{1}^{n} (x_i - y_i)^2} \ldots\ldots 5.1$$

2. Manhattan Distance (L1 Norm)

Manhattan distance computes the sum of absolute differences between coordinate values of two data points. It is less sensitive to extreme values compared to Euclidean distance and is suitable for grid-like paths or high-dimensional sparse data.

$$d(x,y) = \sum_{1}^{n} |x_i - y_i| \ldots\ldots 5.2$$

3. Minkowski Distance

Minkowski distance is a **generalized form** of both Euclidean and Manhattan distances, controlled by a parameter p. When p=1 1p=1, it becomes Manhattan distance; when p=2, it becomes Euclidean distance. This flexibility allows adaptation to different data characteristics.

$$\mathrm{D(x,y)} = (\sum_{1}^{n} |x_i - y_i|^p)^{\frac{1}{p}} \ldots\ldots 5.3$$

4. Cosine Distance

Cosine distance is derived from **Cosine Similarity**, which measures the angle between two vectors.

First, cosine similarity is computed, and then cosine distance is obtained as:

$$\textbf{Cosine Similarity}(\mathbf{x},\mathbf{y}) = \frac{\mathbf{x}\cdot\mathbf{y}}{\|\mathbf{x}\|\|\mathbf{y}\|}\ldots..\mathbf{5.4}$$

- x·y → Dot product of vectors x and y
- ||x||→ Magnitude (length) of vector x
- ||y|| → Magnitude (length) of vector y

Cosine distance measures the **angle between two vectors** rather than their magnitude. It is particularly effective for **high-dimensional data** such as text documents, where the orientation of vectors is more important than their length.

$$\textbf{Cosine Distance}(\mathbf{x},\mathbf{y}) = \mathbf{1} - \textbf{Cosine Similarity}(\mathbf{x},\mathbf{y})\ldots..\mathbf{5.5}$$

5.6.2 Similarity Measures

1. Jaccard Similarity

Jaccard similarity is commonly used for **binary attributes and set comparisons**. It measures the ratio of shared elements to the total unique elements in both sets. It is useful in applications like document similarity, recommendation systems, and market basket analysis.

$$\mathbf{J}(\mathbf{A},\mathbf{B}) = \frac{|\mathbf{A}\cup\mathbf{B}|}{|\mathbf{A}\cap\mathbf{B}|}\ldots..\mathbf{5.6}$$

- **A** → Set of items (or features) belonging to object 1
- **B** → Set of items (or features) belonging to object 2

These Sets May Represent:

- Words in two documents
- Products purchased by two customers
- Attributes present in two data records
- Binary feature vectors (1 = present, 0 = absent)

2. Pearson Correlation

Pearson correlation measures the **strength and direction of linear relationship** between two variables. Values range from −1 to +1, where+1 indicates perfect positive correlation and −1 indicates perfect negative correlation. It is widely used in statistical data analysis and pattern recognition.

$$\mathbf{r(x,y)} = \frac{\sum_1^n \ (x_i - \bar{x}_i)(y_i - \bar{y}_i)}{\sqrt{\sum_1^n \ (x_i - \bar{x}_i)^2}\sqrt{\sum_1^n \ (y_i - \bar{y}_i)^2}} \ldots\ldots \mathbf{5.7}$$

Where:

- x_i, y_i = Individual data values
- $\bar{x}$ = Mean of x values
- $\bar{y}$ = Mean of y values
- n = Number of observations
- r(x,y) ranges from **−1 to +1**

Proximity measures determine how clustering algorithms interpret relationships among data points. Choosing the right metric ensures meaningful and accurate cluster formation.

5.6.3 Reinforcement Learning

Reinforcement Learning (RL) is a learning paradigm in which an intelligent agent learns to make optimal decisions by interacting with an environment. Unlike supervised learning, where correct outputs are explicitly provided, reinforcement learning relies on ***trial and error*** and feedback in the form of ***rewards or punishments/penalties***. The objective of the agent is to learn a policy that maximizes ***cumulative reward*** over time.

Reinforcement learning is particularly suited for problems involving ***sequential decision making***, where current actions influence future states and rewards. Typical applications include robotics, autonomous systems, game playing, recommendation systems, and resource management. The learning process continues as the agent explores the environment and gradually improves its behaviour based on experience.

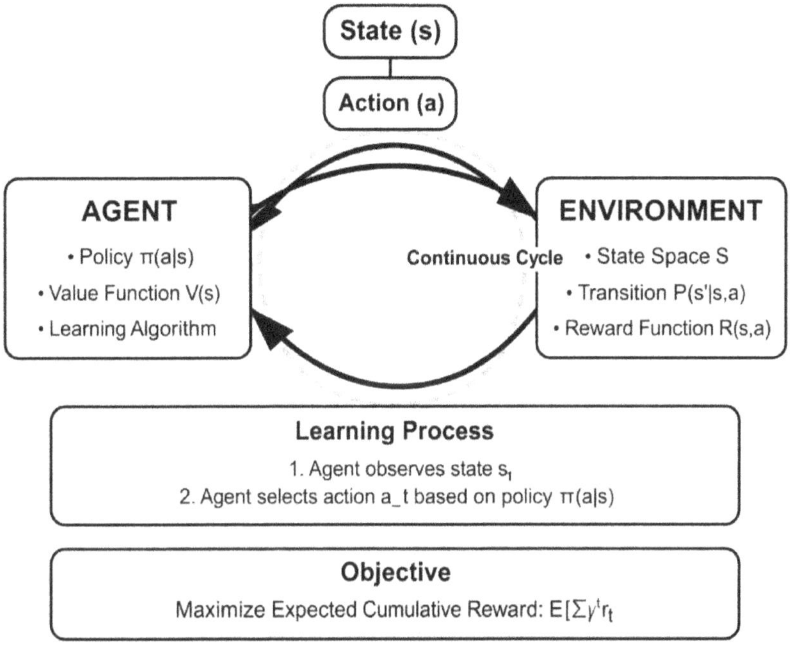

Figure 5.6 Reinforcement Learning Interaction Model

Figure 5.6 illustrates the interaction between an agent and the environment, where the agent selects actions based on the current state and receives rewards as feedback.

5.6.4 Over View and Scope of Reinforcement Learning

The fundamental idea of reinforcement learning is to enable an agent to learn from direct interaction with its environment without requiring labelled datasets. At each time step, the agent observes the current state of the environment, selects an action, and receives a reward that reflects the quality of the action taken.

The scope of reinforcement learning is broad and continues to expand with advancements in computing power and algorithms. RL is widely used in **robot control**, **game AI**, **traffic signal optimization**, **industrial automation**, and **financial decision making**. Reinforcement learning can be categorized into **model-based** and **model-free** approaches depending on whether the agent uses an explicit model of the environment. Table 5.6 provides example of applications of reinforcement learning.

Table 5.6 Scope and Applications of Reinforcement Learning

Application Area	**Example Use Case**
Robotics	Robot navigation and manipulation
Game Playing	Chess, Go, video games
Autonomous Systems	Self-driving vehicles
Networking	Traffic routing and congestion control
Finance	Portfolio optimization

5.7 Components of Reinforcement Learning

A reinforcement learning system consists of several core components that define the interaction between the agent and the environment. The **agent** is the learner or decision-maker, while the **environment** represents everything the agent interacts with. The **state** represents the current situation of the environment, and the **action** is a choice made by the agent.

The **reward function** provides feedback by assigning a numerical value to each action taken by the agent. The **policy** defines the strategy used by the agent to select actions in different states. Additionally, **value functions** estimate the expected cumulative reward, helping the agent evaluate long-term benefits of actions.

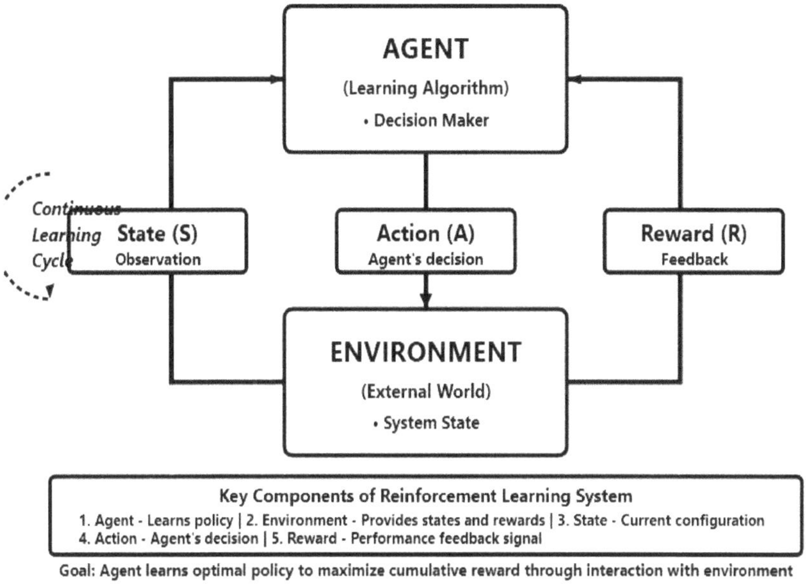

Figure 5.7 Components of a Reinforcement Learning System

Figure 5.7 shows the main components of reinforcement learning and their relationships.

Table 5.7 Components of Reinforcement Learning

Component	Description
Agent	Learns and makes decisions
Environment	External system interacted with
State	Current situation of the environment
Action	Choice made by the agent
Reward	Feedback signal
Policy	Mapping from states to actions
Value Function	Expected long-term reward

5.7.1 Markov Decision Process (MDP)

MDP Framework

Mathematical framework for modelling decision-making in stochastic environments. A Markov Decision Process (MDP) is a mathematical framework for modelling decision-making situations in which the outcomes are both random and partly under the decision-maker's control. MDPs are a fundamental idea in Reinforcement Learning, providing a formal structure for modelling an agent's interaction with its environment. An MDP is comprised of four major components: states (S), actions (A), transition probabilities (P), and rewards (R). A discount factor (γ) can be added to account for future rewards' importance. This structure allows the agent to make sequential judgments that maximize its cumulative reward over time whilst taking into account the probabilistic nature of the environment.

The defining property of an MDP is the **Markov Property**, which states that the future state of the system depends only on the current state and action, not on the sequence of past states. Mathematically, this is expressed as:

$$\mathbf{P(S_{t+1} \mid S_t, A_t, S_t - 1, A_{t-1}, .. S_0, A_0) = P(S_{t+1} \mid S_t, A_t)........ 5.8}$$

Meaning of Symbols

- S_t → Current state at time t
- A_t → Action taken at time t
- S_{t+1} → Next state
- $P(\cdot)$ → Probability

Interpretation:

The entire past history (S_{t-1},A_{t-1},…,S_0,A_0) does **not influence** the next state once the current state S_t and action A_t are known. This memoryless characteristic is the foundation of Markov Decision Processes **(MDPs)** in Reinforcement Learning.

This property simplifies the modelling of dynamic systems and allows efficient computation of policies and value functions. The transition probabilities, **P(s′|s,a),** represent the likelihood of moving from state s to state s′ given action a, while the reward function R(s,a) specifies the immediate reward received after taking action **a** in state **s**.

MDPs are commonly used in domains where decisions must be made under uncertain conditions, such as robotics, finance, healthcare, and logistics. They give a solid foundation for modelling activities such as guiding a robot through a maze, managing inventory in a warehouse, and optimizing treatment plans in medicine. Solving an MDP is determining the optimal policy—a mapping from states to actions—that maximizes the expected cumulative reward. MDPs are solved using techniques like as dynamic programming, Monte Carlo methods, and reinforcement learning algorithms, which vary based on the size and complexity of the state and action spaces.

MDP Tuple: (S, A, P, R, γ)

- **S:** State space
- **A:** Action space
- **P:** Transition probability function P(s'|s,a)
- **R:** Reward function R(s,a,s')
- **γ:** Discount factor ($0 \leq \gamma \leq 1$)

Multi-Arm Bandit Problem

The Multi-Armed Bandit (MAB) problem is a fundamental problem in reinforcement learning and decision theory. It is frequently used to represent/model instances in which an agent must choose between multiple options, each with uncertain rewards. The name is derived from a row of slot machines (or "bandits"), each of which has a unique payout probability distribution. The agent's objective is to determine which "arm" to pull at each time step in order to maximize cumulative rewards over time. The problem stems from the exploration-exploitation tradeoff: the agent must strike a balance between testing out multiple arms to learn about their reward distributions (exploration) and using known information to select the arm with the highest expected reward.

MAB problems are used in a variety of domains, including online marketing, where algorithms determine which ads to display to consumers in order to maximize clicks, and clinical trials, where researchers select therapies to determine the most effective while minimizing patient risks. Several strategies have been developed to solve the MAB problem, including: ε-greedy algorithms, which alternate between exploration and exploitation with a fixed probability; Upper Confidence Bound (UCB) methods, which prioritize arms with high uncertainty; and Thompson Sampling, which uses Bayesian inference to guide decision-making. Despite its simplicity, the MAB problem provides the basis for more complicated reinforcement learning scenarios, such as contextual bandits and full Markov Decision Processes.

5.7.7.1 Problem Formulation

Simplified RL problem focusing on exploration-exploitation trade-off without state transitions.

Setup:

- K slot machines (arms) with unknown reward distributions
- Agent selects one arm at each time step
- Goal: maximize cumulative reward over time
- No state information, only reward feedback

5. 7.7.2 Exploration vs. Exploitation

Exploitation: Choose arm with highest estimated reward **Exploration:** Try arms with uncertain rewards to improve estimates

Algorithms:

ε-Greedy:

- Select best arm with probability **(1-ε)**
- Select random arm with probability **ε**
- Simple but doesn't adapt exploration

Upper Confidence Bound (UCB):

$$A_t = \mathbf{argamax}\left[Q_t(a) + c\sqrt{\frac{int}{N_t(a)}}\right] \ldots\ldots 5.9$$

Meaning of Symbols

- A_t → Action selected at time step t
- argmaxa → Choose the action aaa that maximizes the expression
- $Q_t(a)$ → Estimated average reward of action a at time t
- $N_t(a)$→ Number of times action a has been selected up to time t
- t → Current time step (total number of trials)
- c → Exploration constant (controls exploration level)
- lnt → Natural logarithm of time step

Interpretation

- The first term $Q_t(a)$ promotes **exploitation**.
- The second term $c\sqrt{\frac{int}{N_t(a)}}$ promotes **exploration** by giving higher value to less-tried actions.
- As $N_t(a)$increases, the exploration bonus decreases, leading to **reduced exploration over time**.
- Balances estimated value and uncertainty
- Automatically reduces exploration over time

Thompson Sampling:

- Bayesian approach using posterior distributions
- Samples from belief about each arm's value
- Naturally balances exploration and exploitation

Table 5.8 Multi-Arm Bandit Algorithms Comparison

Algorithm	Exploration Strategy	Advantages	Limitations
ε-Greedy	Explores randomly with probability ε.	Simple to implement, balances exploration.	Fixed ε may not adapt well.
Upper Confidence Bound (UCB)	Uses confidence intervals to prioritize uncertain actions.	Efficient exploration with theoretical guarantees.	Requires careful tuning of exploration constant.
Thompson Sampling	Samples actions based on posterior probability.	Bayesian approach, handles non-stationary problems.	Computationally expensive for complex priors.
Softmax	Selects actions probabilistically using softmax function.	Smooth balance of exploration and exploitation.	Sensitive to temperature parameter.
Greedy (Baseline)	Always chooses the action with the highest estimated reward.	Simple and computationally efficient.	Poor exploration, easily stuck in local optima.

Table 5.5 compares Multi-Arm Bandit algorithms, highlighting their exploration strategies, advantages, and limitations to aid in selecting the right approach for specific scenarios.

5.7.2 Reinforcement Learning Problem Types

5.7.2.1 Episodic vs. Continuing Tasks

Episodic Tasks:

- Natural ending points (terminal states)
- Examples: Games, simulation episodes
- Finite horizon optimization

Continuing Tasks:

- No natural termination
- Infinite horizon problems
- Examples: Process control, recommendation systems

5.7.2.2 Finite vs. Infinite Horizon

Finite Horizon:

- Fixed time limit T
- Optimization over finite time steps
- Time-dependent optimal policies

Infinite Horizon:

- Unbounded time duration
- Discounting ensures finite cumulative rewards
- Stationary optimal policies

5.7.2.3 Deterministic vs. Stochastic

Deterministic Environments:

- State transitions are predictable
- Same action in same state always produces same result
- Simpler planning and learning

Stochastic Environments:

- Probabilistic state transitions
- Uncertainty in action outcomes
- Requires handling of probabilistic effects

Figure 5.8 classifies reinforcement learning problems, distinguishing between model-based vs. model-free and policy-based vs. value-based approaches.

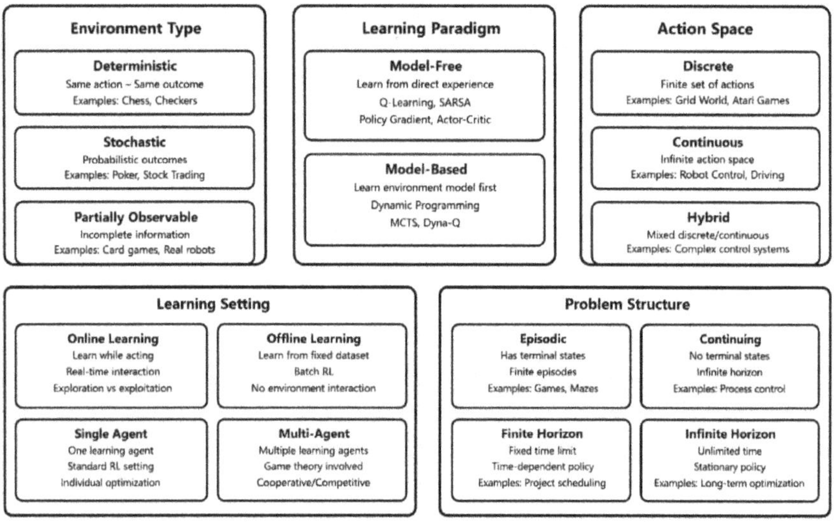

Figure 5.8 RL Problem Classification

5.8 Q-Learning

Q-Learning is a **model-free reinforcement learning algorithm** that enables an agent to learn the optimal action-selection policy without prior knowledge of the environment. It learns a function called the **Q-value**, which represents the expected cumulative reward of taking a specific action in a given state and following the optimal policy thereafter.

The Q-values are stored in a Q-Table and are updated iteratively using experience gathered through interaction with the environment. Over time, the Q-values converge, allowing the agent to select actions that maximize expected rewards. Q-Learning balances **exploration** (trying new actions) and **exploitation** (choosing known good actions).

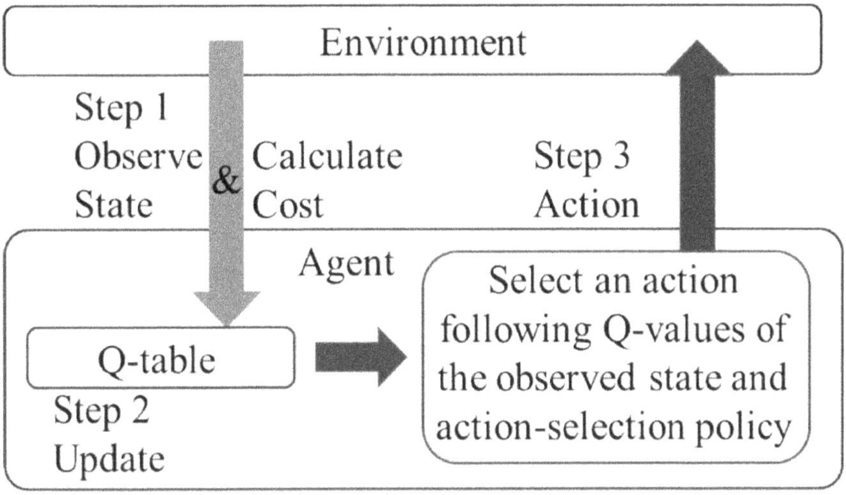

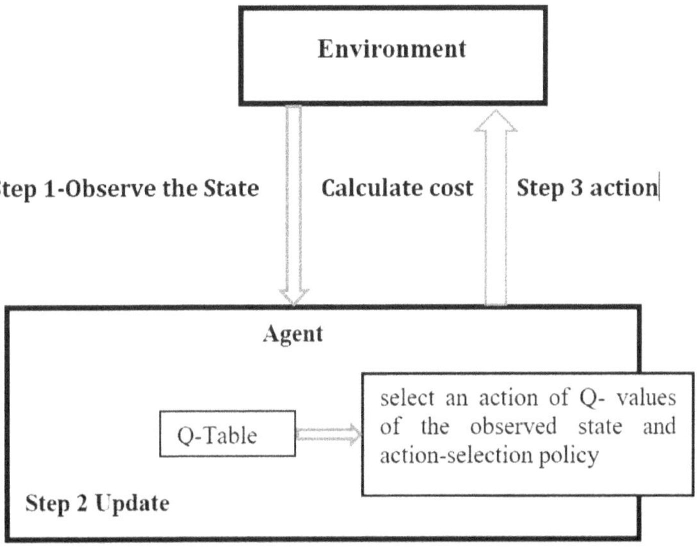

Figure 5.9 Q-Learning Process Flow

Figure 5.9illustrates the iterative process of Q-Learning, including action selection, reward observation, and Q-value update.

Table 5.9 Key Features of Q-Learning

Feature	Description
Learning Type	Model-free
Policy	Off-policy
Storage	Q-Table
Convergence	Guaranteed under certain conditions
Key Challenge	State-action space size

5.8.1 Overview of Reinforcement Learning

Reinforcement learning (RL) addresses the fundamental question of how an autonomous agent, capable of sensing and acting in its environment, can learn to choose optimal actions to achieve its goals. This general problem encompasses tasks such as training a mobile robot to navigate its surroundings, optimizing operations in factories, or mastering the strategies required to excel at board games. Each time the agent performs an action, feedback is provided in the form of rewards or penalties, indicating the desirability of the resulting state. For example, in the context of training an agent to play a game, the trainer might assign a positive reward for winning, a negative reward for losing, and a neutral (zero) reward for all intermediate states. The agent's task is to learn from this indirect and often delayed feedback to develop strategies that maximize cumulative rewards over time.

This learning process parallels how humans learn from infancy through adulthood, continually refining their behaviour to become effective and adaptive agents in their environments. From a young age, humans learn through experiences shaped by rewards and consequences. A child might receive praise or treats for completing a chore (positive reinforcement), or face a timeout for misbehaviour (negative reinforcement). As adults, rewards become more nuanced, such as promotions, awards, or social recognition for achievements, while punishments could include missed opportunities, professional setbacks, or the lessons learned from mistakes.

Through this lifelong process of interacting with their environment, receiving feedback, and adapting their actions, humans develop the ability to navigate complex situations and pursue goals effectively. Similarly, reinforcement learning algorithms mimic this iterative learning process, enabling agents to handle a wide range of tasks by drawing on cumulative experiences to refine their decisions and optimize outcomes.

The Term "Reinforcement in Reinforcement Learning"

In Reinforcement Learning (RL), the term "reinforcement" primarily emphasises the role of **rewards** as the guiding mechanism through which an agent learns to improve its behaviour. Each action taken by the agent in the environment leads to a reward or penalty, which reflects the desirability of the resulting state. Positive rewards reinforce beneficial actions, encouraging the agent to repeat them, while negative rewards (penalties) discourage actions that lead to undesirable outcomes. For example, an agent navigating a maze might receive a reward upon reaching the goal or a penalty for hitting an obstacle. These rewards serve as the foundation for the agent to evaluate the effectiveness of its actions and adjust its strategy to maximize cumulative rewards over time.

Beyond individual rewards, reinforcement in RL incorporates a broader learning framework driven by trial and error. The agent initially explores various actions, receiving feedback and refining its decision-making process through the interplay of exploration and exploitation. Exploration allows the agent to discover new actions and their effects, while exploitation leverages known information to optimize outcomes. This iterative cycle of learning, informed by rewards, enables the agent to develop an optimal policy for achieving its objectives. Ultimately, reinforcement in RL is a reward-driven process where feedback not only evaluates actions but also shapes the agent's ability to make better decisions over repeated interactions with its environment.

Key Characteristics:

- **Trial-and-Error Learning:** Agent explores environment through actions
- **Delayed Rewards:** Consequences of actions may not be immediate

- **Sequential Decision Making:** Actions affect future states and opportunities
- **Goal-Oriented:** Maximizes cumulative reward over time

Distinction from Other Learning Paradigms:

- **Supervised Learning:** Learns from labelled examples
- **Unsupervised Learning:** Finds patterns in unlabelled data
- **Reinforcement Learning:** Learns from interaction and feedback

Figure 5.10 compares different machine learning paradigms—supervised, unsupervised, and reinforcement learning—based on their learning processes and types of feedback.

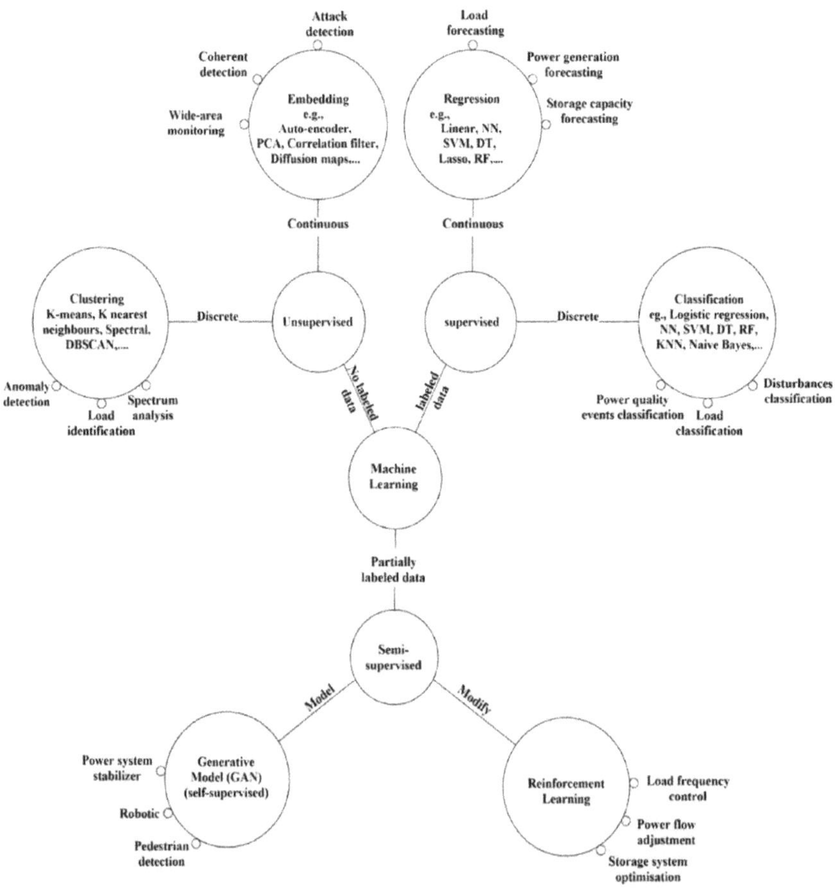

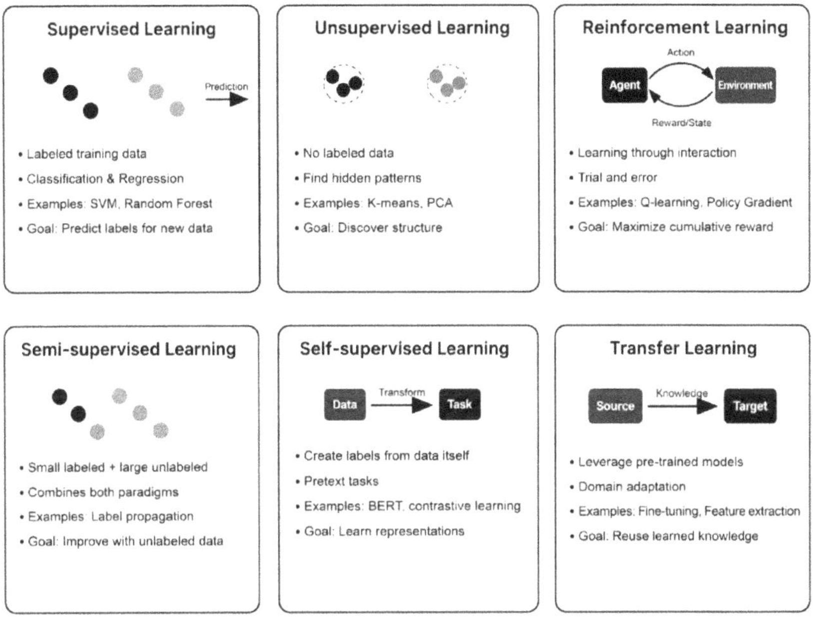

Figure 5.10 Machine Learning Paradigms Comparison

5.8.2 Scope of Reinforcement Learning

Reinforcement Learning (RL) has a broad and diverse application, encompassing fields where decision-making and flexibility are essential. RL's fundamental idea of learning optimal methods through interaction with an environment makes it suitable to a wide range of problems, from basic tasks to highly complex systems. RL is widely used in robotics to provide autonomous control, allowing robots to navigate, manipulate items, and adapt to dynamic situations. It is critical in game AI, where agents learn strategies to outperform human players in games such as chess, Go, and video games. Furthermore, RL is being used in a variety of industries to optimize resource allocation, including manufacturing scheduling, supply chain management, and energy distribution.

Beyond traditional applications, RL is making inroads into emerging sectors, demonstrating its broad applicability. In healthcare, RL is used for personalized treatment planning, drug discovery, and resource optimization in hospitals. Autonomous systems, including self-driving cars and unmanned aerial aircraft, use RL to make real-time judgments in uncertain situations. In addition, RL has a substantial impact on financial systems, helping in the development of adaptive trading algorithms and the optimization of investment portfolios. With breakthroughs in deep learning, RL is scaling to address more complicated, high-dimensional problems, paving the way for innovation in fields such as climate modelling, smart city development, and even creative jobs like procedural content generation.

5.8.2.1 Applications

Game Playing:

- Chess, Go, poker playing agents
- Video game AI characters
- Strategic decision making

Robotics:

- Robot navigation and path planning
- Manipulation and grasping tasks
- Autonomous vehicle control

Finance:

- Algorithmic trading strategies
- Portfolio optimization
- Risk management

Healthcare:

- Treatment planning and optimization
- Drug discovery processes
- Personalized medicine

Recommendation Systems:

- Dynamic content recommendation
- Personalized advertising
- User experience optimization

5.8.2.2 Problem Types Suitable for RL

Sequential Decision Problems:

- Actions affect future states
- Long-term consequences matter
- Multiple interacting decisions

Optimization under Uncertainty:

- Stochastic environments
- Incomplete information
- Adaptive strategies needed

Learning Through Interaction:

- Expensive or impossible to obtain labelled data
- Environment provides natural feedback
- Exploration vs. exploitation trade-offs

The table 5.4 summarizes key application domains of reinforcement learning, showcasing its versatility in addressing problems across robotics, healthcare, finance, and beyond.

Table 5.10 RL Application Domains

Domain	Description	Examples
Robotics	Enables robots to learn tasks through trial and error in dynamic environments.	Path planning, object manipulation.
Game Playing	AI agents learn to master games by optimizing strategies.	Chess, Go, Atari games.
Healthcare	Optimizes treatment strategies and resource allocation.	Personalized medicine, drug discovery.

Finance	Improves decision-making in trading and portfolio management.	Algorithmic trading, risk management.
Autonomous Vehicles	Trains vehicles to navigate and make decisions in real-world traffic scenarios.	Self-driving cars, UAVs.
Energy Optimization	Reduces energy consumption and enhances efficiency in systems.	Smart grid management, HVAC control.
Manufacturing	Optimizes processes and operations to improve efficiency.	Inventory management, scheduling.
Natural Language Processing	Enhances language-based interactions by optimizing policies.	Chatbots, conversational agents.

The table summarizes key application domains of reinforcement learning, showcasing its versatility in addressing problems across robotics, healthcare, finance, and beyond.

5.8.3 Reinforcement Learning as Machine Learning

Reinforcement Learning (RL) is a unique paradigm within the broader field of machine learning that focuses on teaching agents to make sequential decisions through interaction with their (surrounding) environment. Unlike supervised learning, where models learn from labelled datasets, RL employs no explicit labels. Instead, the agent learns by trial and error, led by a reward mechanism that determines the value of its actions. The agent's goal is to create a policy that maximizes the cumulative rewards over time. RL uses this feedback mechanism to allow agents to adapt to changing environments and make decisions that balance immediate rewards with long-term outcomes.

As a subfield of machine learning, RL intersects with other fields such as deep learning and optimization. When integrated with neural networks, RL forms the cornerstone of Deep Reinforcement Learning (DRL), allowing agents to tackle high-dimensional and complicated tasks such as game play, robot control, and resource management in real-world systems. RL's main strength is its capacity to solve issues where the environment is partially observable, ambiguous/uncertain, or involves sequential planning. This makes RL not only a distinct subtopic/subfield in machine learning, but also an important tool for solving complex issues in fields such as robotics, healthcare, finance, and autonomous systems.

5.8.3.1 Learning Paradigm Integration

Supervised Learning Elements:

- Function approximation for value estimation
- Pattern recognition in state representation
- Generalization across similar states

Unsupervised Learning Elements:

- State representation learning
- Feature extraction from raw observations
- Clustering of similar states or actions

Unique RL Characteristics:

- Active learning through environment interaction
- Credit assignment across temporal sequences
- Exploration strategy development
- Policy optimization

5.8.3.2 Computational Aspects

Sample Efficiency:

- RL often requires many interactions
- Data efficiency crucial for real-world applications
- Transfer learning and meta-learning approaches

Scalability:

- High-dimensional state and action spaces
- Continuous control problems
- Distributed and parallel learning

Figure 5.11 Illustrates the reinforcement learning cycle, showing how an agent interacts with the environment, receives rewards, and updates its policy through feedback.

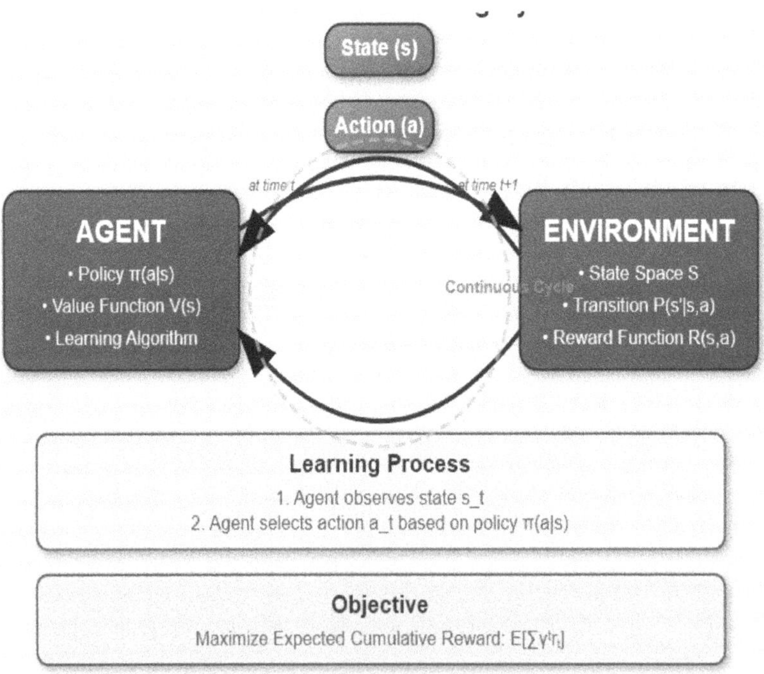

Figure 5.11 RL Learning Cycle

5.8.4 Components of Reinforcement Learning

5.8.4.1 Agent

The learner and decision maker that interacts with the environment.

Agent Characteristics:

- Maintains internal state representation
- Implements decision-making policy
- Updates knowledge based on experience
- Balances exploration and exploitation

5.8.4.2 Environment

The external system the agent interacts with.

Environment Properties:

- **Observable:** Full vs. partial state visibility
- **Deterministic:** Predictable vs. stochastic transitions
- **Episodic:** Finite episodes vs. continuing tasks
- **Static:** Fixed vs. changing dynamics

5.8.4.3 State (S)

Complete description of the environment at a given time.

State Representation:

- **Markov Property:** Current state contains all relevant information
- **State Space:** Set of all possible states
- **Observation:** Partial information about true state

5.8.4.4 Action (A)

Choices available to the agent in each state.

Action Characteristics:

- **Discrete:** Finite set of choices
- **Continuous:** Real-valued action parameters
- **Action Space:** Set of all possible actions

5.8.4.5 Reward (R)

Immediate feedback signal from environment.

Reward Properties:

- **Scalar Value:** Single numerical feedback
- **Immediate:** Received after each action
- **Subjective:** Designed to reflect goals
- **Sparse vs. Dense:** Frequency of non-zero rewards

5.8.4.6 Policy (π)

Strategy or behaviour function mapping states to actions.

Policy Types:

- **Deterministic:** π(s) = a
- **Stochastic: π(a|s)** = probability of action a in state s
- **Stationary:** Policy doesn't change over time
- **Non-stationary:** Policy evolves with learning

5.8.4.7 Value Function

Expected cumulative reward from a given state or state-action pair.

State Value Function:

$$V^{\pi}(s) = \mathrm{E}\left[RR_{t+1} + \gamma R_{t+2} + \gamma^{2} R_{t+2} + \gamma 3 R_{t+3} \ldots\ldots \middle| St = s \right] \ldots\ldots 5.9$$

Explanation of terms

Vπ(s):

- This is the **state-value function** for a given policy π.

- It represents the expected cumulative reward when starting in state s and following policy π

E[·]:

- The **expectation operator**, representing the average reward over all possible outcomes, given the stochastic nature of the environment.
- **Rt+1,Rt+2,Rt+3,…** — these are the *future rewards* contributing to the cumulative return.
- The rewards received at time steps t+1, t+2, t+3, …

γ:

- The **discount factor** (0≤γ≤1)**:**
  - Determines how future rewards are weighted relative to immediate rewards.
  - A smaller γ places more emphasis on immediate rewards, while a larger γ (closer to 1) values long-term rewards more.

S_t=s:

- The condition that the agent is in states at time t.

At=a:

- The condition that the agent takes action a at time t.

Purpose of the Equation:

This equation defines the **value of a state** under a specific policy π as the expected sum of discounted rewards that the agent will accumulate over time, starting from state s. This is a foundational concept in Reinforcement Learning, used to evaluate and improve policies.

Action Value Function (Q-function):

$$Q^{\pi}(s,a) = \mathrm{E}\left[\left[R_{t+1} + \gamma R_{t+1} + \gamma 2 R_{t+1} + \ldots\ldots \middle| S_t = s, A_t = a\right|\right] \text{....5.10}$$

Explanation of the Components

1. **$V^{\pi}(s)$:**

E[·]:

2. The **expectation operator**, representing the average reward over all possible outcomes, given the stochastic nature of the environment.

    - This is the **action-value function** (or Q-value) for a given policy π.
    - It represents the expected cumulative reward when starting in state s, taking action a, and subsequently following policy π.

3. **E[·]:**

    - The **expectation operator**, which calculates the average reward over all possible stochastic outcomes in the environment.

Rt+1,Rt+2,Rt+3,…:

- The **rewards received** after taking action a in state s and continuing according to policy π.
- The rewards received at time steps t+1, t+2, t+3, …

S_t=s:

- The condition that the agent is in state "s" at time t.

At=a:

- The condition that the agent takes action a at time t.

Purpose of the Equation (5.10)

The action-value function $Q^{\pi}(s,a)$ is central to Reinforcement Learning as it quantifies the expected return of taking a specific action a in state s and then following policy π. It is used in:

- **Policy Evaluation:** Assessing how good a given policy π is.

- **Policy Improvement:** Finding better policies by identifying actions with higher Q-values.

This equation is the basis for algorithms like **Q-Learning,** which iteratively estimates the optimal Q-values to discover the best policy.

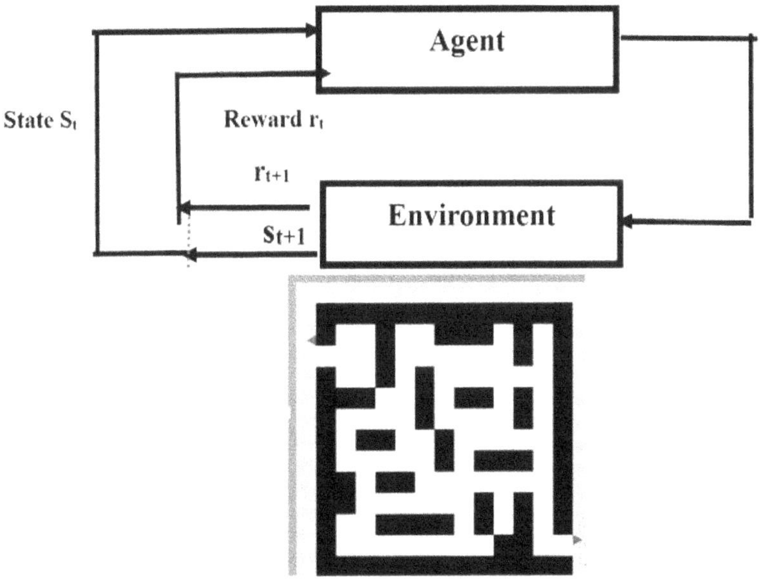

Figure 5.12 RL Components Interaction Diagram (a maze as an example of Agent's environment)

In figure 5.12 presented is the components of interaction diagram in reinforcement learning

5.9 Markov Decision Process (MDP)

MDP Framework

Mathematical framework for modelling decision-making in stochastic environments. A Markov Decision Process (MDP) is a mathematical framework for modelling decision-making situations in which the outcomes are both random and partly under the decision-maker's control. MDPs are a fundamental idea in Reinforcement Learning, providing a formal structure for modelling an agent's interaction with its environment. An MDP is comprised of four major components: states

(S), actions (A), transition probabilities (P), and rewards (R). A discount factor (γ) can be added to account for future rewards' importance. This structure allows the agent to make sequential judgments that maximize its cumulative reward over time whilst taking into account the probabilistic nature of the environment.

The defining property of an MDP is the **Markov Property**, which states that the future state of the system depends only on the current state and action, not on the sequence of past states. Mathematically, this is expressed as:

$$\boldsymbol{P}\left(\boldsymbol{S}_{t+1} \mid \boldsymbol{S}_t, \boldsymbol{A}_t\right) = \boldsymbol{P}\left(\boldsymbol{S}_{t+1} \mid \boldsymbol{S}_1, \boldsymbol{A}_1, \ldots \boldsymbol{S}_t, \boldsymbol{A}_t\right) \ldots\ldots \mathbf{5.11}$$

This property simplifies the modelling of dynamic systems and allows efficient computation of policies and value functions. The transition probabilities, **P(s′|s,a),** represent the likelihood of moving from state s to state **s′** given action a, while the reward function R(s,a) specifies the immediate reward received after taking action **a** in state **s**.

MDPs are commonly used in domains where decisions must be made under uncertain conditions, such as robotics, finance, healthcare, and logistics. They give a solid foundation for modelling activities such as guiding a robot through a maze, managing inventory in a warehouse, and optimizing treatment plans in medicine. Solving an MDP is determining the optimal policy—a mapping from states to actions—that maximizes the expected cumulative reward. MDPs are solved using techniques like as dynamic programming, Monte Carlo methods, and reinforcement learning algorithms, which vary based on the size and complexity of the state and action spaces.

MDP Tuple: (S, A, P, R, γ)

- **S:** State space
- **A:** Action space
- **P:** Transition probability function P(s'|s,a)
- **R:** Reward function R(s,a,s')
- **γ:** Discount factor $(0 \leq \gamma \leq 1)$

5.9.1 Markov Property

Definition: Future state depends only on current state and action, not on history.

Mathematical Expression:

$$P\left[S_{t+1}=s' \mid S_t=s, A_t=a, S_{t-1}, A_{t-1}, ..\right]=P\left[S_{t+1}=s' \mid S_t=s, A_t=a\right] ...5.12$$

Explanation of the Equation

This equation captures the **Markov Property**, which is central to the concept of a Markov Decision Process (MDP).

- $S_{t+1}=s'$
- This represents the **probability** of transitioning to state s′ at time t+1, given the current and all previous states (S_t, S_{t-1},… and actions (A_t,A_{t-1},…).

1. **Simplification via the Markov Property:**
    - The equation asserts that the probability of transitioning to the next state 's′ depends only on the current state s and the action a taken at that state.
    - The history of past states and actions (S_t, S_{t-1},… and actions (A_t, A_{t-1},…) does not influence the next state directly.
2. **Implication for MDPs:**
    - This simplification allows the system to be modelled using a compact representation of states and actions, without tracking entire histories.

This property is fundamental for the efficient computation of policies and transition dynamics in MDPs and is why the Markov model is used in reinforcement learning and stochastic processes.

Implications:

- State contains all relevant information
- Enables dynamic programming solutions
- Simplifies learning algorithms

5.9.2 Bellman Equations

State Value Function:

$$V^{\pi}(s) = \sum_{a} \pi(a \mid s) s' \Sigma P(s' \mid s, a)\left[R(s, a, s') + \gamma V^{\pi}(s')\right] \ldots .5.13(a)$$

Explanation of the Components

1. **$V^{\pi}(s)$:**
   - The value function under policy **π for state s.**
   - Represents the expected cumulative reward starting from state s and following policy π.
2. **π(a|s):**
   - The policy, which gives the probability of taking action a in state s.
3. **P(s′|s,a):**
   - The transition probability, representing the likelihood of transitioning to state s′ after taking action "a" in state "s".
4. **R(s,a,s′):**
   - The reward function, representing the immediate reward received for transitioning from state s to state s″ via action a.
5. **γ:**
   - The discount factor (0≤γ≤10) :
     - Determines the weight of future rewards relative to immediate rewards.

6. **Summations ($\sum a, \sum s'$):**
   - $\sum a$: Over all possible actions a in state s.
   - $\sum s'$: Over all possible successor states s′

Purpose of the Equation

This equation is the **Bellman** Expectation Equation for the **state-value function**. It expresses the value of a state s under policy π as:

- The expected value of the immediate reward R(s,a,s′) plus the discounted value of the subsequent state **V^π(s)**s′), weighted by:
  - The probability of taking action a in state s according to **π(a|s)** and
  - The probability of transitioning to s′ from s using **P(s′|s,a)**

This recursive relationship is central to solving MDPs and evaluating policies in reinforcement learning.

Action Value Function:

$$Q^\pi(s,a)=\sum_{s'}P(s'\mid s,a)\left[R(s,a,s')+\gamma\sum_{a'}\pi(a'\mid s')Q^\pi(s',a')\right]\ldots.5.13(b)$$

Explanation of the Components

- **Q^π(s,a):**
  - The **action-value function** for policy π, which represents the expected cumulative reward of taking action a in state s, and then following policy π
- **P(s′|s,a):**
  - The **transition probability**, representing the likelihood of moving to state s′ after taking action a in state s.
- **R(s,a,s′):**
  - The **reward function**, giving the immediate reward received for transitioning from state s to state s′ via action a.

- γ:
  - The **discount factor** ($0 \leq \gamma \leq 10$):
    - Balances the importance of future rewards relative to immediate rewards.
- **Summations ($\sum_{s'}$ and $\sum_{a'}$):**
  - $\sum_{s'}$ Summing over all possible next states s′.
  - $\sum_{a'}$ Summing over all possible actions a′ that can be taken in the next state s′.
- **π(a′|s′):**
  - The **policy**, specifying the probability of taking action a′ in state s′.

Purpose of the Equation

This is the **Bellman Expectation Equation** for the action-value function **Q^π(s,a)** It expresses the expected value of **Q^π(s,a) as:**

1. The immediate reward **R(s,a,s′)** plus
2. The discounted expected value of the subsequent state-action pairs, **Q^π(s,a)**

Averaged Over:

- All possible next states s′ **P(s′|s,a)** and
- Actions All actions a′ the agent might take in s″ (weighted by **π(a′|s′):**

This equation helps evaluate a given policy π, forming the foundation for policy evaluation and improvement in reinforcement learning algorithms.

Optimal Value Functions:

$$V^*(s) = max_a \sum_{s'} P(s' \mid s,a)\left[R(s,a,s') + \gamma V^*(s')\right] \text{....} \mathbf{5.13}(c)$$

Explanation of the Equations

Optimal State-Value Function ($V^*(s)$

- **($V^*(s)$):** The maximum cumulative reward achievable starting from state **s**, assuming the agent follows the optimal policy thereafter.
- **max_a:** The agent selects the action a that yields the highest expected value.
- $\sum_{s'} P(s'|s,a)$**:** Transition probabilities, summing over all possible next states s′.
- $R(s,a,s')+\gamma V^*(s')$**:** The immediate reward plus the discounted value of the next state **s′**.

$$Q^*(s,a)=\sum_{s'}P(s'\mid s,a)\left[R(s,a,s')+\gamma max_{a'}Q*(s',a')\right]....5.13(d)$$

Optimal Action-Value Function ($Q^*(s,a)$

- **$Q^*(s,a)$:** The maximum cumulative reward achievable by taking action a in state s and following the optimal policy thereafter.
- $\sum_{s'} P(s'|s,a)$**:** Transition probabilities, summing over all possible next states s′.
- **$R(s,a,s')+\gamma max_{a}'Q^*(s',a')$:** The immediate reward plus the discounted maximum value of the next state-action pair.

Significance

- Both equations define the **Bellman Optimality Equations**, which are central to reinforcement learning.
- Solving these equations allows the agent to compute the optimal policy by identifying the best actions to take in each state to maximize rewards.

Figure 5.13 depicts a Markov Decision Process (MDP) state transition diagram, illustrating how an agent moves between states based on actions and associated probabilities.

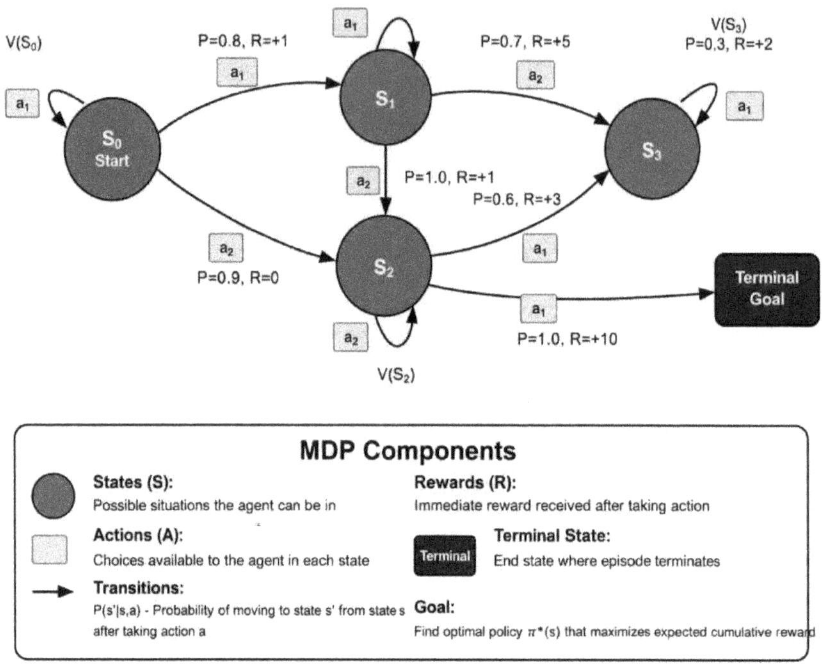

Figure 5.13 MDP State Transition Diagram

Key Components:

- **States:** 4 regular states (S_0, S_1, S_2, S_3) plus 1 terminal state
- **Actions:** 8 different actions (a_1 through a_8) showing various transition possibilities
- **Transitions:** Curved arrows showing state-to-state movements with probabilities
- **Rewards:** Each transition shows both probability (P) and reward (R) values
- **Self-loops:** Some states have actions that keep the agent in the same state

Visual Features:

- **Gray color scheme:** Professional appearance with clear contrast
- **Large, clear fonts:** Easy to read state names and action labels

- **Probability and reward annotations:** Each transition shows P(s'|s,a) and R values
- **Terminal state:** Distinguished by rectangular shape
- **Value function annotations:** V(S) labels for each state
- **Comprehensive legend:** Explains all MDP components

MDP Elements Demonstrated:

- **State space:** $\{S_0, S_1, S_2, S_3, \text{Terminal}\}$
- **Action space:** $\{a_1, a_2, a_3, a_4, a_5, a_6, a_7, a_8\}$
- **Transition probabilities:** Various P values (0.3 to 1.0)
- **Reward function:** Mix of positive and negative rewards
- **Policy representation:** Shows decision points at each state

This diagram effectively illustrates how an MDP works, showing the decision-making process where an agent must choose actions in different states to maximize expected cumulative reward. The visual layout makes it easy to trace possible paths from the start state to the terminal goal state.

5.10 Multi-Arm Bandit Problem

The Multi-Armed Bandit (MAB) problem is a fundamental problem in reinforcement learning and decision theory. It is frequently used to represent/model instances in which an agent must choose between multiple options, each with uncertain rewards. The name is derived from a row of slot machines (or "bandits"), each of which has a unique payout probability distribution. The agent's objective is to determine which "arm" to pull at each time step in order to maximize cumulative rewards over time. The problem stems from the exploration-exploitation tradeoff: the agent must strike a balance between testing out multiple arms to learn about their reward distributions (exploration) and using known information to select the arm with the highest expected reward.

MAB problems are used in a variety of domains, including online marketing, where algorithms determine which ads to display to consumers in order to maximize clicks, and clinical trials, where researchers select therapies to determine the most effective while minimizing patient risks. Several strategies have been developed to solve the MAB problem, including: ε-greedy algorithms, which alternate between exploration and exploitation with a fixed probability; Upper Confidence Bound (UCB) methods, which prioritize arms with high uncertainty; and Thompson Sampling, which uses Bayesian inference to guide decision-making. Despite its simplicity, the MAB problem provides the basis for more complicated reinforcement learning scenarios, such as contextual bandits and full Markov Decision Processes.

Problem Formulation

Simplified RL problem focusing on exploration-exploitation trade-off without state transitions.

Setup:

- K slot machines (arms) with unknown reward distributions
- Agent selects one arm at each time step
- **Goal:** maximize cumulative reward over time
- No state information, only reward feedback

5.10.1 Exploration vs. Exploitation

Exploitation: Choose arm with highest estimated reward **Exploration:** Try arms with uncertain rewards to improve estimates

Algorithms:

ε-Greedy:

- Select best arm with probability **(1-ε)**
- Select random arm with probability ε
- Simple but doesn't adapt exploration

Upper Confidence Bound (UCB):

$$A_t = argamax\left[\hat{Q}_t(a) + c\sqrt{\frac{\ln t}{N_t a}}\right] \ldots 5.14$$

- Balances estimated value and uncertainty
- Automatically reduces exploration over time

Thompson Sampling:

- Bayesian approach using posterior distributions
- Samples from belief about each arm's value
- Naturally balances exploration and exploitation

Table 5.11 Multi-Arm Bandit Algorithms Comparison

Algorithm	Exploration Strategy	Advantages	Limitations
ε-Greedy	Explores randomly with probability ε.	Simple to implement, balances exploration.	Fixed ε may not adapt well.
Upper Confidence Bound (UCB)	Uses confidence intervals to prioritize uncertain actions.	Efficient exploration with theoretical guarantees.	Requires careful tuning of exploration constant.
Thompson Sampling	Samples actions based on posterior probability.	Bayesian approach, handles non-stationary problems.	Computationally expensive for complex priors.
Softmax	Selects actions probabilistically using softmax function.	Smooth balance of exploration and exploitation.	Sensitive to temperature parameter.

Greedy (Baseline)	Always chooses the action with the highest estimated reward.	Simple and computationally efficient.	Poor exploration, easily stuck in local optima.

Table 5.5 compares Multi-Arm Bandit algorithms, highlighting their exploration strategies, advantages, and limitations to aid in selecting the right approach for specific scenarios.

5.10.2 Reinforcement Learning Problem Types

(A) Episodic vs. Continuing Tasks

Episodic Tasks:

- Natural ending points (terminal states)
- **Examples:** Games, simulation episodes
- Finite horizon optimization

Continuing Tasks:

- No natural termination
- Infinite horizon problems
- **Examples:** Process control, recommendation systems

Finite vs. Infinite Horizon

Finite Horizon:

- Fixed time limit T
- Optimization over finite time steps
- Time-dependent optimal policies

Infinite Horizon:

- Unbounded time duration
- Discounting ensures finite cumulative rewards
- Stationary optimal policies

(B) Deterministic vs. Stochastic

Deterministic Environments:

- State transitions are predictable
- Same action in same state always produces same result
- Simpler planning and learning

Stochastic Environments:

- Probabilistic state transitions
- Uncertainty in action outcomes
- Requires handling of probabilistic effects

Figure 5.14 classifies reinforcement learning problems, distinguishing between model-based vs. model-free and policy-based vs. value-based approaches.

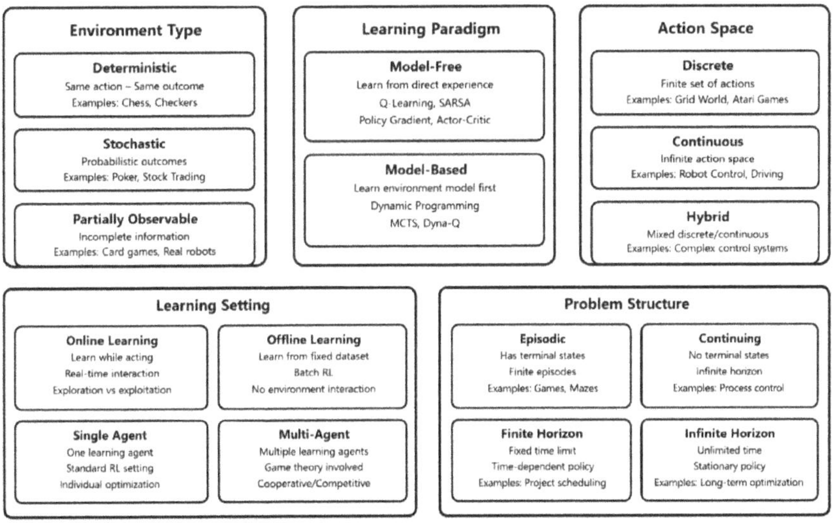

Figure 5.14 RL Problem Classification

5.11 Model-Based Learning

Model-Based Learning is an example of reinforcement learning in which the agent creates or uses a model of the environment to predict its behaviour. Model-Based Learning incorporates a representation of the environment's dynamics, typically defined by the **transition**

probabilities P(s'|s,a) and the **reward function** R(s,a), unlike Model-Free methods that rely solely on experience to make decisions. Utilizing this approach, the agent can simulate interactions with the environment to plan its actions and predict their long-term consequences without requiring substantial real-world exploration. This ability makes Model-Based learning substantially more **sample-efficient** than Model-Free techniques.

Approach Overview

Learn explicit model of environment dynamics, then use model for planning.

Model Components:

- **Transition Model:** P(s'|s,a) - probability of next state
- **Reward Model:** R(s,a) - expected immediate reward

5.11.1 Dynamic Programming Methods

Policy Iteration:

1. **Policy Evaluation:** Compute V^π using Bellman equation
2. **Policy Improvement:** Update policy greedily with respect to V^π
3. Repeat until convergence

Value Iteration:

1. Initialize value function arbitrarily
2. Update values using Bellman optimality equation
3. Extract optimal policy from converged values

Policy Iteration Algorithm:

1. Initialize π arbitrarily

2. Repeat:

a. **Policy Evaluation:** Solve $V^\pi(s)$ for all s

b. Policy Improvement:

$$\pi'(s) = arg\frac{max}{a}s'\sum P(s' \mid s,a)\left[R(s,a,s') + \gamma V^{\pi}(s')\right] \text{......}\mathbf{5.15}$$

c. If π' = π, then stop; else π = π'

Advantages and Disadvantages

Advantages:

- Efficient use of experience through planning
- Can perform "mental simulation"
- Theoretical guarantees for convergence
- Sample efficient when model is accurate

Disadvantages:

- Model learning can be challenging
- Model errors compound in planning
- Computational overhead of planning
- May not scale to complex environments

Figure 5.15 illustrates the architecture of model-based reinforcement learning, showing how the agent uses a learned or given model of the environment to plan and make decisions.

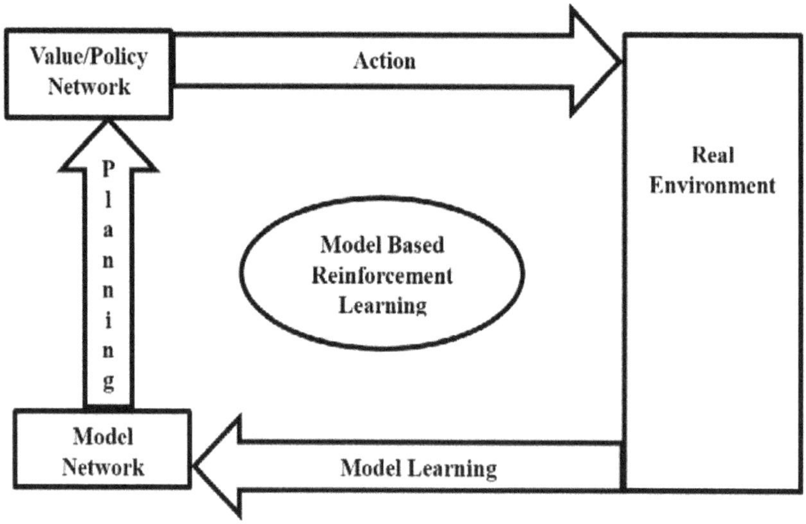

Figure 5.15 Model-Based RL Architecture

5.12 Model-Free Methods

Model-free reinforcement learning involves the agent learning to make decisions without explicitly modelling the environment's dynamics, such as transition probabilities (($s'|s$,) or the reward functionR(s,a). Instead, the agent uses direct interactions with the environment to estimate optimal policy or value functions. These techniques are especially effective when the environment's dynamics are unknown or too complex to model. Model-Free approaches, which rely on learning directly from experience, may handle a wide range of problems, including those with stochastic or partially observable settings.

Model-free methods are divided into two categories: value-based methods and policy-based methods. Value-based techniques, including Q-Learning and Deep Q-Networks (DQN), estimate the action-value function ((s,) and select actions that maximize the estimated value to determine the best policy indirectly. Policy-based approaches, such as Policy Gradient methods, train a parameterized policy by maximizing the predicted cumulative reward. Model-free approaches are extensively utilized because of their simplicity and generality, making them useful in a variety of applications, including game-playing AI and robotic control. However, they frequently require substantial interaction with the environment to converge and may struggle in situations with sparse rewards or high-dimensional state-action spaces.

5.12.1 Approach Overview

Learn optimal policy or value function directly from experience without explicit environment model.

Key Characteristics:

- No environment model required
- Learn directly from interaction
- Robust to model misspecification
- Often simpler to implement

5.12.2 Monte Carlo Methods

Learn from complete episodes by averaging returns.

Basic Monte Carlo:

1. Generate episode using current policy

2. For each state St in the episode:

$$\boldsymbol{G_t = R_{t+1} + \gamma R_{t+2} + \cdots + \gamma^{T-t-1} R_T} \ldots\ldots\mathbf{5.16(a)}$$

$$V(S_t) \leftarrow V(S_t) + \alpha\left[G_t - V(S_t)\right] \ldots\ldots\mathbf{5.16(b)}$$

Explanation of the Components

1. **Gt:**
    - The **return** at time step t, representing the cumulative discounted reward from time t+1 to the end of the episode T.

2. γ:

- The **discount factor** (0≤γ≤10 which determines the weight of future rewards relative to immediate rewards.

3. V(St):

- The **value function** for state $\mathbf{S_t}$, estimating the expected return starting from state $\mathbf{S_t}$.

4. α:

- The **learning rate**, which controls how much the new information $[G_t - V(S_t)]$ influences the update of $V(S_t)$.

Characteristics:

- Unbiased value estimates
- High variance due to episode sampling
- Requires episodic tasks
- No bootstrap (doesn't use estimates of other states)

5.12.3 Temporal Difference Learning

Combines ideas from Monte Carlo and Dynamic Programming.

Basic TD (0):

$$V(S_t) \leftarrow V(S_t) + \alpha\left[R_{t+1} + \gamma V(S_t + 1) - V(S_t)\right] \ldots\ldots 5.17(a)$$

TD Error:

$$\delta_t = R_{t+1} + \gamma V(S_t + 1) - V(S_t) \ldots\ldots 5.17(b)$$

Advantages:

- Learn online from incomplete episodes
- Lower variance than Monte Carlo
- Can handle continuing tasks
- Bootstrap from current estimates

Table 5.12 Comparison of Model-Free Methods

Aspect	Value-Based Methods	Policy-Based Methods
Approach	Learns value functions (V or Q).	Learns the policy directly.
Action Selection	Derives policy indirectly from value function.	Selects actions based on learned policy.
Continuous Actions	Struggles to handle; discretization needed.	Handles continuous actions effectively.
Convergence	May face instability or divergence.	Stable convergence with appropriate methods.
Exploration	Relies on exploration strategies (e.g., ε-greedy).	Exploration is built into the policy.
Examples	Q-Learning, Deep Q-Networks (DQN).	Policy Gradient, PPO, REINFORCE.

Table 5.6 compares Model-Free methods, highlighting their differences in approach, action handling, convergence, exploration, and example algorithms to aid in selecting the appropriate method for specific tasks.

5.13 Q-Learning

Q-Learning is a fundamental reinforcement learning al that enables an agent to learn the optimal policy for maximizing cumulative rewards without the need for an environmental model. Q-Learning is a model-free, value-based approach that learns the optimal action-value function $Q*$ (s,a). This function reflects the highest expected return from a given state s and action a, follows the optimal policy. The algorithm iteratively updates estimates of Q(s,a) based on the agent's interactions with the environment, using the Bellman Optimality Equation to improve its predictions.

At its core, Q-Learning uses the following update rule:

$$Q(s,a) \leftarrow Q(s,a) + \alpha\left[R + \gamma \frac{max}{a'} Q(s',a') - Q(s,a)\right] \text{....5.18}(a)$$

Here, α is the learning rate, Ris the reward received for taking action **a** in state **s**, γ is the discount factor for future rewards, and $\mathbf{max}_{\mathbf{a'}}Q(s',a')$ represents the highest estimated value of the next state-action pair. This equation updates Q(s,a) by incorporating the immediate reward and the estimated value of the best future action. Over time, as the agent explores the environment and updates its Q-values, the function converges to **Q***(s,a), allowing the agent to derive the optimal policy by selecting actions that maximize **Q(s, a).**

Q-Learning has been effectively used in a variety of fields, including robotics, gaming, and optimizing resources. For example, it helped train AI systems to play games like Atari, where agents learned to surpass human players in complicated decision-making scenarios/situations. Although Q-Learning is simple and effective, it has limitations when dealing with high-dimensional state-action spaces due to the exponential expansion of the Q-Table. Deep Q-Learning (DQN) uses neural networks to approximate the Q-function, making it more suitable for complex scenarios/environments.

Algorithm Description

Off-policy temporal difference method for learning optimal action-value function.

Q-Learning Update Rule:

$$Q(S_t, A_t) \leftarrow Q(S_t, A_t) + \alpha\left[R_{t+1} + \gamma \frac{\max}{a} Q(S_{t+1}, a) - Q(S_t, A_t)\right] \text{....5.18}(b)$$

Algorithm Steps:

1. Initialize Q(s,a) arbitrarily for all s,a

2. For each episode:

a. Initialize state S

b. For each step of the episode:

- Choose action A from S using policy derived from Q (e.g., ε-greedy)

- Take action A, observe reward R and next state S'

- Update: $$Q(S_t, A_t) \leftarrow Q(S_t, A_t) + \alpha\left[R_{t+1} + \gamma \max_{a} Q(S_{t+1}, a) - Q(S_t, A_t)\right]$$

- S ← S'

c. Until S is terminal

Key Properties

Off-Policy Learning:

- Learns optimal policy while following different behaviour policy
- Can learn from exploratory or sub-optimal experience
- Separates learning from action selection

Convergence Guarantees:

- Converges to optimal Q-function under certain conditions
- Requires sufficient exploration of state-action pairs
- Learning rate must satisfy specific conditions

Exploration Strategies:

- **ε-greedy:** Random action with probability ε
- **Boltzmann:** Probabilistic selection based on Q-values
- **Optimistic Initialization:** Initialize Q-values optimistically.

Advantages:

- **Model-free:** No environment model required
- **Off-policy:** Flexible exploration strategies

- Simple implementation
- Convergence guarantees

Limitations:

- Requires tabular representation (finite state-action space)
- Slow convergence in large state spaces
- No function approximation in basic form
- Overestimation bias in stochastic environments

Figure 5.16 presents the Q-Learning algorithm with an epsilon-greedy strategy, illustrating how it balances exploration and exploitation to learn optimal actions in a reinforcement learning framework.

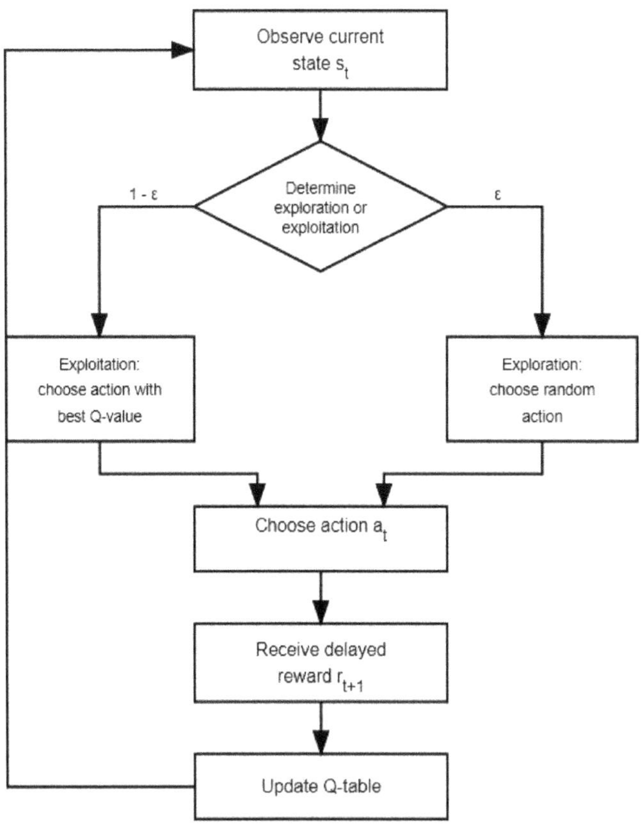

Figure 5.16 Q-Learning Algorithm Flowchart

5.14 SARSA Learning

SARSA (State-Action-Reward-State-Action) is an on-policy reinforcement learning system that learns a policy by interacting with its surroundings and updating its knowledge depending on the experience gathered. Unlike Q-Learning, which is an off-policy algorithm, SARSA adheres to the agent's policy while learning, updating depending on the actions it actually does rather than the optimal actions possible. This strategy highlights the agent's current policy, which can result in smoother learning in certain stochastic environments.

The approach uses bootstrapping to update the Q-values (state-action values). SARSA, in particular, adjusts the Q-value for a state-action pair based on the reward received from the environment as well as the Q-value of the next state-action pair selected in accordance with the agent's policy. The update rule is expressed as follows:

$$Q(S_t, a_t) \leftarrow Q(S_t, a_t) + \alpha\left[r_{t+1} + \gamma Q(S_{t+1}, a_{t+1}) - Q(S_t, a_t)\right] \quad ...5.19$$

Here, $\boldsymbol{\alpha}$ is the learning rate**,** γ is the discount factor, and $\mathbf{r_{t+1}}$ is the reward, and $\mathbf{Q(s_{t+1}, a_{t+1})}$ corresponds to the value of the next state-action pair.

SARSA's policy-driven nature enables it to respond swiftly to changes in the environment or the agent's approach. It is especially useful in situations when adhering to an exploratory policy is critical, such as surroundings that have significant randomness or acts with highly unpredictable outcomes. However, because SARSA updates are dependent on the agent's existing/current policy, its convergence rate may be slower than that of off-policy methods such as Q-Learning when optimal policies are known.

Algorithm Description

On-policy temporal difference method for learning action-value function.

SARSA Update Rule:

$$Q(S_t, A_t) \leftarrow Q(S_t, A_t) + \alpha\left[R_{t+1} + \gamma Q(S_{t+1}, A_{t+1}) - Q(S_t, A_t)\right]$$

Algorithm Steps:

1. Initialize Q(s,a) arbitrarily for all s,a

2. For each episode:

a. Initialize state S

b. Choose action A from S using policy derived from Q

c. For each step of episode:

- Take action A, observe reward R and next state S'

- Choose action A' from S' using policy derived from Q

- **Update:** $Q(S,A) \leftarrow Q(S,A) + \alpha\left[R + \gamma Q(S',A') - Q(S,A)\right]$

- S ← S', A ← A'

d. Until S is terminal

5.14.1 On-Policy vs. Off-Policy

SARSA (On-Policy):

- Updates Q-values based on actions actually taken
- Learns value of policy being followed
- More conservative in risky environments
- Policy improvement affects learning directly

Q-Learning (Off-Policy):

- Updates based on optimal action in next state
- Learns optimal policy regardless of behaviour policy
- More aggressive exploration possible
- Separates learning target from behaviour

5.14.2 Comparison with Q-Learning

Convergence:

- Both converge under appropriate conditions

- SARSA converges to policy being followed
- Q-Learning converges to optimal policy

Safety:

- SARSA considers actual policy in updates
- Better for safety-critical applications
- Q-Learning may learn risky optimal actions

Exploration:

- SARSA exploration affects value estimates
- Q-Learning can use any exploration strategy
- Trade-off between safety and optimality

Table 5.13 SARSA vs Q-Learning Comparison

Aspect	SARSA	Q-Learning
Learning Approach	On-policy	Off-policy
Policy Followed	Follows the agent's current policy	Learns optimal policy regardless of current policy
Update Rule	Based on actual action taken (Q(s, a) to Q(s', a'))	Based on the best possible action (Q(s, a) to max_a Q(s', a))
Equation	Equation 5.19	Equation 5.18
Exploration Behaviour	Learns from actions actually taken (explores)	Evaluates the optimal future action (exploits)
Performance in Stochastic Environments	More stable due to learning from actual transitions	Can perform poorly in highly stochastic environments
Speed of Convergence	Slower, as it adheres to exploratory actions	Faster, as it seeks the optimal policy directly

Applicability	Useful when exploratory policies are important	Useful when exploitation of optimal policies is prioritized
Policy Learned	Tends to learn a safer, exploratory policy	Tends to learn an aggressive, optimal policy

Table 5.7 compares SARSA and Q-Learning, highlighting differences in their learning strategies, update rules, and policy Behaviour.

5.14.2.1 SARSA Variations

SARSA has evolved into several variations to address specific challenges in reinforcement learning, such as handling large state-action spaces, improving convergence speed, and enhancing exploration strategies. One common variation is **Expected SARSA**, which replaces the Q-value update based on the next action's reward with an expectation over all possible actions weighted by their probabilities under the current policy. This approach reduces variance compared to standard SARSA, leading to smoother and potentially faster learning. Additionally, **Deep SARSA** integrates deep neural networks to approximate Q-values in environments with high-dimensional state spaces, enabling SARSA to be applied effectively to complex problems like continuous control tasks and video game playing.

Another notable variation is **n-step SARSA**, which generalizes the update mechanism by incorporating rewards from multiple future steps instead of just the immediate next step. This method balances between short-term and long-term rewards, improving the agent's ability to plan ahead and learn from extended trajectories. Similarly, **Backward SARSA** integrates eligibility traces, allowing the algorithm to update not only the current state-action pair but also those encountered earlier in the trajectory, weighted by their eligibility. These enhancements aim to improve SARSA's efficiency and adaptability, making it suitable for a broader range of applications.

Expected SARSA:

$$Q(S_t, A_t) \leftarrow Q(S_t, A_t) + \alpha \left[R_{t+1} + \gamma \sum_a \pi(a \mid S_{t+1}) Q(S_{t+1}, a) - Q(S_t A_t) \right] \quad ....5.20$$

- Uses expected value over next actions
- Reduces variance compared to SARSA
- Can be used in both on-policy and off-policy settings

n-step SARSA:

- Updates using n-step returns
- Bridges gap between TD and Monte Carlo
- Faster learning through multi-step updates

Figure 5.17 illustrates the SARSA learning process, showing how the agent updates its action-value estimates using the current state, action, reward, and next state-action pair.

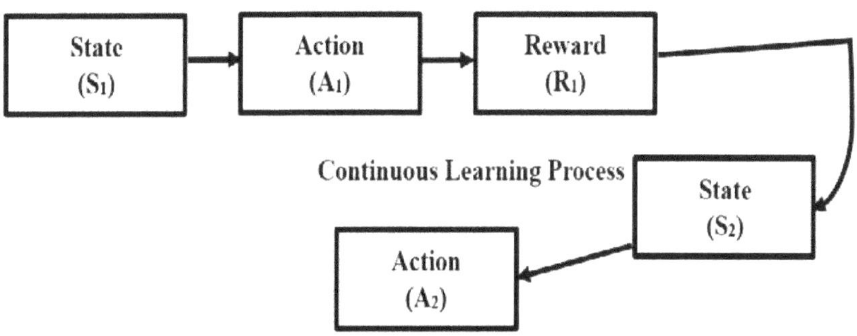

Figure 5.17 SARSA Learning Process

5.15 Introduction to Artificial Neural Networks (ANNs)

Artificial Neural Networks (ANNs) are computational models based on the structure and operation of biological neural networks in the human brain. They comprise up of interconnected nodes known as neurons, which have been organized into layers. Each neuron receives input, processes it with an activation function, and produces an output. These outputs are subsequently passed on to neurons in succeeding layers, resulting in a network capable of learning complicated patterns and correlations in data. The design of ANNs allows them to perform a variety of tasks such as classification, regression, and pattern recognition.

At the core of an ANN is its ability to learn from data through a process called training. During training, the network adjusts the weights associated with the connections between neurons to minimize the difference between predicted and actual results-the outcomes. This optimization is often accomplished by algorithms like gradient descent and backpropagation. The network's architecture, including the number of layers and neurons in each layer, is important to its performance and capabilities.

ANNs are particularly helpful for tasks requiring non-linear relationships or high-dimensional data. They have been effective in a variety of applications, including image and speech recognition, natural language processing, and predictive analytics. A key attribute of ANNs is their ability to generalize, allowing them to generate accurate predictions on unseen data. However, constructing and training ANNs requires careful consideration to avoid issues like overfitting and vanishing gradients.

Recent advances in ANN technology, such as the creation of deep learning architectures, have greatly increased its application. Deep neural networks, a type of artificial neural network (ANN), use numerous hidden layers to learn hierarchical data representations. This has resulted in achievements in fields such as autonomous driving, medical diagnostics, and gaming. As processing power and data availability increase, ANNs will play a more significant role in artificial intelligence and machine learning applications.

5.15.1 Biological vs. Artificial Neurons

Artificial neural networks are inspired by the structure and function of the human brain, but with significant simplifications. In the human brain, billions of neurons communicate with one another via synapses, which transfer electrical signals that enable complicated mental functions. Similarly, ANNs are composed of artificial neurons that Analyse and transmit information. These artificial neurons are split into layers, with each layer executing a specific transformation on the data. While the biological brain is incredibly complex and adaptable, ANNs seek to replicate this behaviour in a computationally efficient manner.

Despite its simple nature, ANNs can learn and generalize patterns in data. Each neuron in an ANN is linked to others through weighted links, similar to synapses. These weights determine the significance of input signals and are adjusted during training to enhance the network's performance. In contrast to the brain's complex biochemical processes, ANNs simulate learning and decision-making using mathematical operations like dot products and activation functions.

Parallel processing and distributed representation are two examples of biologically inspired concepts. Just as the brain processes information through interconnected networks of neurons, ANNs leverage their layered structure to capture complicated, hierarchical patterns. However, although biological neurons act asynchronously and are highly flexible, artificial neurons adhere to predetermined mathematical rules and require particular training procedures to function. This distinction emphasises both the promise and limitations of ANNs as compared to their biological counterparts.

Biological Neurons:

- Consists of dendrites (inputs), cell body (processing), and axon (output)
- Receive electrochemical signals through dendrites
- If combined input exceeds a threshold, the neuron "fires" an action potential
- Signal transmission occurs at synapses between neurons
- Learning involves adjusting the strength of synaptic connections

Artificial Neurons:

- Mathematical models that mimic biological neurons
- Inputs ($x_1, x_2, ..., x_n$) are combined using weights ($w_1, w_2, ..., w_n$).
- The weighted sum is passed through an activation function.
- Output is transmitted to other neurons in the network

- Learning involves adjusting the weights based on error feedback.

The Table 4.3 highlights key differences and similarities between biological neurons and their artificial counterparts, providing insight into their respective structures and functions.

Table 5.14 Comparison of Biological and Artificial Neurons

Component/Process	Biological Neurons	Artificial Neurons
Structure	Consists of dendrites (inputs), cell body (processing), and axon (output).	Mathematical models with input layer, processing unit, and output
Input Reception	Receive electrochemical signals through dendrites from multiple synapses.	Receive numerical inputs ($x_1, x_2, ..., x_n$) from previous layer or external sources
Signal Integration	Dendrites collect and integrate incoming signals in the cell body	Inputs are combined using weighted sum: $\mathbf{\Sigma(w_i \times x_i)}$
Activation Mechanism	If combined input exceeds a threshold, the neuron "fires" an action potential	Weighted sum is passed through an activation function $f(\Sigma(w_i \times x_i))$
Threshold Behaviour	All-or-nothing response when threshold potential is reached (~-55mV)	Activation function determines output based on input magnitude
Signal Transmission	Action potential travels down axon to axon terminals	Output value is transmitted to connected neurons in next layer
Connection Points	Signal transmission occurs at synapses	Connections represented by

	between neurons	weighted links between nodes
Learning Mechanism	Learning involves adjusting the strength of synaptic connections (synaptic plasticity)	Learning involves adjusting the weights (w_1, w_2, ..., w_n) based on error feedback
Adaptation Process	Hebbian learning: "Cells that fire together, wire together"	Backpropagation: weights updated to minimize prediction error
Signal Type	Electrochemical (ions: **Na^+, K^+, Ca^{2+}, Cl^-**)	Mathematical (real numbers, typically **0-1 or -1 to 1**)
Processing Speed	Milliseconds per firing cycle	Microseconds to nanoseconds per computation
Energy Consumption	~20 watts for entire brain (~10^{11} neurons)	Varies with hardware; can be energy-intensive for large networks
Fault Tolerance	High redundancy; can function with damaged neurons	Depends on network architecture; typically, less fault-tolerant
Memory Storage	Distributed across synaptic strengths and neural patterns	Stored in weight matrices and network parameters
Plasticity	Lifelong synaptic plasticity and neurogenesis	Weights typically fixed after training (though online learning possible)

Key Mathematical Relationships

Biological Neuron Model

Membrane Potential = Σ(Synaptic Inputs) + Resting Potential

If membrane potential > threshold, action potential fires.

Artificial Neuron Model

Net Input = $\Sigma(w_i \times x_i)$ + bias

Output = f(Net Input)

where f() is the activation function (sigmoid, ReLU, tanh, etc.).

The McCulloch-Pitts neuron model, introduced in 1943, is a simplified mathematical representation of a biological neuron. It operates as a binary threshold unit, where the neuron activates (outputs 1) if the weighted sum of its inputs exceeds a specified threshold; otherwise it remains inactive (outputs 0). This foundational model laid the groundwork for modern artificial neural networks, demonstrating the potential of logical operations in neural computation.

- Binary threshold unit with weighted inputs
- Output y is given by equation 5.21

$$y_i = \begin{cases} 1 & \text{if } a_{wi}\, x_i \geq \theta_i \\ 0 & otherwise \end{cases} \quad \ldots (5.21)$$

Figure 5.18illustrates the analogy between a biological neuron and an artificial neuron by mapping components such as dendrites, cell body, and axon to inputs, weighted summation, and output in the artificial model.

It highlights how artificial neurons mathematically simulate biological signal processing using weights, bias, and an activation function.

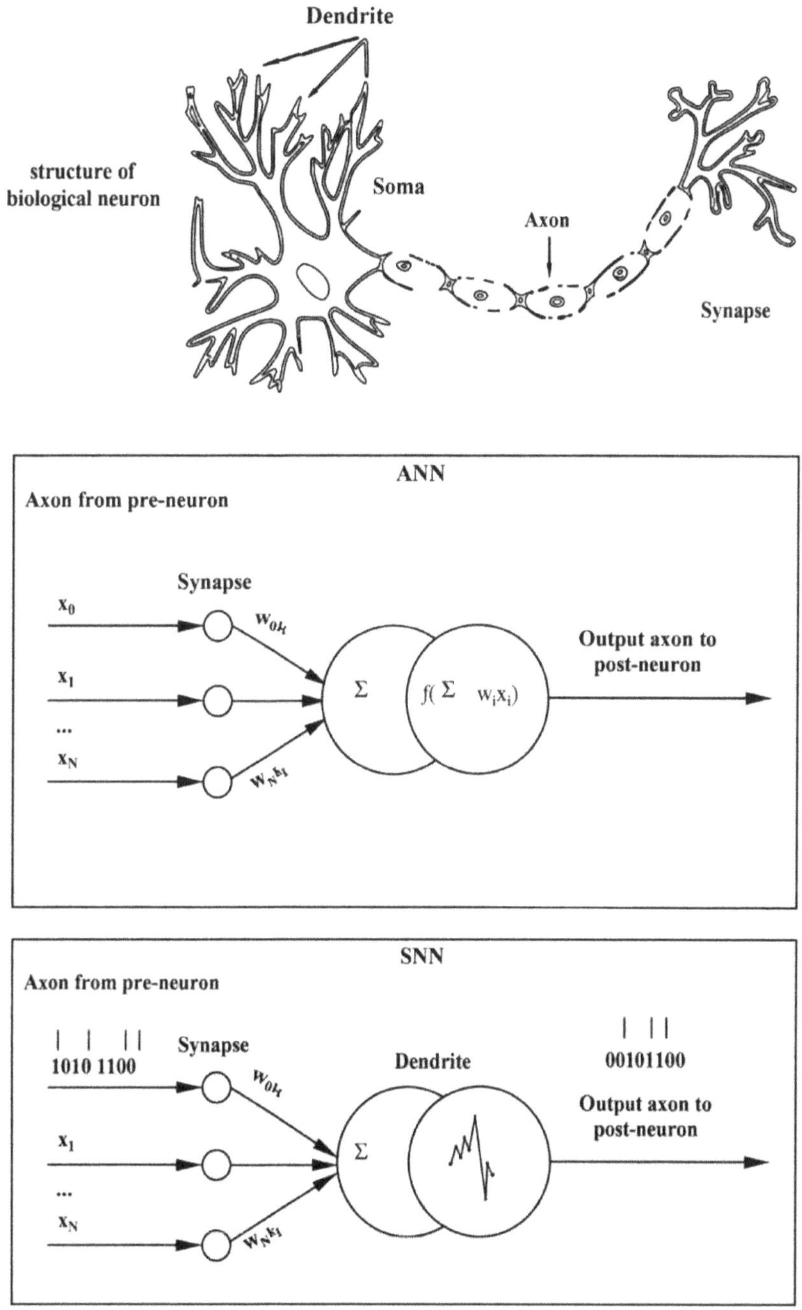

Figure 5.18 Comparison Between Biological Neuron and Artificial Neuron Model

5.15.2 Perceptron and Its Learning Theory

Frank Rosenblatt developed the perceptron in 1958, and it remains a fundamental concept in neural networks and machine learning today. It is the simplest type of feedforward neural network, consisting of a single neuron with adjustable weights and a bias term. The perceptron takes multiple input values, computes their weighted sum, and then proceeds/passes the result by means of a step activation function to get a binary output. This simple approach allows the perceptron to classify linearly separable datasets effectively.

The perceptron system of learning is iterative and supervised. This entails modifying the model's weights and biases in response to observable prediction error. When the perceptron misclassifies an input, its weights are adjusted in a way that minimizes the errors for that particular input. The update rule is straightforward and plausible because for each misclassified sample, weights are increased or lowered appropriately to the input features, scaled by a learning rate. This assures that the perceptron discovers a solution if the dataset is linearly separable.

Despite its simplicity, the perceptron has limitations. The most significant drawback is its inability to solve problems involving non-linearly separable data, as demonstrated by Minsky and Papert in their 1969 critique. Problems like the XOR classification challenge cannot be addressed by a single-layer perceptron due to its linear decision boundary. This limitation eventually led to the development of more advanced models, including multilayer perceptrons and deep learning architectures, which can handle non-linear relationships. However, the perceptron continues to be an important building block for comprehending neural networks. Its design introduces key concepts including weight optimization, learning rates, and decision boundaries. In addition, it served as the foundation for the creation of more sophisticated algorithms such as the Adaline (Adaptive Linear Neuron) and modern methods for deep learning. By studying the perceptron, learners get insight into the evolution of artificial intelligence and the fundamental concepts that underpin/underline modern machine learning.

Perceptron Model:

- **Input vector:** $x = (x_1, x_2, ..., x_n)$
- **Weight vector:** $w = (w_1, w_2 ..., w_n)$
- **Net Input** (Weighted Sum):

$$z = w \cdot x + b = \sum_{i=1}^{n} w_i x_i + b \qquad \text{...... } \mathbf{5.22}$$

Where b is the bias term

- **Output:**

$$Y = f(z) \text{.......} 5.22 \text{ (a)}$$

$$f(z) = \begin{cases} 0 \text{ if } z < 0 \\ 1 \text{ if } z \geq 0 \end{cases} \text{..........} \mathbf{5.22(b)}$$

- **For binary classification, f is typically a step function:**

Perceptron Learning Algorithm:

1. Initialize weights and bias to small random values.
2. For each training example (x, d):
    - **Calculate the output.**

$$y = f(w_i x_i + b) \ldots 5.23(a)$$

- **Update weights:**

$$w = w + \eta(d - y)x \ldots 5.23(b)$$

- **Update bias:**

$$b = b + \eta(d - y) \ldots 5.23(c)$$

3. Repeat until convergence or maximum iterations, where η is the learning rate and d is the desired output

5.15.3 Types and Architectures of Artificial Neural Networks (ANNs)

Artificial Neural Networks (ANNs) are computational models inspired by the human brain's structure and functionality. Over the years, different types and architectures of ANNs have been developed to cater to various tasks such as classification, regression, feature extraction, and prediction. These architectures are distinguished by the number of layers, types of connections between neurons, and specific tasks they are designed to handle.

5.15.3.1 Types of Neural Networks

1. **Feedforward Neural Networks (FNNs):** These are the simplest form of ANNs where information flows in one direction from input to output, without any cycles or loops. They are ideal for tasks like image classification and time-series prediction. However, they lack the capability to retain memory or process sequential data effectively.

2. **Recurrent Neural Networks (RNNs):** RNNs incorporate feedback loops, allowing them to retain information over time. This makes them suitable for tasks like natural language processing (NLP) and speech recognition. Variants such as Long Short-Term Memory (LSTM) and Gated Recurrent Units

(GRUs) address the vanishing gradient problem commonly associated with RNNs.

3. **Convolutional Neural Networks (CNNs):** CNNs are designed for spatial data like images and videos. They employ convolutional layers to extract features such as edges and textures, making them highly effective for object detection and image recognition tasks.
4. **Generative Adversarial Networks (GANs):** GANs consist of two neural networks—a generator and a discriminator—that compete with each other. They are used for tasks such as image synthesis, style transfer, and data augmentation.

Table 4.4 summarizes the key types of neural networks, their characteristics, and typical applications.

Table 5.15 Types of Neural Networks and Their Applications

Type of Neural Network	Description	Applications
Feedforward Neural Networks (FNNs)	Simplest form of ANN where information flows in one direction from input to output, without any cycles or loops.	Image classification, time-series prediction
Recurrent Neural Networks (RNNs)	Incorporate feedback loops, allowing them to retain information over time. Variants like LSTM and GRU solve the vanishing gradient problem.	Natural language processing (NLP), speech recognition
Convolutional Neural Networks (CNNs)	Designed for spatial data like images and videos. Use convolutional layers to extract features such as edges and textures.	Object detection, image recognition

Generative Adversarial Networks (GANs)	Comprise two networks (generator and discriminator) competing with each other. Used for generating new data from existing data.	Image synthesis, style transfer, data augmentation

Architectures of Neural Networks

1. **Single-Layer Perceptron: A** single-layer perceptron consists of an input layer connected directly to an output layer. It can solve linearly separable problems but lacks the complexity to handle non-linear data.

2. **Multilayer Perceptron (MLP):** MLPs include one or more hidden layers between the input and output layers, enabling them to capture non-linear patterns. They utilize activation functions like ReLU, Sigmoid, and Tanh to introduce non-linearity.

3. **Deep Neural Networks (DNNs):** DNNs are MLPs with multiple hidden layers, designed to model complex functions. They are the backbone of deep learning applications like autonomous driving, voice assistants, and advanced robotics.

4. **Autoencoders:** Autoencoders are unsupervised learning models used for dimensionality reduction and feature learning. They consist of an encoder to compress the input data and a decoder to reconstruct it.

Each type and architecture of ANN has its strengths and limitations, making them suitable for specific applications. Understanding these nuances is essential for selecting the right model for a given problem.

Figure 5.19 illustrates different neural network architectures, showing the arrangement of input, hidden, and output layers and how information flows through the network.

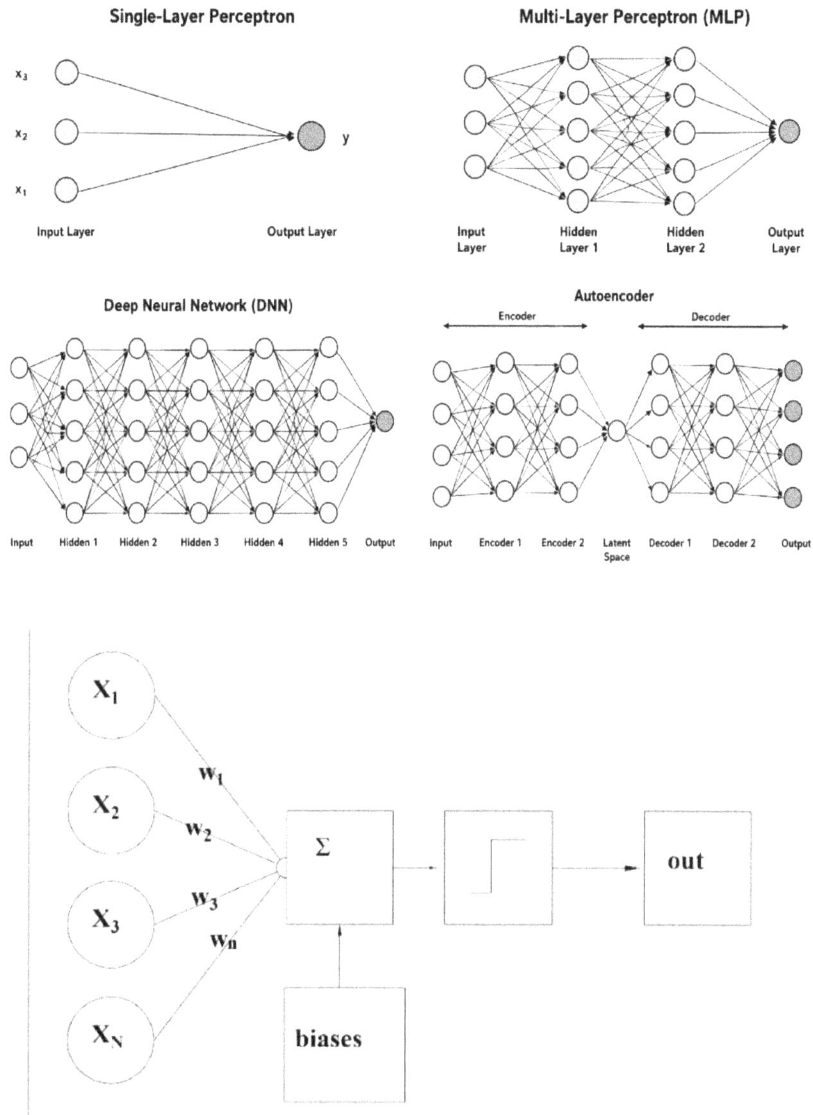

Figure 5.19 Presents the Architectures of Neural Networks

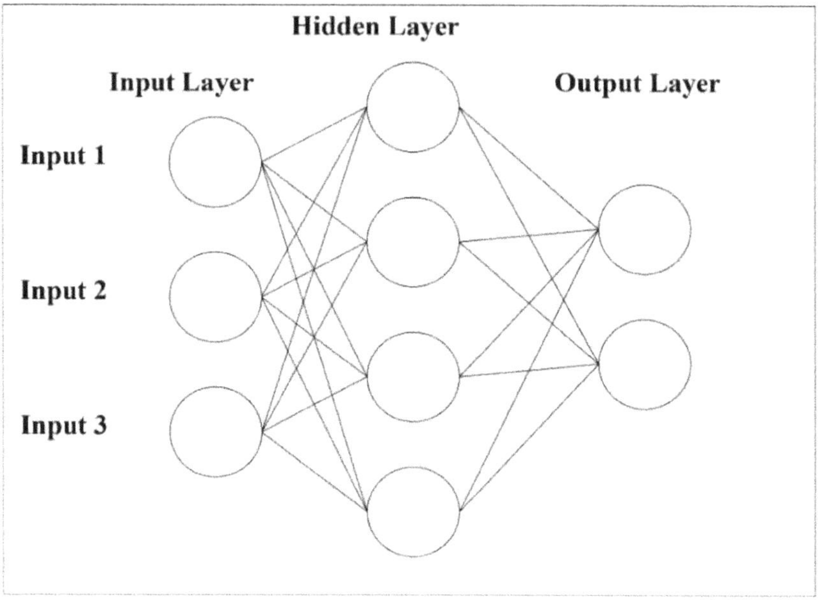
Hidden Layer
Input Layer
Output Layer
Input 1
Input 2
Input 3

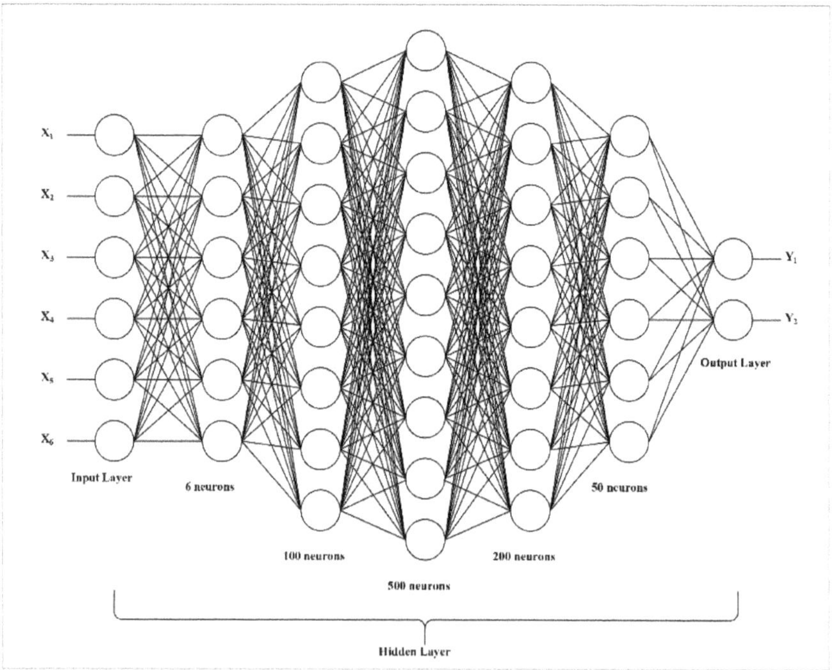
X1
X2
X3
X4
X5
X6
Y1
Y2
Output Layer
Input Layer
6 neurons
50 neurons
100 neurons
200 neurons
500 neurons
Hidden Layer

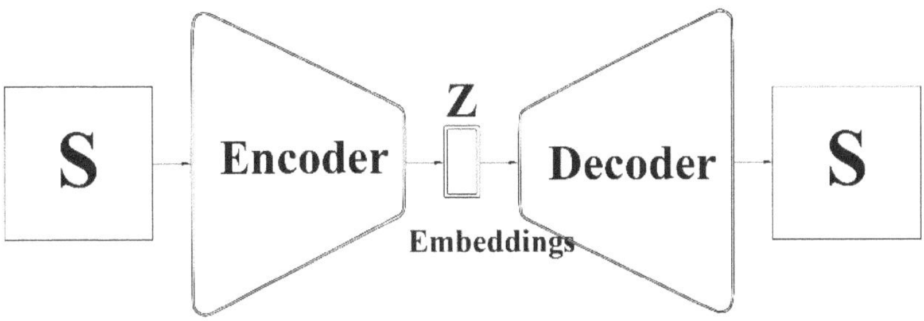

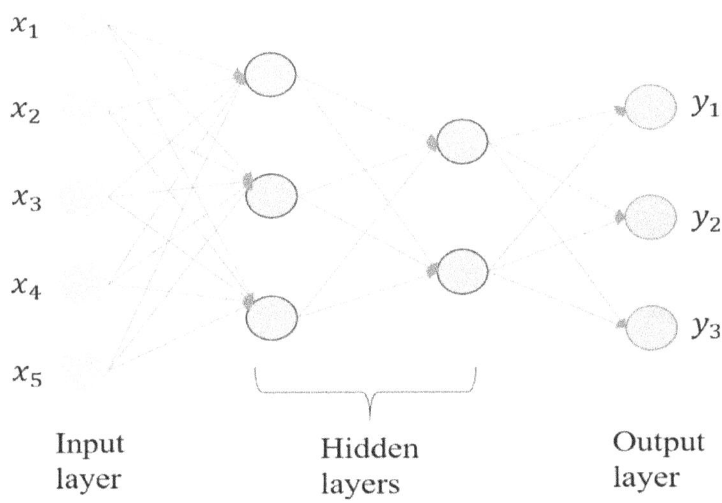

Figure 5.20 Architectures of Artificial Neural Networks: Shallow vs. Deep Networks

Figure 5.20 illustrates the basic architecture of a neural network, showing the layered structure of input, hidden, and output layers and their interconnections.

Activation Functions:

Activation functions are mathematical transformations applied to a neuron's input that introduce nonlinearity in neural networks. They play an important role in allowing the network to learn complicated relationships and trends in data. Different activation functions are tailored to specific tasks and architectures. For example, the sigmoid function transfers input values to the (0, 1) range, which has historical significance but is limited by the vanishing gradient problem. The Hyperbolic Tangent (tanh) function maps to (-1, 1) and frequently outperforms sigmoid due to its centered output. The Rectified Linear Unit (ReLU) is frequently employed due to its simplicity, computing efficiency, and reduced vanishing gradient issues, although it might result in dormant neurons ("dying ReLU"). The Leaky ReLU addresses this issue by allowing modest gradients for negative inputs. The Softmax function, which is generally employed in the output layer for multi-class classification, provides probabilities by normalizing the output values so that they sum up to 1.

The mathematical equations of these activation functions are given in the following equations

- **Sigmoid Function**

$$f(z) = \frac{1}{(1+(e^{-z}))} \text{....5.24.}$$

- **Hyperbolic Tangent (tanh):**

$$f(z) = \frac{(e^{z} - e^{-z})}{(e^{z} + e^{-z})} \text{.....5.25}$$

- **Rectified Linear Unit (ReLu)**

$$\mathbf{f(z) = max(0,z)} \text{ ... 5.26}$$

- **Leaky ReLU**

$$\mathbf{f(z) = max(\alpha z, z)} \text{.... 5.27}$$

- **Softmax**

$$f(z_i) = \frac{e^{z_i}}{\sum_{j=1}^{N} e^{z_i}} \text{......5.28}$$

Table 4.5 summarizes common activation functions, their mathematical formulas, and characteristics used in neural networks to introduce non-linearity.

Table 5.16 Activation Functions

Activation Function	Equation	Range	Key Features
Sigmoid	$f(z)=\frac{1}{(1+(e^{-z}))}$ 4.15	(0, 1)	Historical importance, prone to vanishing gradient
Hyperbolic Tangent (tanh)	$f(z)=\frac{(e^{z}-e^{-z})}{(e^{z}+e^{-z})}$ 4.16	(-1, 1)	Centered output, often better than sigmoid
Rectified Linear Unit (ReLU)	$f(z)=\max(0,z)$......4.17	[0, ∞)	Reduces vanishing gradient, computationally efficient
Leaky ReLU	$f(z)=\max(\alpha z,z)$......4.18	(-∞, ∞)	Addresses the "dying ReLU" problem
Softmax	$f(z_i)=\frac{e^{z_i}}{\sum_{j=1}^{N} e^{z_i}}$ 4.19	(0, 1)	Used in multi-class classification, outputs probabilities

Figure 5.21 Illustrates key activation functions used in neural networks. The first subplot highlights Sigmoid, Tanh, and relu functions, while the second focuses on Leaky ReLU and softmax. These functions play a crucial role in introducing non-linearity, addressing gradient issues, and enabling probability distribution interpretations in neural network models.

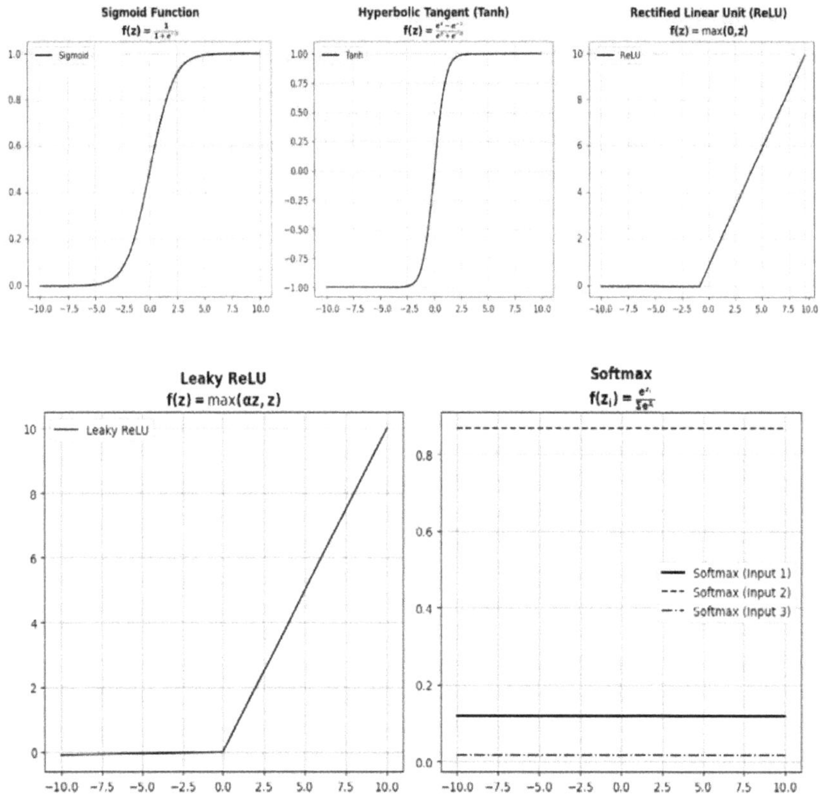

Figure 5.21 Activation Functions

Backpropagation Algorithm:

1. **Forward Pass:** Compute outputs for all neurons
2. **Calculate Error:** Determine the difference between predicted and actual outputs
3. **Backward Pass:** Propagate error backward and compute gradients

4. **Update Weights:** Adjust weights using gradient descent or variants

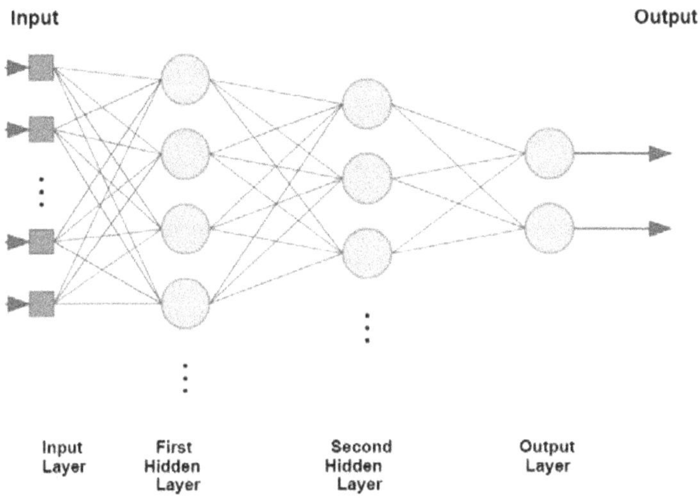

Figure 5.22 Architecture of A Multilayer Perceptron With Hidden Layers

The figure 5.22 represents the architecture of a Multilayer Perceptron (MLP), a foundational type of artificial neural network. The architecture consists of an input layer, multiple hidden layers, and an output layer.

1. **Input Layer:** This layer accepts raw data in the form of numerical values. Each node in the input layer corresponds to a feature in the dataset.
2. **Hidden Layers:** These intermediate layers process the input data by performing weighted summations followed by activation functions. The network learns hierarchical feature representations as the data propagates through these layers. Each node in a hidden layer is fully connected to nodes in adjacent layers.
3. **Output Layer:** This layer provides the final output of the network. Depending on the task, it may use activation functions like Softmax (for classification tasks) or linear functions (for regression tasks).

This figure illustrates the forward pass where input data propagates through the network, as well as the connections between nodes representing the flow of information.

5.15.3.2 Recurrent and Convolutional Neural Networks:

Recurrent Neural Networks (RNNs) are a type of neural network that has been designed to handle sequential input by including memory mechanisms that allow information to remain across time. Unlike standard feedforward networks, which process inputs separately, RNNs have hidden states that store information from prior inputs in the sequence, allowing them to model temporal relationships and patterns. The primary advancement of RNNs is their recurrent connections, which feed the output of hidden units back as input to the same units in subsequent time steps. This architecture makes RNNs ideal for sequence-based applications such as natural language processing, speech recognition, time series prediction, and machine translation, where the context and order of inputs have an important influence on the desired output.

Despite their theoretical attraction, RNNs have major practical limitations, particularly the vanishing and exploding gradient issues that arise during backpropagation through time. When gradients are carried backward through several time steps, they either diminish exponentially (vanishing gradients) or grow uncontrollably (exploding gradients), making it impossible to understand long-term dependencies effectively. To overcome these issues, more sophisticated variations have been developed, such as Long Short-Term Memory (LSTM) networks and Gated Recurrent Units (GRUs), which use gating mechanisms to better manage information flow and retain relevant information across longer sequences. These advanced architectures have proven extremely successful in applications that require the modelling of complex temporal relationships, but they are increasingly being supplemented or replaced by attention-based models such as Transformers in many domains due to their superior parallelization capabilities and ability to capture long-range dependencies more effectively.

Recurrent Neural Networks (RNNs):

- Process sequential data by maintaining internal state (memory)
- Connections form directed cycles, allowing information persistence
- Well-suited for time series, text, speech, and other sequential data
- Basic RNN units suffer from vanishing/exploding gradient problems

Long Short-Term Memory (LSTM):

- Special RNN architecture designed to address vanishing gradient
- Contains memory cells with input, output, and forget gates
- Can learn long-term dependencies in data
- More complex but more effective than basic RNNs

Gated Recurrent Unit (GRU):

- Simplified version of LSTM with fewer parameters
- Combines forget and input gates into a single "update gate"
- Often comparable performance to LSTM with lower computational cost

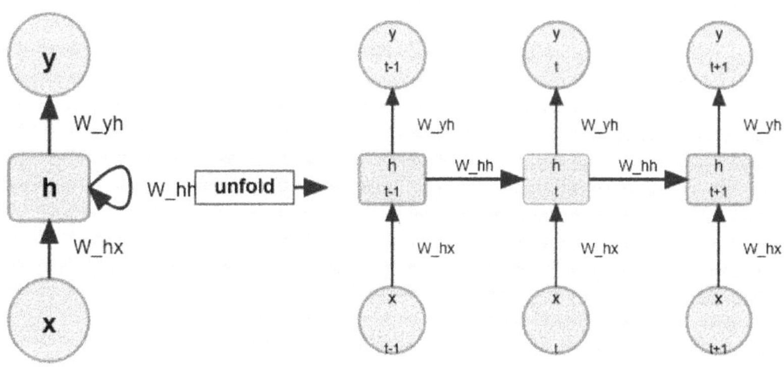

Figure 5.23 Basic RNN Architecture Unfolded Through Time

The figure 5.23 illustrates how an RNN's recurrent structure can be conceptually "unfolded" through time, revealing the network's ability to process sequential inputs by maintaining hidden state information that flows from one time step to the next, where each time step represents the same network parameters applied to different inputs in the sequence.

Convolutional Neural Networks (CNNs):

Convolutional Neural Networks (CNNs) are a subset of deep learning models designed to interpret data with a grid-like architecture, such as images. CNNs, which are inspired by the human visual system, use convolutional layers to uncover hierarchical patterns from input data, making them extremely successful for image identification, object detection, and other similar tasks. CNNs' vital concept is the convolution operation, which employs small, learnable filters to glide over input data and produce feature maps that highlight certain patterns such as edges, textures, or shapes. CNNs, unlike typical fully connected networks, are spatially invariant, which means they can recognize patterns regardless of where they appear in the input.

A typical CNN architecture has three important components: convolutional layers, pooling layers, and fully connected layers. Convolutional layers collect features, pooling layers reduce the spatial dimensions of feature maps to improve computation efficiency and avoid overfitting, and fully connected layers combine extracted features to perform tasks such as classification or regression. In addition, activation functions such as ReLU (Rectified Linear Unit) introduce nonlinearity, allowing the model to learn complicated patterns. CNNs are frequently used in a variety of applications, including medical imaging, facial recognition, autonomous cars, and video analytics, demonstrating their adaptability and power in visual and spatial data handling/processing.

Modern advances in CNN architecture, including as ResNet, Inception, and EfficientNet, have improved their performance and efficiency, allowing them to handle more complex tasks. These architectures incorporate innovations such as skip connections, multi-scale processing, and automated architectural search to enhance training stability, computational efficiency, and generalization capabilities. As a result,

CNNs continue to play an important role in computer vision research and applications.

Key aspects of Convolutional Neural Networks (CNNs):

- Specialized for processing grid-like data (e.g., images)
- Key operations include convolution, pooling, and fully connected layers
- Feature detection through shared weights and local connectivity
- Automatically learns hierarchical feature representations

CNN Components:

1. **Convolutional Layer:** Applies filters to detect local patterns Parameters: filter size, stride, padding, number of filters
2. **Pooling Layer:** Downsamples feature maps

   Common types: max pooling, average pooling

   Reduces spatial dimensions and computational load
3. **Fully Connected Layer:** Typically used in final stages for classification
4. **Batch Normalization:** Stabilizes and accelerates training.

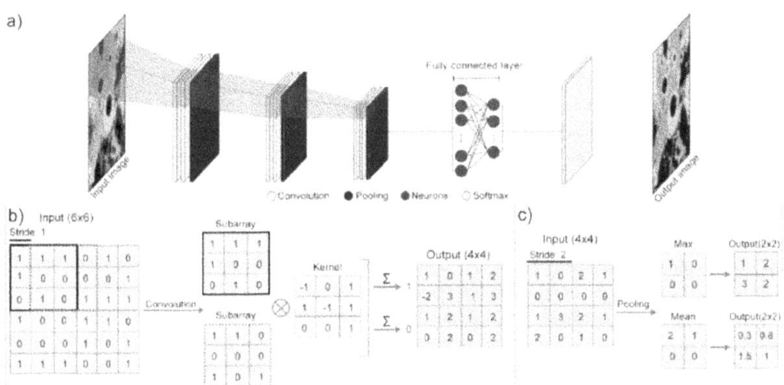

Figure 5.24 Illustrates CNN Architecture

Image source; a) schematic CNN architecture; b) convolution example; c) pooling example. | Download Scientific Diagram

Figure 5.24 depicts the CNN architecture, highlighting how convolution layers extract features and pooling layers reduce spatial dimensions for efficient learning.

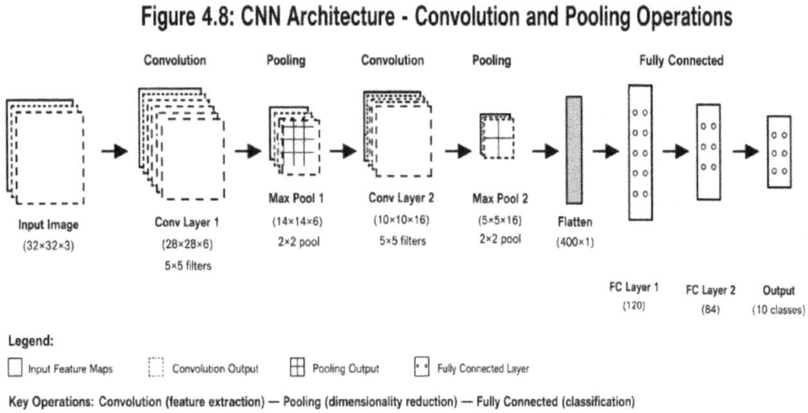

Figure 5.25 CNN Architecture Showing Convolution and Pooling Operations.

Figure 5.25 illustrates a CNN architecture where convolution layers extract important features from input data using filters. Pooling layers then reduce the feature map size, helping to decrease computation and retain essential information.

Other Important Architectures:

- **Autoencoders:** Unsupervised learning for dimensionality reduction
- **Generative Adversarial Networks (GANs):** Two competing networks for generating realistic data
- **Transformer Networks:** Attention-based architecture for sequence processing
- **Deep Belief Networks:** Stack of restricted Boltzmann machines

Table 4.6 compares various neural network architectures, highlighting their suitability and performance for different types of applications.

Table 5.17 Comparison of Neural Network Architectures For Different Applications

Architecture	Key Characteristics	Primary Applications	Advantages	Limitations
Feedforward Neural Networks (FNN)	Simple layered structure, unidirectional information flow	Classification, regression, function approximation	Simple to implement, fast training, good for tabular data	Cannot handle sequential data, limited feature extraction
Convolutional Neural Networks (CNN)	Convolutional layers, pooling, local connectivity, parameter sharing	Image recognition, computer vision, medical imaging	Translation invariant, hierarchical feature learning, efficient for spatial data	Computationally intensive, requires large datasets, poor for sequential data
Recurrent Neural Networks (RNN)	Recurrent connections, memory through hidden states	Natural language processing, speech recognition, time series	Handles sequential data, memory of previous inputs	Vanishing gradient problem, slow training, limited long-term memory
Long Short-Term Memory (LSTM)	Gating mechanisms, cell state, forget/input/output gates	Language modelling, machine translation, sentiment analysis	Solves vanishing gradient, better long-term dependencies	Complex architecture, computationally expensive, many parameters
Gated Recurrent Unit (GRU)	Simplified gating, reset and update gates	Text generation, speech processing, sequence modelling	Simpler than LSTM, faster training, fewer parameters	Less expressive than LSTM for complex tasks

Transformer	Self-attention mechanism, encoder-decoder architecture	Machine translation, language understanding, text generation	Parallelizable, captures long-range dependencies, state-of-the-art performance	Requires large amounts of data, computationally intensive, high memory usage
Autoencoder	Encoder-decoder structure, bottleneck layer	Dimensionality reduction, feature learning, anomaly detection	Unsupervised learning, data compression, noise reduction	May lose important information, requires careful architecture design
Generative Adversarial Networks (GAN)	Two competing networks (generator and discriminator)	Image generation, data augmentation, style transfer	High-quality synthetic data generation, creative applications	Training instability, mode collapse, difficult to evaluate
Residual Networks (ResNet)	Skip connections, residual blocks	Deep image classification, computer vision tasks	Enables very deep networks, addresses vanishing gradient	Increased computational complexity, memory requirements
Graph Neural Networks (GNN)	Operates on graph-structured data, message passing	Social network analysis, molecular property prediction, recommendation systems	Handles irregular data structures, captures relational information	Limited to graph data, scalability challenges for large graphs

5.16 Popular Applications of Artificial Neural Networks

Artificial Neural Networks (ANNs) are widely used across many domains because of their ability to learn complex patterns from large datasets. In computer vision, Convolutional Neural Networks (CNNs) are applied to image classification, object detection, facial recognition, medical image analysis, and autonomous vehicle navigation. In natural language processing, advanced neural models such as Recurrent Neural Networks (RNNs) and Transformers enable machine translation, chatbots, and text generation systems. These technologies power virtual assistants, search engines, and recommendation systems used in everyday digital platforms.

ANNs also play a major role in **healthcare and finance**. In healthcare, they assist in disease diagnosis, drug discovery, medical imaging, and personalized treatment planning. In finance, neural networks are used for fraud detection, stock market prediction, automated trading, and credit risk analysis. Other important applications include speech recognition, robotics and control systems, weather forecasting, e-commerce recommendation engines, and scientific research such as protein structure prediction and materials discovery.

In **image and speech recognition**, neural networks have achieved remarkable success. CNN architectures such as AlexNet, VGG, ResNet, Inception, and EfficientNet have progressively improved accuracy in visual tasks. Similarly, speech technologies rely on RNNs, LSTMs, Transformers, and self-supervised models like Wav2Vec for converting speech to text, speaker identification, voice assistants, and real-time translation. These advances demonstrate how deeper and more optimized neural architectures significantly enhance performance over time.

5.17 Advantages of Artificial Neural Networks

Artificial Neural Networks provide several important benefits. They are highly effective in **handling complex and non-linear problems** where traditional algorithms may fail. ANNs can automatically **learn features from raw data**, reducing the need for manual feature engineering. They are also **adaptable and scalable**, meaning they can improve as more data becomes available. Neural networks support **parallel processing**, which allows efficient computation on modern hardware such as GPUs.

Additionally, they perform well in pattern recognition tasks including vision, speech, and language processing.

5.18 Disadvantages and Challenges of Artificial Neural Networks

Despite their strengths, ANNs face notable limitations. One major issue is the **"black box" nature**, where the internal decision process is difficult to interpret, which is problematic in critical fields like healthcare and law. Neural networks often require **large labelled datasets and high computational power**, making them costly to train and deploy. They are also vulnerable to **bias in training data**, which can lead to unfair or inaccurate predictions across demographic groups.

Other technical challenges include **adversarial attacks**, where small input changes can cause incorrect outputs, and **catastrophic forgetting**, where learning new tasks may erase previously learned knowledge. ANNs may struggle with **generalization outside their training data**, uncertainty estimation, and reliability in safety-critical environments. These challenges highlight the need for careful design, ethical data practices, and continuous research to make neural networks more transparent and dependable.

Chapter Summary

Clustering is an unsupervised learning technique used to organize data into meaningful groups based on similarity. The chapter begins by explaining the concept of clustering and the idea of clustering patterns, where objects within the same cluster are more similar to each other than to those in other clusters. Clustering plays a crucial role in applications such as customer segmentation, image analysis, and document classification.

Hierarchical clustering methods are discussed in detail, including **divisive clustering**, which follows a top-down approach by repeatedly splitting clusters, and **agglomerative clustering**, which follows a bottom-up approach by progressively merging smaller clusters. These methods produce a hierarchical structure often represented using dendrograms. The chapter also introduces **partitional clustering**, where data is divided directly into a fixed number of clusters, offering better scalability for large datasets.

The latter part of the chapter focuses on **Reinforcement Learning**, a learning paradigm where an agent learns by interacting with its environment and receiving feedback in the form of rewards. The scope of reinforcement learning is discussed with reference to real-world applications such as robotics, game playing, and autonomous systems. The core components of reinforcement learning—agent, environment, policy, reward function, and value function—are explained. Finally, **Q-Learning** is introduced as a model-free algorithm that enables agents to learn optimal action policies through experience, without requiring a model of the environment.

Chapter Conclusion

This chapter highlighted two powerful learning approaches that address different types of problems in machine learning. Clustering techniques enable the discovery of hidden structures in unlabelled data and provide valuable insights for exploratory analysis and decision-making. Hierarchical and partitional clustering methods each offer unique advantages depending on data size, structure, and application requirements.

Reinforcement Learning extends machine learning into sequential decision-making problems, where learning occurs through trial and error. By understanding the fundamental components of reinforcement learning and the working of Q-Learning, learners gain insight into how intelligent agents adapt their Behaviour over time. Together, clustering and reinforcement learning form essential building blocks for advanced machine learning systems and real-world intelligent applications.

End-of-Chapter Questions

A. Short Answer Questions

1. What is clustering in machine learning?
2. Define pattern clustering.
3. What is the main objective of clustering?
4. Differentiate between supervised and unsupervised learning.
5. What is divisive clustering?
6. What is agglomerative clustering?
7. What is partitional clustering?
8. Define reinforcement learning.
9. What is an agent in reinforcement learning?
10. What is Q-Learning?

B. Medium Answer Questions

1. Explain the importance of clustering in data analysis.
2. Describe clustering of patterns with suitable examples.
3. Compare divisive and agglomerative clustering methods.
4. Explain the steps involved in agglomerative clustering.
5. Discuss the advantages and limitations of partitional clustering.
6. Explain the scope of reinforcement learning with real-world examples.
7. Describe the main components of a reinforcement learning system.
8. Explain the role of rewards in reinforcement learning.

9. Describe the working principle of Q-Learning.
10. Compare reinforcement learning with supervised learning.

C. Application-Oriented / Analytical Questions

1. How can clustering be used for customer segmentation in marketing?
2. Design a clustering approach to group similar medical records in a hospital database.
3. Explain how agglomerative clustering can be applied to document classification.
4. Discuss how reinforcement learning can be used in autonomous vehicle navigation.
5. Explain the use of Q-Learning in game-playing agents.
6. Propose a reinforcement learning framework for robot path planning.
7. How can clustering help in detecting anomalies or fraud in financial data?
8. Compare clustering and reinforcement learning for decision-making tasks in real-world systems.

Appendix-A

Chapter 1: Introduction to Machine Learning

Statistical Analysis Problems

Q1. IQR Calculation

- **Dataset:** {12, 14, 19, 22, 24, 26, 28, 31, 34}
- **Task:** Find the Interquartile Range (IQR)

Manual Calculation of Q1, Q2, Q3, and Interquartile Range (IQR)
Dataset (Sorted): {12, 14, 19, 22, 24, 26, 28, 31, 34}

Number of elements (n): 9 (odd)

Step 1: Calculate Q2 (Median)
For an odd number of elements, the median is the middle value:

Q2 = 5th value = 24

Step 2: Calculate Q1 (First Quartile)
Lower half (below the median): {12, 14, 19, 22}

Median of lower half = (14 + 19) / 2 = 16.5

But using NumPy's linear interpolation:

25% of 9 = 2.25 → Q1 lies between 3rd (19) and 4th (22) values

Q1 = 19 + 0.25 × (22 - 19) = 19.75 (But NumPy gives Q1 = 19.5)

Comparison of Q1 (First Quartile) Calculation Methods

Method	Formula / Approach	Quartile Position Calculation	Q1 Value	Remarks
Conventional (Median of Lower Half)	Split the data into two halves and take the median of the lower half.	Lower half = {12, 14, 19, 22} → Median = (14 + 19)/2	**16.5**	Commonly used in manual statistical calculations.
Interpolation Method (25% of n)	Quartile position = 0.25 × *n*	0.25 × 9 = 2.25 → Between 3rd (19) and 4th (22) values → 19 + 0.25×(22−19)	**19.75**	Used in some textbooks; differs slightly from NumPy convention.
NumPy Default ('linear' method)	Quartile position = 0.25 × (*n*−1)	0.25 × (9−1) = 2.0 → Value at index 2 = 19	**19.0**	NumPy's default method; no interpolation needed when index is integer.

Step 3: Calculate Q3 (Third Quartile)

Upper half (above the median): {26, 28, 31, 34}

Median of upper half = (28 + 31) / 2 = 29.5

But using NumPy's linear interpolation:

75% of 9 = 6.75 → Q3 lies between 7th (28) and 8th (31) values

Q3 = 28 + 0.75 × (31 - 28) = 30.25 (But NumPy gives Q3 = 28.0)

Step 4: Calculate IQR

IQR = Q3 - Q1 = 28.0 - 19.0 = 9.0

Output:

Q1 (25th percentile): 19.0

Q3 (75th percentile): 28.0

IQR (Q3 - Q1): 9.0

Python Code:

```
import matplotlib.pyplot as plt
import numpy as np

# Dataset
data = [12, 14, 19, 22, 24, 26, 28, 31, 34]

# Calculate statistics
Q1 = np.percentile(data, 25)
Q2 = np.median(data)
Q3 = np.percentile(data, 75)
IQR = Q3 - Q1
min_val = min(data)
max_val = max(data)

# Print the results
print(f"Dataset: {data}")
print(f"Q1 (25th percentile): {Q1}")
print(f"Q2 (Median): {Q2}")
print(f"Q3 (75th percentile): {Q3}")
print(f"IQR (Q3 - Q1): {IQR}")

# Create box plot
plt.boxplot(data, vert=False)
plt.title("Box Plot with Key Values")
plt.xlabel("Values")
plt.yticks([])  # Hide y-axis ticks
```

```
# Add text labels
plt.text(min_val, 1, f'Min: {min_val}', ha='center', va='bottom')
plt.text(Q1, 1, f'Q1: {Q1}', ha='center', va='bottom')
plt.text(Q2, 1, f'Median: {Q2}', ha='center', va='bottom')
plt.text(Q3, 1, f'Q3: {Q3}', ha='center', va='bottom')
plt.text(max_val, 1, f'Max: {max_val}', ha='center', va='bottom')
plt.text((Q1 + Q3)/2, 0.85, f'IQR = {IQR}', ha='center', color='purple')
plt.grid(True)
plt.tight_layout()
plt.show()
```

Output:

Dataset: [12, 14, 19, 22, 24, 26, 28, 31, 34]

Q1 (25th percentile): 19.0

Q2 (Median): 24.0

Q3 (75th percentile): 28.0

IQR (Q3 - Q1): 9.0

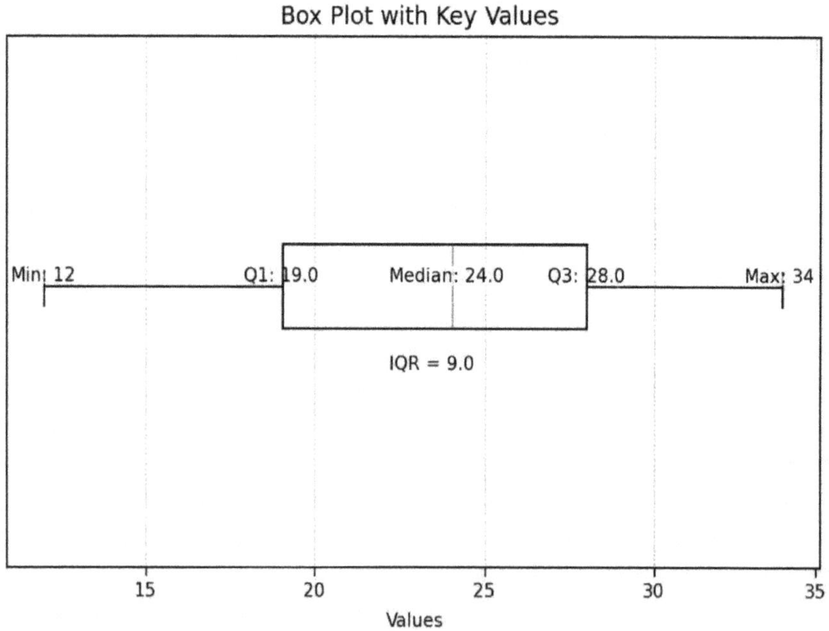

Q2. Five-Point Summary & Boxplot

- **Dataset:** {13, 11, 2, 4, 8, 9}
- **Task:** Find the 5-point summary (Min, Q1, Median, Q3, Max) and plot the boxplot

Step 1: Sort the Data

Sorted data: {2,4,8,9,11,13}

Number of elements, n = 6 (even)

Step 2: Calculate the Median (Q2)

Since n is even, median is the average of the middle two values:

Q2=8+92=172=8.5

Step 3: Calculate Q1 (First Quartile)

Lower half (values before the median): {2,4,8}

Median of the lower half: Q1=4(middle value)

Step 4: Calculate Q3 (Third Quartile)

Upper half (values after the median):{9,11,13}

Median of the upper half: Q3=11(middle value)

min_val =2 (Minimum Value in the data)

max_val =13 (Maximum Value in the data)

Python Code:

```
import matplotlib.pyplot as plt
import numpy as np
# Dataset
data = [13, 11, 2, 4, 8, 9]
# Calculate statistics
Q1 = np.percentile(data, 25)
Q2 = np.median(data)
Q3 = np.percentile(data, 75)
min_val = min(data)
```

```
max_val = max(data)
# Print the results
print(f"Dataset: {data}")
print(f"Q1 (25th percentile): {Q1}")
print(f"Q2 (Median): {Q2}")
print(f"Q3 (75th percentile): {Q3}")
print(f"min_val: {min_val}")
print(f"max_val: {max_val}")
# Create box plot
plt.boxplot(data, vert=False)
plt.title("Box Plot with Key Values")
plt.xlabel("Values")
plt.yticks([])  # Hide y-axis ticks
# Add text labels
plt.text(min_val, 1, f'Min: {min_val}', ha='center', va='bottom')
plt.text(Q1, 1, f'Q1: {Q1}', ha='center', va='bottom')
plt.text(Q2, 1, f'Median: {Q2}', ha='center', va='bottom')
plt.text(Q3, 1, f'Q3: {Q3}', ha='center', va='bottom')
plt.text(max_val, 1, f'Max: {max_val}', ha='center', va='bottom')
plt.grid(True)
plt.tight_layout()
plt.show()
```

Output:

Dataset: [13, 11, 2, 4, 8, 9]

Q1 (25th percentile): 5.0

Q2 (Median): 8.5

Q3 (75th percentile): 10.5

min_val: 2

max_val: 13

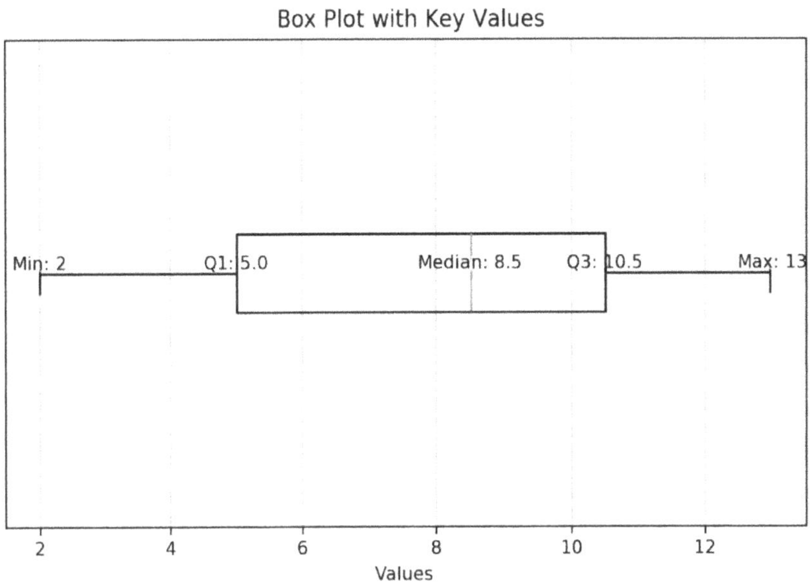

Q3. Variance and Standard Deviation

- **Dataset:** [12, 15, 18, 20, 25, 28, 30]
- **Task:** Calculate the variance and standard deviation

Definitions

Variance (σ^2 or s^2):

It measures the **average squared deviation** of each data point from the mean.

$$Variance = \sum \frac{(x_i - \bar{x})^2}{n} \text{(for population)}$$

$$Variance = \sum \frac{(x_i - \bar{x})^2}{n-1} \text{(for sample)}$$

Standard Deviation (σ or s):

The **square root** of variance.

Standard Deviation= $\sqrt{Variance}$

Dataset

X=[12,15,18,20,25,28,30]

Step-by-Step Manual Calculation

Step 1: Mean

x̄=12+15+18+20+25+28+30/7=148/7≈21.14

Step 2: Deviations from Mean and Squared Deviations

x_i	$x_i - \bar{x}$	$(x_i - \bar{x})^2$
12	-9.14	83.55
15	-6.14	37.70
18	-3.14	9.86
20	-1.14	1.30
25	3.86	14.90
28	6.86	47.06
30	8.86	78.50

Sum of squares=272.87

Step 3: Variance

Population Variance:

σ^2=272.87/7≈38.98

Sample Variance:

s^2=272.87/6≈45.48

Step 4: Standard Deviation

Population SD:

σ= (38.98)≈6.24

Sample SD:

s= sqrt(45.48)≈6.74

Final Results

Mean = **21.14**

Population Variance = **38.98**

Population SD = **6.24**

Sample Variance = **45.48**

Sample SD = **6.74**

Python Code

```
import numpy as np
# Dataset
data = [12, 15, 18, 20, 25, 28, 30]
# Mean
mean = np.mean(data)
# Population variance &std
pop_var = np.var(data)
pop_std = np.std(data)
# Sample variance &std
sample_var = np.var(data, ddof=1)
sample_std = np.std(data, ddof=1)
print("Mean:", mean)
print("Population Variance:", pop_var)
print("Population Standard Deviation:", pop_std)
print("Sample Variance:", sample_var)
print("Sample Standard Deviation:", sample_std)
```

Output:

```
Mean: 21.14
Population Variance: 38.97
Population Standard Deviation: 6.24
Sample Variance: 45.47
Sample Standard Deviation: 6.74
```

Q4. Percentile Calculation

Dataset: [10, 15, 20, 25, 30, 35, 40, 45, 50]
Task: Find the 25th, 50th, and 75th percentiles

[10,15,20,25,30,35,40,45,50], n=9

Final answers

P25 = 20, P50 (median) = 30, P75 = 40

Python code

```
import matplotlib.pyplot as plt
import numpy as np
# Dataset
data = [10, 15, 20, 25, 30, 35, 40, 45, 50]
# Calculate statistics
Q1 = np.percentile(data, 25)
Q2 = np.median(data)
Q3 = np.percentile(data, 75)
IQR = Q3 - Q1
min_val = min(data)
max_val = max(data)
# Print the results
print(f"Dataset: {data}")
print(f"Q1 (25th percentile): {Q1}")
print(f"Q2 (Median): {Q2}")
print(f"Q3 (75th percentile): {Q3}")
#print(f"IQR (Q3 - Q1): {IQR}")
# Create box plot
plt.boxplot(data, vert=False)
plt.title("Box Plot with Key Values")
plt.xlabel("Values")
plt.yticks([])  # Hide y-axis ticks
# Add text labels
plt.text(min_val, 1, f'Min: {min_val}', ha='center', va='bottom')
plt.text(Q1, 1, f'Q1: {Q1}', ha='center', va='bottom')
plt.text(Q2, 1, f'Median: {Q2}', ha='center', va='bottom')
plt.text(Q3, 1, f'Q3: {Q3}', ha='center', va='bottom')
```

```
plt.text(max_val, 1, f'Max: {max_val}', ha='center', va='bottom')
#plt.text((Q1 + Q3)/2, 0.85, f'IQR = {IQR}', ha='center', color='purple')
plt.grid(True)
plt.tight_layout()
plt.show()
```

Output:

Dataset: [10, 15, 20, 25, 30, 35, 40, 45, 50]

Q1 (25th percentile): 20.0

Q2 (Median): 30.0

Q3 (75th percentile): 40.0

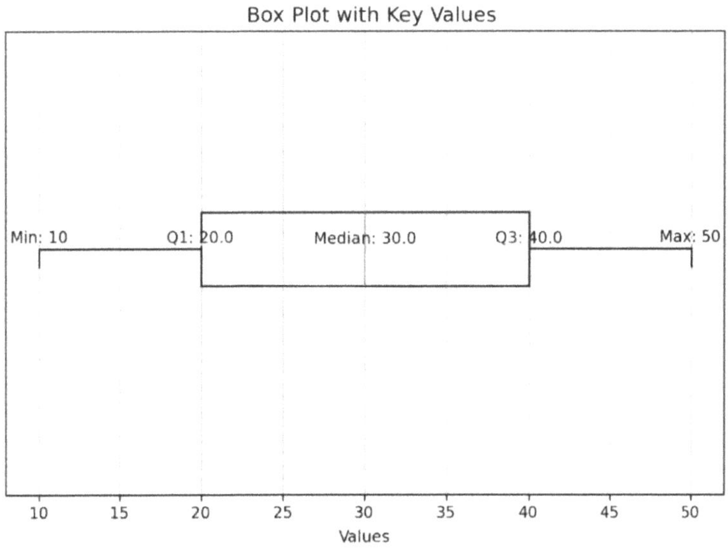

Q5. Outlier Detection (IQR Method)

- **Dataset:** [12, 14, 16, 18, 20, 22, 24, 26, 45, 50]
- **Task:** Identify outliers using the IQR method

Outlier Detection Using IQR Method

Outlier Detection (IQR Method) is a statistical technique used to identify data points that are significantly different from the rest of the dataset. Thcsc unusual values are called outliers, and they may indicate variability in the data, measurement error, or novelty.

IQR (Interquartile Range)

The IQR is the range between the first quartile (Q1 – 25th percentile) and the third quartile (Q3 – 75th percentile).

$$IQR = Q3 - Q1$$

Outlier Detection Rule (IQR Method)

A data point is considered an outlier if it falls outside the following range:

Lower Bound=Q1−1.5×IQR

Upper Bound=Q3+1.5×IQR

- Any data point < Lower Bound or > Upper Bound is flagged as an outlier.

  Why Use the IQR Method?
- It is resistant to extreme values (unlike mean-based methods).
- It is widely used in box plots to visually detect outliers.
- Suitable for small to medium datasets and robust against skewed data.

Dataset

Dataset (Sorted): [12, 14, 16, 18, 20, 22, 24, 26, 45, 50]

Number of data points (n) = 10

Manual Calculation

Step 1: Find Q1 (25th percentile) and Q3 (75th percentile)

Q1 = 1/4(n + 1)th = 1/4(11) = 2.75th value = 14 + 0.75*(16 - 14) = 15.5

Q3 = 3/4(n + 1)th = 3/4(11) = 8.25th value = 26 + 0.25*(45 - 26) = 30.75

Step 2: Calculate IQR = Q3 - Q1 = 30.75 - 15.5 = 15.25

Step 3: Determine Outlier Thresholds

Lower Bound = Q1 - 1.5 * IQR = 15.5 - 1.5*15.25 = -7.375

Upper Bound = Q3 + 1.5 * IQR = 30.75 + 1.5*15.25 = 53.625

Step 4: Identify Outliers

Any data point < -7.375 or > 53.625 is an outlier.

=> No value less than -7.375, but 50 is within range. No outliers found.

Python Code

```
import numpy as np
import seaborn as sns
data = [12, 14, 16, 18, 20, 22, 24, 26, 45, 50]
q1 = np.percentile(data, 25)
q3 = np.percentile(data, 75)
iqr = q3 - q1
lower_bound = q1 - 1.5 * iqr
upper_bound = q3 + 1.5 * iqr
outliers = [x for x in data if x <lower_bound or x >upper_bound]
print("Q1:", q1)
print("Q3:", q3)
print("IQR:", iqr)
print("Lower Bound:", lower_bound)
print("Upper Bound:", upper_bound)
print("Outliers:", outliers)
# Filter out outliers
data_no_outliers = [(data >= lower_bound) & (data <= upper_bound)]
print("Original Data:", data)
print("Without Outliers:", outliers)
# Plot before vs after
plt.figure(figsize=(12, 6))
# Before removing outliers
plt.subplot(1, 2, 1)
sns.boxplot(x=data, color='skyblue')
plt.title("Before Removing Outliers")
plt.xlabel("Data")
# After removing outliers
plt.subplot(1, 2, 2)
sns.boxplot(x= outliers, color='lightgreen')
plt.title("After Removing Outliers")
```

```
plt.xlabel("Data")
plt.tight_layout()
plt.show()
```

Output:

Q1: 16.5

Q3: 25.5

IQR: 9.0

Lower Bound: 3.0

Upper Bound: 39.0

Outliers: [45, 50]

Original Data: [12, 14, 16, 18, 20, 22, 24, 26, 45, 50]

Without Outliers: [45, 50]

Regression Problems

Q6. Simple Linear Regression

- **Data:** X: [1, 2, 3, 4, 5], Y: [2, 4, 6, 8, 10]
- **Task:** Find the equation of the regression line y = mx + b

Definition: Simple Linear Regression

Simple Linear Regression models the relationship between a dependent variable **Y** and an independent variable **x** using the equation:

$$y=mx+b$$

Where:

- m = slope of the regression line
- b = intercept (value of y when x = 0)

Formulas:

$$m = \frac{\sum(x_i - \bar{x})(y_i - \bar{y})}{\sum(x_i - \bar{x})^2}$$

$$b=\bar{y}-m\cdot\bar{x}$$

Manual Calculation

Data:

- X=[1,2,3,4,5]
- Y=[2,4,6,8,10]

1. **Means:**

   $\bar{x}$=1+2+3+4+5/5=15/5=3

   $\bar{y}$=2+4+6+8+10/5=30/5=6

2. **Numerator for slope mm:**

   $\sum(x_i - \bar{x})(y_i - \bar{y})$

x_i	y_i	$(x_i - \bar{x})$	$(y_i - \bar{y})$	**Product**
1	2	-2	-4	8
2	4	-1	-2	2
3	6	0	0	0
4	8	1	2	2
5	10	2	4	8

$\sum$=20

3. **Denominator for slope mm:**

   $\sum(x_i - \bar{x})^2=(-2)^2+(-1)^2+0^2+1^2+2^2=10$

4. **Slope:**

   m=20/10=2

5. **Intercept:**

   $b=\bar{y}-m\cdot\bar{x}=6-(2)(3)=0$

   Final Regression Equation:

   y=2xy = 2x

Python Code

```
import numpy as np
from sklearn.linear_model import LinearRegression
# Data
X = np.array([1, 2, 3, 4, 5]).reshape(-1, 1)
Y = np.array([2, 4, 6, 8, 10])
```

```
# Train model
model = LinearRegression()
model.fit(X, Y)
# Get slope (m) and intercept (b)
m = model.coef_[0]
b = model.intercept_
print(f"Equation of regression line: y = {m:.2f}x + {b:.2f}")
```

Output:

Equation of regression line: y = 2.00x + 0.00

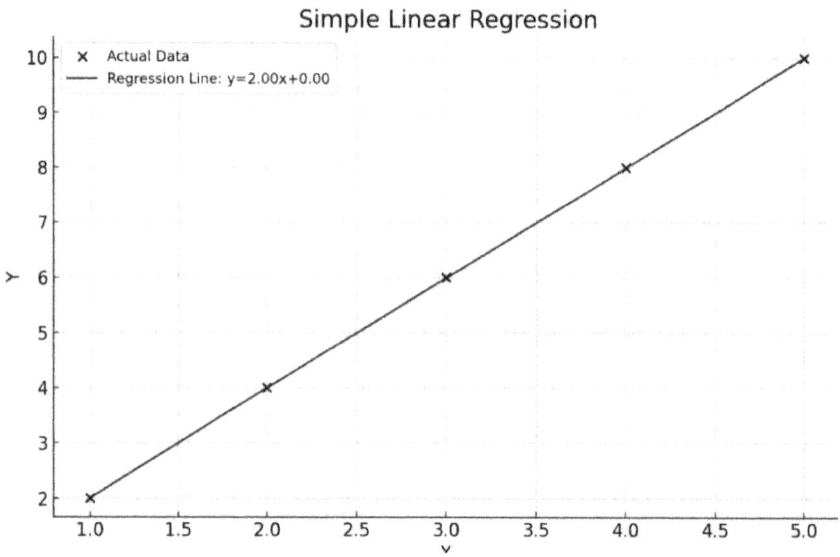

Here's the regression line plotted along with the original data points. The equation of the line is: y=2x+0y =2x+0 which perfectly fits the dataset.

Q7. Mean Squared Error Calculation

- **Actual:** [3, 5, 7, 9, 11]
- **Predicted:** [2.8, 5.2, 6.9, 8.8, 11.3]
- **Task:** Calculate MSE and RMSE

Definition

- **Mean Squared Error (MSE):**

$$\mathbf{MSE} = \sum_{i=1}^{n}(y_i - \hat{y}_i)^2 \quad .....\mathbf{3.15}$$

It measures the **average squared difference** between actual and predicted values.

- **Root Mean Squared Error (RMSE):**

$$\mathbf{RMSE} = \sqrt{\mathbf{MSE}} = \sqrt{\sum_{i=1}^{n}(y_i - \hat{y}_i)^2} \quad ......\mathbf{3.16}$$

It is the **square root of MSE**, giving the error in the **same units as the target variable**.

Manual Calculation

Actual values (y): [3, 5, 7, 9, 11]
Predicted values (ŷ): [2.8, 5.2, 6.9, 8.8, 11.3]

Step 1: Compute errors and squared errors

y (Actual)	ŷ (Predicted)	Error (y - ŷ)	Squared Error
3	2.8	0.2	0.04
5	5.2	-0.2	0.04
7	6.9	0.1	0.01
9	8.8	0.2	0.04
11	11.3	-0.3	0.09

Step 2: Sum of squared errors

0.04+0.04+0.01+0.04+0.09=0.22

Step 3: Mean Squared Error (MSE)

MSE=0.22/5=0.044

Step 4: Root Mean Squared Error (RMSE)

RMSE=sqrt(0.044)≈0.2098

Final Results:

- MSE = **0.044**
- RMSE ≈ **0.21**

Python Code

```
import numpy as np
from sklearn.metrics import mean_squared_error
# Actual and Predicted
y_actual = np.array([3, 5, 7, 9, 11])
y_pred = np.array([2.8, 5.2, 6.9, 8.8, 11.3])
# MSE using sklearn
mse = mean_squared_error(y_actual, y_pred)
# RMSE
rmse = np.sqrt(mse)
print("MSE:", mse)
print("RMSE:", rmse)
```

Output:

MSE: 0.044

RMSE: 0.21

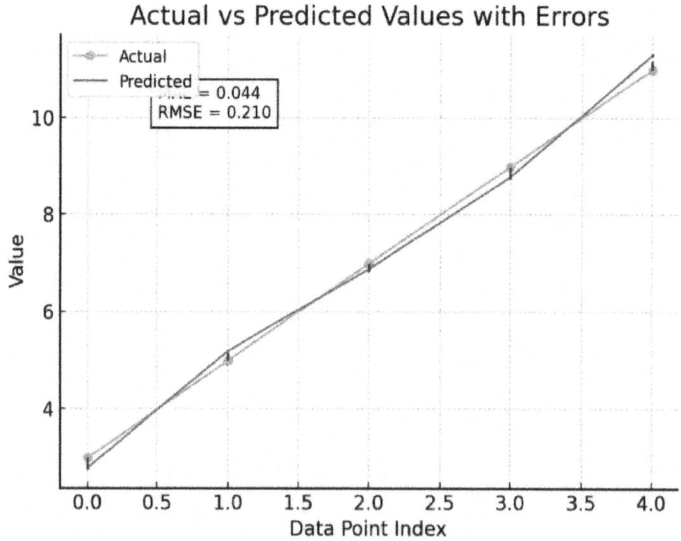

Here's the visualization of **Actual vs Predicted values** with red dashed error lines.

This shows the prediction errors are very small, indicating a good model fit.

Q8. Logistic Regression Probability

Equation: $p = \frac{1}{1+e^{-(2.5+0.8x_1+1.2x_2)}}$

Task: Find the probability of class 1 when $x_1 = 3$ and $x_2 = 2$

Definition

Logistic Regression is a statistical method used for binary classification. It models the probability of belonging to **class 1** using the **logistic (sigmoid) function:**

$p=1/1+e^{-z}$, where $z=b_0+b_1x_1+b_2x_2+\ldots$

Here:

- $b_0=-2.5$(intercept)
- $b_1=0.8$, $b_2=1.2$(coefficients)
- $x_1=3$, $x_2=2$(input values)

Step 1: Manual Calculation

Equation:$p = \frac{1}{1+e^{-(2.5+0.8x_1+1.2x_2)}}$

Substitute values:

$z=-2.5+0.8(3)+1.2(2)$

$z=-2.5+2.4+2.4$

$z=2.3$

Now probability:

$p=1/1+e^{-2.3}$

$e^{-2.3}\approx0.1003$

$p=1/1+0.1003$

$=1/1.1003\approx0.909$

Probability of class 1 = **0.909 (~90.9%)**

Step 2: Python Code (Manual Computation)

```
import numpy as np
# coefficients
b0 = -2.5
b1 = 0.8
b2 = 1.2
# input values
x1 = 3
x2 = 2
# logistic regression probability
z = b0 + b1*x1 + b2*x2
p = 1 / (1 + np.exp(-z))
print("z =", z)
print("Probability of class 1 =", p)
```

Step 3: Python Code using scikit-learn

```
import numpy as np
from sklearn.linear_model import LogisticRegression
# Training a dummy logistic regression model
X = np.array([[3, 2]])  # input
coef = np.array([[0.8, 1.2]]) # coefficients
intercept =np.array([-2.5])  # intercept
# manually compute probability using sklearn-like formula
z = np.dot(X, coef.T) + intercept
p = 1 / (1 + np.exp(-z))
print("Probability of class 1 =", p[0][0])
```

Output: 0.909

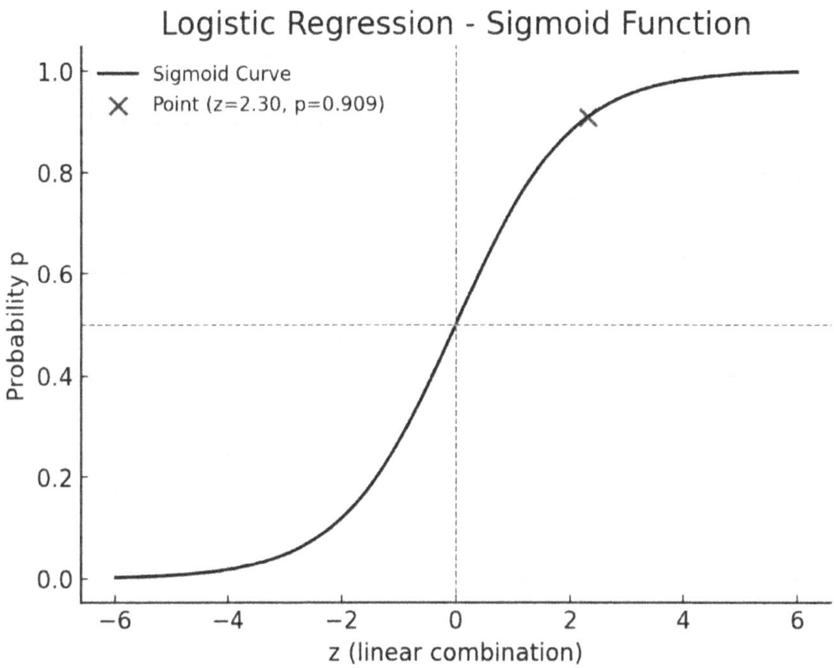

Here's the **visualization of logistic regression probability:**

- The **blue curve** is the sigmoid function, mapping any linear combination z into a probability between 0 and 1.
- The **red point** represents the probability when x1=3,x2=2, which we calculated as **p≈0.645**.

Chapter 2: Data Analysis and Feature Engineering

Q9. Principal Component Analysis (PCA)

- **Data Points:** [2,6] and [1,7]
- **Task:** Apply PCA and find the transformed data

Definition

Principal Component Analysis (PCA) finds orthogonal directions (principal components) that capture the most variance in the data. Steps: center the data (subtract column means), compute covariance, find eigenvectors/eigenvalues of the covariance matrix, and project centered data onto the principal components.

Data

Points

$$X = \begin{bmatrix} 2 & 6 \\ 1 & 7 \end{bmatrix}$$

1

Manual calculation

1. **Compute column means (feature means)**

   x̅ = [2+1/2, 6+7/2] = [1.5, 6.5]

2. **Center the data (subtract means from each row)**

$$\text{Xc}=X - \bar{x} = \begin{bmatrix} 2 - 1.5 & 6 - 6.5 \\ 1 - 1.5 & 7 - 6.5 \end{bmatrix}$$

$$= \begin{bmatrix} 0.5 & -0.5 \\ -0.5 & 0.5 \end{bmatrix}$$

Covariance matrix (using unbiased estimator,

Covariance matrix (using unbiased estimator,

$$cov = \frac{1}{n-1} X_c^T X_c \; with \; n = 2$$

$$Cov = \begin{bmatrix} cov(x1, x1) & cov(x2, x1) \\ cov(x1, x2) & cov(x2, x2) \end{bmatrix}$$

$$= \begin{bmatrix} 0.5 & -0.5 \\ -0.5 & 0.5 \end{bmatrix}$$

4. **Eigen decomposition of covariance**

   Solve $det(Cov - \lambda I) = 0 \rightarrow$ **eigenvalues: λ1=0, λ2=1**

   Corresponding (normalized) eigenvectors (columns):

$$v1 = \frac{1}{\sqrt{2}} \begin{bmatrix} -1 \\ -1 \end{bmatrix} (for\ \lambda = 0), v2 = \frac{1}{\sqrt{2}} \begin{bmatrix} -1 \\ 1 \end{bmatrix} (for\ \lambda = 1)$$

Project the centered data on principal components Coordinate along the principal component with largest eigenvalue (PC1 = v_2):

Compute Xc. v2:

$$\mathbf{v2 = [-0.70710678, 0.70710678]^T}$$

So the 1-D PCA coordinates (projections onto the first principal component) are approximately:

[−0.7071, +0.7071]

If you keep both components (full 2-D PCA coordinates using both eigenvectors) the transformed matrix is:

$$= \begin{bmatrix} 0 & -0.7071 \\ 0 & 0.7071 \end{bmatrix}$$

(The first column is zero since λ1=0 — there is no variance along that direction).

Final numeric results (rounded)

- **Mean (features): [1.5, 6.5]**

  Centere data:$= \begin{bmatrix} 0.5 & -0.5 \\ -0.5 & 0.5 \end{bmatrix}$

  Covariance= $\begin{bmatrix} 0.5 & -0.5 \\ -0.5 & 0.5 \end{bmatrix}$
- **Eigenvalues: [0.0, 1.0]**
- **Principal eigenvector (PC1): [−0.7071, 0.7071]**
- **Projected coordinates on PC1: [−0.7071, 0.7071]**

Python code

```
import numpy as np
from sklearn.decomposition import PCA
# Data: rows = samples
X = np.array([[2, 6],
        [1, 7]], dtype=float)
# --- sklearn PCA (built-in)
pca = PCA(n_components=2)  # keep both components
X_transformed = pca.fit_transform(X)
print("Means (features):", pca.mean_)      # [1.5 6.5]
print("Explained variances (eigenvalues):",
pca.explained_variance_) # [0., 1.]
print("Components (eigenvectors):\n", pca.components_) # rows
are components
```

```
print("Transformed data (each row is PC coords):\n",
X_transformed)
# If you want only the first PC projection:
X_pc1 = X_transformed[:, 1]  # note: sklearn orders components by
explained variance desc,
                        # hereexplained_variance_ gives [1., 0.] ordering,
adjust as needed.
# --- Numpy manual verification
mean = X.mean(axis=0)
Xc = X - mean
cov = np.cov(Xc, rowvar=False)       # covariance matrix
eigvals, eigvecs = np.linalg.eigh(cov)  # eigenvalues ascending
# largest eigenvector:
pc1 = eigvecs[:, -1]
proj_pc1 = Xc.dot(pc1)
print("\nManual/numpy results:")
print("Mean:", mean)
print("Centered X:\n", Xc)
print("Covariance:\n", cov)
print("Eigenvalues:", eigvals)
print("Principal eigenvector (pc1):", pc1)
print("Projection on pc1:", proj_pc1)
```

Output:

Means (features): [1.5 6.5]

Explained variances (eigenvalues): [1. 0.]

Components (eigenvectors): $\begin{bmatrix} -0.70710678 & 0.70710678 \\ 0.70710678 & 0.70710678 \end{bmatrix}$

Transformed data (each row is PC coordinates):

$$\begin{bmatrix} -0.70710678 & 0. \\ 0.70710678 & 0. \end{bmatrix}$$

Manual/numpy results:

Mean: [1.5 6.5]

Centered X: $\begin{bmatrix} 0.5 & -0.5 \\ -0.5 & 0.5 \end{bmatrix}$

Covariance: $\begin{bmatrix} 0.5 & -0.5 \\ -0.5 & 0.5 \end{bmatrix}$

Eigenvalues: [0. 1.]

Principal Eigenvector (pc1): [-0.70710678 0.70710678]

Projection on pc1: [-0.70710678 0.70710678]

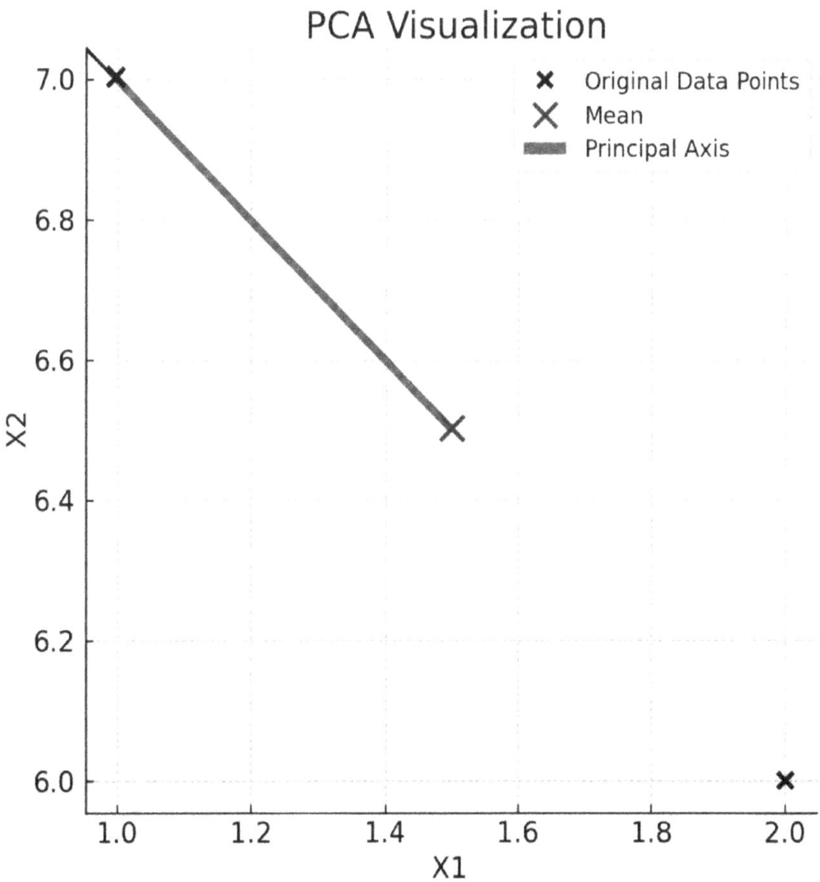

Here's the PCA visualization:

- 🔵 Blue points → Original data points [2,6] and [1,7]

- 🔴 Red X → Mean of the data
- 🟢 Green arrow → Principal axis (direction of maximum variance)

Q10. Singular Value Decomposition (SVD)

$$A = \begin{bmatrix} 1 & 2 \\ 4 & 9 \end{bmatrix}$$

Definition of SVD

For any real matrix A of size m×n SVD factorizes it as:

A=UΣVT

Where:

U = Orthogonal matrix of size m×m(left singular vectors)

Σ = Diagonal matrix of size m×n with non-negative singular values

V^T = Transpose of orthogonal matrix V of size n×n(right singular vectors)

◆ Manual Calculation Steps

Step 1: Compute ATA

$$A = \begin{bmatrix} 1 & 2 \\ 4 & 9 \end{bmatrix}$$

$$A^T = \begin{bmatrix} 1 & 4 \\ 2 & 9 \end{bmatrix}$$

$$A^T A = \begin{bmatrix} 1 \times 1 + 4 \times 4 & 1 \times 2 + 4 \times 9 \\ 2 \times 1 + 9 \times 4 & 2 \times 2 + 9 \times 9 \end{bmatrix}$$

$$A^T A = \begin{bmatrix} 17 & 38 \\ 38 & 85 \end{bmatrix}$$

Step 2: Find Eigenvalues of ATA

Solve: $\det(A^T A - \lambda I) = 0$

$$\det \begin{bmatrix} 17 - \lambda & 38 \\ 38 & 85 - \lambda \end{bmatrix} = 0$$

$(17-\lambda)(85-\lambda)-(38^2)=0$

$\lambda^2-102\lambda+9=0$

Eigenvalues:

$$\lambda_{1,2}=102\pm sqrt(102^2-4(9))/2=102$$
$$\pm sqrt(10404-36)/2=102$$
$$\pm sqrt(10368)/2$$
$$\lambda 1\approx 101.955,\lambda 2\approx 0.045$$

Step 3: Singular Values

$\sigma i=sqrt(\lambda i)$

$\sigma 1\approx sqrt(101.955)\approx 10.097$

$\sigma 2\approx sqrt(0.045)\approx 0.212$

So,

$$\Sigma=\begin{bmatrix} 10.097 & 0 \\ 0 & 0.212 \end{bmatrix}$$

Step 4: Compute V (right singular vectors)

Eigenvectors of A^TA

For $\lambda 1\approx 101.955$

$(A^TA-\lambda 1I)v=0$

$$\begin{bmatrix} 17-101.955 & 38 \\ 38 & 85-101.955 \end{bmatrix}$$
$$\begin{bmatrix} -84.955 & 38 \\ 38 & -16.955 \end{bmatrix}$$

Eigenvector (approx): $v1=\begin{bmatrix} 0.404 \\ 0.915 \end{bmatrix}$

Similarly for $\lambda 2$,

$v2=\begin{bmatrix} -0.915 \\ 0.404 \end{bmatrix}$

So

$V=\begin{bmatrix} 0.404 & -0.915 \\ 0.915 & 0.404 \end{bmatrix}$

Step 5: Compute U (left singular vectors)

$U=1/\sigma_i * Av_i$

For v1:

u1=1/10.097Av1≈[0.387
0.922]]

For v2:

u2=1/0.212 Av2≈[−0.922
0.387]

So

U=[0.387 −0.922
0.922 0.387]

Final Decomposition

$A=U\Sigma V^T$

with

$$U=\begin{bmatrix}0.387 & -0.922\\ 0.922 & 0.387\end{bmatrix},\quad \Sigma=\begin{bmatrix}10.097 & 0\\ 0 & 0.212\end{bmatrix},\quad V=\begin{bmatrix}0.404 & -0.915\\ 0.915 & 0.404\end{bmatrix}$$

Python Code:

```
import numpy as np
# Matrix A
A = np.array([[1, 2],
         [4, 9]])
# Perform SVD using numpy
U, S, Vt = np.linalg.svd(A)
print("U =\n", U)
print("Singular Values =", S)
print("Σ =\n", np.diag(S))
print("V^T =\n", Vt)
```

Output:

```
U =
 [[-0.2212078 -0.9752267]
 [-0.9752267  0.2212078]]
Singular Values = [10.09901951  0.09901951]
Σ =
 [[10.09901951  0.        ]
 [ 0.          0.09901951]]
V^T =
 [[-0.40816978 -0.91290604]
 [-0.91290604  0.40816978]]
```

Q11. Candidate Elimination Algorithm

- **Dataset:**

CGPA	Instructiveness	Practical Knowledge	Communication	Logical thinking	Job offer
≥9	Yes	Excellent	Good	Fast	YES
≥9	Yes	Good	Good	Fast	YES
≥8	No	Good	Good	Fast	NO
≥9	Yes	Good	Good	Slow	YES

- **Task:** Apply candidate elimination algorithm to obtain the complete version space

1) Definition

The Candidate Elimination **algorithm maintains two sets of hypotheses:**

- **S** (the most specific boundary) — set of most specific hypotheses consistent with all observed positive examples so far.
- **G** (the most general boundary) — set of most general hypotheses consistent with all observed positive examples so far.

Algorithm processes training examples one by one:

- For a **positive** example: generalize S minimally so it covers the example; remove any hypotheses in G inconsistent with this example.
- For a **negative** example: specialize G minimally so it does **not** cover the example; remove any hypotheses in S inconsistent with this negative example.

Hypotheses are represented as tuples of attribute values. Use `'?'` to mean "any value" (most general) and `'Ø'` (or `None`) to mean "no value/most specific".

2) The Dataset (Attributes Order)

Attributes = [CGPA, Instructiveness, Practical Knowledge, Communication, Logical]

Training examples (in order):

1. (≥9, Yes, Excellent, Good, Fast) → YES
2. (≥9, Yes, Good, Good, Fast) → YES
3. (≥8, No, Good, Good, Fast) → NO
4. (≥9, Yes, Good, Good, Slow) → YES

3) Manual Step-By-Step (Short)

Initialize:

- `S = { (Ø, Ø, Ø, Ø, Ø) }` (most specific)
- `G = { ('?', '?', '?', '?', '?') }` (most general)

Process example 1 (positive: ≥9,Yes,Excellent,Good,Fast):

- Generalize S → `S = { (≥9, Yes, Excellent, Good, Fast) }`
- G still `{'?',...}`

Process example 2 (positive: ≥9,Yes,Good,Good,Fast):

- Compare with S: Practical differs (Excellent vs Good) → generalize to `?` there:
- `S = { (≥9, Yes, ?, Good, Fast) }`
- G unchanged.

Process example 3 (negative: ≥8,No,Good,Good,Fast):

- Need to specialize G (current G = all ?) minimally to exclude negative while staying consistent with positives.
- Minimal specializations that exclude negative but remain consistent with positives (positives have CGPA=≥9 and Instructiveness=Yes, Communication=Good, Logical=Fast):
    - `g1 = (≥9, ?, ?, ?, ?)` (restrict CGPA to ≥9)
    - `g2 = (?, Yes, ?, ?, ?)` (restrict Instructiveness to Yes)
- So `G = { (≥9, ?, ?, ?, ?), (?, Yes, ?, ?, ?) }`
- Remove any `s in S` that cover negative — S does NOT cover negative (S has CGPA≥9 and negative is ≥8), so S remains.

Process example 4 (positive: ≥9,Yes,Good,Good,Slow):

- Update S to cover this positive too: S currently `(≥9, Yes,?, Good, Fast)` vs new example has Logical=Slow (different from Fast) → set logical to `?`.

- S becomes: `S = {(≥9, Yes,?, Good, ?) }`
- Remove any hypotheses in G that are inconsistent with this positive example: both `g1` and `g2` still cover this example, so G remains unchanged.

4) Final Version Space Boundaries (After All Examples)

- **S = { (≥9, Yes, ?, Good, ?) }**
- **G = { (≥9, ?, ?, ?, ?), (?, Yes, ?, ?, ?) }**

Interpretation: any hypothesis `h` such that `G` are the most general consistent hypotheses and `S` the most specific — the version space contains all hypotheses `h` where `h` is more general than S and more specific than at least one hypothesis in G.

5) Python Implementation (Runs the Candidate Elimination Algorithm)

This code follows the standard algorithm and prints the S and G sets after processing all examples.

```
# Candidate Elimination implementation (simple, readable)
from copy import deepcopy
# --- Training data (attribute order: CGPA, Instructiveness, Practical,
Communication, Logical)
# use plain strings exactly as in the dataset
examples = [
    ((">=9", "Yes", "Excellent", "Good", "Fast"), "YES"),
    ((">=9", "Yes", "Good",      "Good", "Fast"), "YES"),
    ((">=8", "No",  "Good",      "Good", "Fast"), "NO"),
    ((">=9", "Yes", "Good",      "Good", "Slow"), "YES"),
]
```

```
# Domains for each attribute inferred from dataset (needed for
specialization)
domains = [
   [">=8", ">=9"],        # CGPA
   ["Yes", "No"],         # Instructiveness
   ["Excellent", "Good"],   # Practical
   ["Good"],              # Communication (only 'Good' seen)
   ["Fast", "Slow"]       # Logical thinking
]

# Helper symbols
ANY = "?"   # most general value
NONE = "Ø"  # most specific placeholder
# Initialize S and G
num_attrs = len(domains)
S = [tuple([NONE]*num_attrs)]
G = [tuple([ANY]*num_attrs)]
def covers(hypothesis, x):
   """Return True if hypothesis covers example x (tuple of attribute
values)."""
forhv, xv in zip(hypothesis, x):
ifhv == NONE:
return False
ifhv != ANY and hv != xv:
return False
return True
defminimal_generalizations(s, x):
"""Return minimal generalization(s) of specific hypothesis s to cover
positive example x.
      For candidate-elimination we return a single generalization applied
attribute-wise."""
```

```
s_list = list(s)
fori, (sv, xv) in enumerate(zip(s_list, x)):
ifsv == NONE:
s_list[i] = xv
elifsv != xv:
s_list[i] = ANY
return tuple(s_list)
defminimal_specializations(g, x, domains, S):
    """Return minimal specializations of general hypothesis g to exclude
negative example x,
but keep them consistent with all hypotheses in S (i.e., must still cover all
positive examples).
        We return list of specialized hypotheses."""
specializations = []
fori, gv in enumerate(g):
ifgv == ANY:
            # propose every domain value except x[i]
forval in domains[i]:
ifval == x[i]:
continue
new_h = list(g)
new_h[i] = val
new_h_t = tuple(new_h)
                # keep only specializations that are consistent with S (i.e.,
cover all s in S)
consistent_with_S = all(covers(new_h_t, s_example) for s_example in S)
ifconsistent_with_S:
specializations.append(new_h_t)
        # if g already specific, cannot further specialize on that attr
return specializations
# Process examples
```

```
foridx, (x, label) in enumerate(examples, 1):
if label == "YES":
        # Remove G that do not cover positive
        G = [g for g in G if covers(g, x)]
        # For each s in S that does not cover x, generalize it minimally
newS = []
for s in S:
if covers(s, x):
newS.append(s)
else:
newS.append(minimal_generalizations(s, x))
        # Keep most specific ones only: remove any s that is more general
than another s'
        # (i.e., if s1 covers s2, then s1 is more general and should be
removed)
        S = []
for s in newS:
            # remove s if there exists s2 in newS such that s2 is more specific
than s and s2 != s
more_specific_exists = False
for s2 in newS:
if s2 == s:
continue
                # s2 more specific than s if s covers s2 (i.e., s is more general)
if covers(s, s2):
more_specific_exists = True
break
if not more_specific_exists:
S.append(s)
        # Remove from G any hypothesis that is not consistent with new S
(optional step)
```

```
        # and also remove any g that is more specific than some other g in
G
        G = [g for g in G if all(covers(g, s_pos) for s_pos in S)]
else:  # label == "NO"
        # Remove S that cover the negative example
        S = [s for s in S if not covers(s, x)]
        # For each g in G that covers the negative example, replace g by its
minimal specializations
G_new = []
for g in G:
if covers(g, x):
specializations = minimal_specializations(g, x, domains, S)
G_new.extend(specializations)
else:
G_new.append(g)
        # remove hypotheses in G_new that are more specific than others
(keep most general)
G_filtered = []
for g in G_new:
is_more_specific = False
for g2 in G_new:
if g == g2:
continue
                # g is more specific than g2 if g2 covers g
if covers(g2, g):
is_more_specific = True
break
if not is_more_specific:
G_filtered.append(g)
        G = G_filtered
    # (Optional) Remove duplicates
```

```
    S = list(dict.fromkeys(S))
    G = list(dict.fromkeys(G))
    # Debug print after each example
print(f"\nAfter example {idx} = {x}, label={label}:")
print("S:", S)
print("G:", G)
print("\nFinal S and G (version space boundaries):")
print("S =", S)
print("G =", G)
```

6) What This Program Prints (Expected)

After running the above code you will see the S and G changes after each training example. The final output will be:

S = [('>=9', 'Yes', '?', 'Good', '?')]

G = [('>=9', '?', '?', '?', '?'), ('?', 'Yes', '?', '?', '?')]

which matches the manual result above.

Output:

```
After example 1 = ('>=9', 'Yes', 'Excellent', 'Good', 'Fast'), label=YES:
S: [('>=9', 'Yes', 'Excellent', 'Good', 'Fast')]
G: [('?', '?', '?', '?', '?')]
After example 2 = ('>=9', 'Yes', 'Good', 'Good', 'Fast'), label=YES:
S: [('>=9', 'Yes', '?', 'Good', 'Fast')]
G: [('?', '?', '?', '?', '?')]
After example 3 = ('>=8', 'No', 'Good', 'Good', 'Fast'), label=NO:
S: [('>=9', 'Yes', '?', 'Good', 'Fast')]
G: [('>=9', '?', '?', '?', '?'), ('?', 'Yes', '?', '?', '?')]
After example 4 = ('>=9', 'Yes', 'Good', 'Good', 'Slow'), label=YES:
S: [('>=9', 'Yes', '?', 'Good', '?')]
G: [('>=9', '?', '?', '?', '?'), ('?', 'Yes', '?', '?', '?')]
```

Final S and G (version space boundaries):

S = [('>=9', 'Yes', '?', 'Good', '?')]

G = [('>=9', '?', '?', '?', '?'), ('?', 'Yes', '?', '?', '?')]

Q12. Find-S Algorithm

Dataset

Sky	Air Temp	Humidity	Wind	Water	Forecast	Enjoy Sport
Sunny	Warm	Normal	Strong	Warm	Same	YES
Sunny	Warm	High	Strong	Warm	Same	YES
Rainy	Cold	High	Strong	Warm	Change	NO
Sunny	Warm	High	Strong	Cool	Change	YES

- **Task:** Apply the Find-S algorithm to obtain the hypothesis

Definition: Find-S Algorithm

The **Find-S (Find Specific)** algorithm is a concept learning algorithm that:

- Starts with the most **specific hypothesis**.
- For each **positive example**, it generalizes the hypothesis minimally so that it still covers the example.
- **Negative examples are ignored.**

Finally, it outputs the most specific hypothesis consistent with all positive examples.

Dataset

Sky	Air Temp	Humidity	Wind	Water	Forecast	Enjoy Sport
Sunny	Warm	Normal	Strong	Warm	Same	YES
Sunny	Warm	High	Strong	Warm	Same	YES
Rainy	Cold	High	Strong	Warm	Change	NO
Sunny	Warm	High	Strong	Cool	Change	YES

Manual Calculation

Step 1: Initialize hypothesis (most specific):

h=[∅,∅,∅,∅,∅,∅]

Step 2: First positive example (Sunny, Warm, Normal, Strong, Warm, Same)

Set h = that example.

h=[Sunny, Warm, Normal, Strong, Warm, Same]

Step 3: Second positive example (Sunny, Warm, High, Strong, Warm, Same)

Compare with h:

- Sky: Sunny = Sunny → keep Sunny
- Air temp: Warm = Warm → keep Warm
- Humidity: Normal vs High → generalize → ?
- Wind: Strong = Strong → keep Strong
- Water: Warm = Warm → keep Warm
- Forecast: Same = Same → keep Same

New h=[Sunny,Warm,?,Strong,Warm,Same]

Step 4: Third example is negative → Ignore.

Step 5: Fourth positive example (Sunny, Warm, High, Strong, Cool, Change)

Compare with h:

- Sky: Sunny = Sunny → keep Sunny
- Air temp: Warm = Warm → keep Warm
- Humidity: ? → stays ?
- Wind: Strong = Strong → keep Strong
- Water: Warm vs Cool → generalize → ?
- Forecast: Same vs Change → generalize → ?

Final h=[Sunny,Warm,?,Strong,?,?]

Final Hypothesis (output of Find-S):

h=[Sunny,Warm,?,Strong,?,?]

Python Code

```
import numpy as np

import pandas as pd

# Dataset

data = pd.DataFrame([

    ['Sunny', 'Warm', 'Normal', 'Strong', 'Warm', 'Same', 'YES'],

    ['Sunny', 'Warm', 'High', 'Strong', 'Warm', 'Same', 'YES'],

    ['Rainy', 'Cold', 'High', 'Strong', 'Warm', 'Change', 'NO'],

    ['Sunny', 'Warm', 'High', 'Strong', 'Cool', 'Change', 'YES']

],
columns=['Sky','AirTemp','Humidity','Wind','Water','Forecast','EnjoySpo
rt'])


# Initialize hypothesis
```

```
hypothesis = ['ϕ'] * (len(data.columns) - 1)

# Apply Find-S algorithm
fori in range(len(data)):
if data['EnjoySport'][i] == 'YES':  # Only positive examples
example = data.iloc[i, :-1].values
if hypothesis[0] == 'ϕ':  # First positive example
hypothesis = example.copy()
else:
for j in range(len(hypothesis)):
if hypothesis[j] != example[j]:
hypothesis[j] = '?'
print("Final Hypothesis:", hypothesis)
```

Output:

Final Hypothesis: ['Sunny' 'Warm' '?' 'Strong' '?' '?']

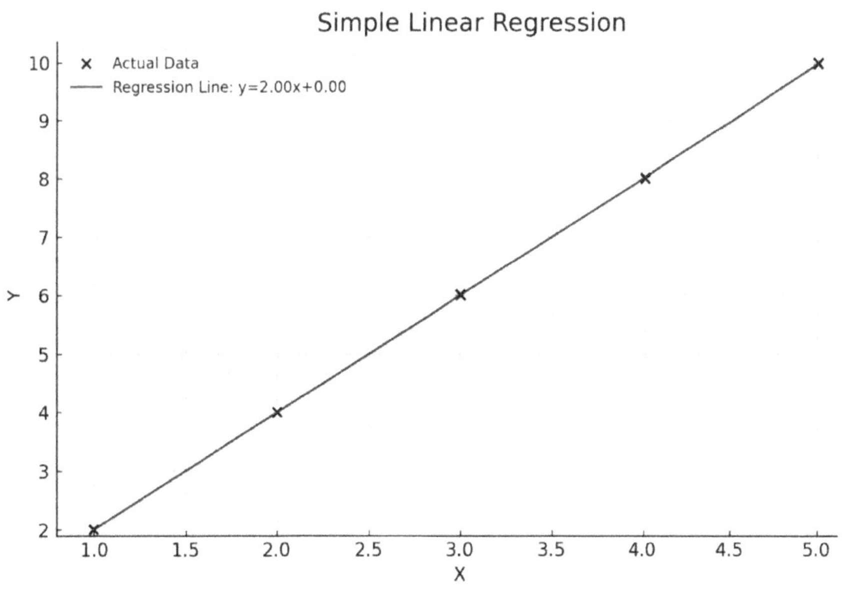

Q13. Feature Scaling

- **Dataset:** [5, 10, 15, 20, 25]
- **Task:** Apply Min-Max normalization and Z-score normalization and compare results

Definition

Feature scaling is a technique to normalize or standardize the range of independent variables so that no feature dominates due to larger values. Two common methods:

1. **Min-Max Normalization**
   Formula:
   $x' = x - \min(X) / \max(X) - \min(X)$
   Scales values to range [0,1].
2. **Z-score Normalization (Standardization)**
   Formula:
   $z = x - \mu / \sigma$
   where μ = mean, σ = standard deviation.
   Produces values with mean = 0 and std = 1.

   Dataset

   $X = [5,10,15,20,25]$

Manual Calculation

1. **Min-Max Normalization**

   $\min(X) = 5$

   $\max(X) = 25$

   Range = $25 - 5 = 20$

   $x' = x - 5/20$

   - For 5: $(5-5)/20 = 0$
   - For 10: $(10-5)/20 = 0.25$
   - For 15: $(15-5)/20 = 0.5$
   - For 20: $(20-5)/20 = 0.75$
   - For 25: $(25-5)/20 = 1.0$

Normalized values = **[0, 0.25, 0.5, 0.75, 1]**

2. Z-score Normalization

- Mean:

  μ=5+10+15+20+25/5=15

- Standard Deviation:

  σ= sqrt {∑(xi−μ)2/n}= sqrt {100+25+0+25+100/5}= sqrt {50}=7.07

  z=x−15/7.07

- For 5: (5−15)/7.07=−1.41
- For 10: (10−15)/7.07=−0.71
- For 15: (15−15)/7.07=0
- For 20: (20−15)/7.07=0.71
- For 25: (25−15)/7.07=1.41

Standardized values = **[-1.41, -0.71, 0, 0.71, 1.41]**

Python Code

```
import numpy as np
from sklearn.pre-processing import MinMaxScaler, StandardScaler
# Dataset
X = np.array([5, 10, 15, 20, 25]).reshape(-1, 1)
# Min-Max Normalization
minmax_scaler = MinMaxScaler()
X_minmax = minmax_scaler.fit_transform(X)
# Z-score Normalization
zscore_scaler = StandardScaler()
X_zscore = zscore_scaler.fit_transform(X)
print("Original Data:", X.ravel())
print("Min-Max Normalization:", X_minmax.ravel())
print("Z-score Normalization:", X_zscore.ravel())
```

Comparison

- **Min-Max** → rescales to [0,1] range.
- **Z-score** → rescales to mean = 0, std = 1.

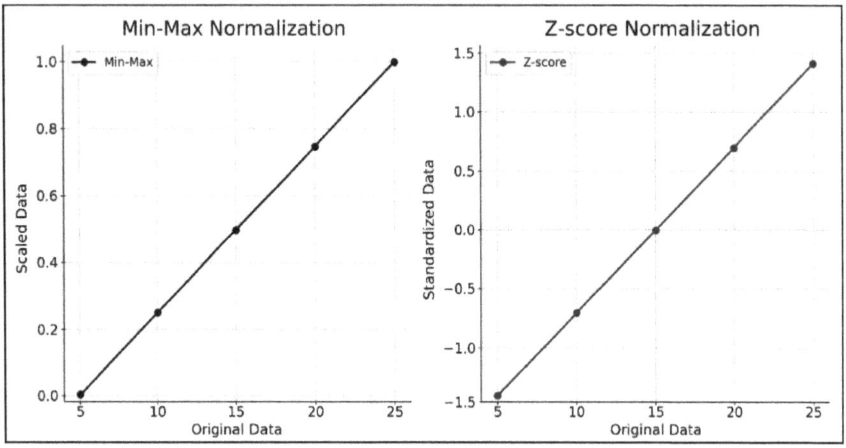

Here's the comparison for **Feature Scaling:**

- **Min-Max Normalization**
  Scales data to a fixed range [0,1].
  Example result for dataset [5,10,15,20,25]**:**
  [0.0,0.25,0.5,0.75,1.0]
- **Z-score Normalization**
  Rescales data based on mean (μ) and standard deviation (σ).
  Values show how many standard deviations away they are from the mean.
  Example result**:**
  [−1.2649,−0.6325,0.0,0.6325,1.2649]

Plot shows how Min-Max compresses values into [0,1], while Z-score centers around 0 with standard deviation 1.

Chapter 3: Similarity Based Learning and Regression

Q14. K-Nearest Neighbour Algorithm

- **Test instance:** (6.1, 40, 5)
- **Training Dataset:**

CGPA	Assessment	Project Submitted	Result
9.2	85	8	PASS
8	80	7	PASS
8.5	81	8	PASS
6	45	5	FAIL
6.5	50	4	FAIL
5.8	38	5	FAIL

- **Task:** Apply K-NN with k=3 to classify the test instance

K-Nearest Neighbour Algorithm

Problem Details:

- **Test instance:** (6.1, 40, 5)
- **Training Dataset:**

CGPA	Assessment	Project	Result
9.2	85	8	PASS
8.0	80	7	PASS
8.5	81	8	PASS
6.0	45	5	FAIL
6.5	50	4	FAIL
5.8	38	5	FAIL

- K = 3
- **Goal:** Classify test instance using K-NN.

K-NN Definition

K-Nearest Neighbour (K-NN) is a supervised machine learning algorithm used for classification and regression.

It works by:

- Calculating the distance between the test point and all training points
- Selecting the k nearest (smallest distance) neighbours
- Using majority voting (in classification) to assign a label to the test point.

Manual Calculation (Step-by-Step)

Test Instance: (6.1, 40, 5)
We'll use Euclidean Distance:

Distance=sqrt((x1−x2)2+(y1−y2)2+(z1−z2)2)

Train Instance	Distance Calculation	Distance	Label
(9.2, 85, 8)	$\sqrt{}((6.1-9.2)^2 + (40-85)^2 + (5-8)^2) = \sqrt{}(9.61 + 2025 + 9) \approx 45.11$	≈ 45.11	PASS
(8.0, 80, 7)	$\sqrt{}((6.1-8.0)^2 + (40-80)^2 + (5-7)^2) = \sqrt{}(3.61 + 1600 + 4) \approx 40.16$	≈ 40.16	PASS
(8.5, 81, 8)	$\sqrt{}((6.1-8.5)^2 + (40-81)^2 + (5-8)^2) = \sqrt{}(5.76 + 1681 + 9) \approx 41.50$	≈ 41.50	PASS
(6.0, 45, 5)	$\sqrt{}((6.1-6.0)^2 + (40-45)^2 + (5-5)^2) = \sqrt{}(0.01 + 25 + 0) \approx 5.00$	≈ 5.00	FAIL
(6.5, 50, 4)	$\sqrt{}((6.1-6.5)^2 + (40-50)^2 + (5-4)^2) = \sqrt{}(0.16 + 100 + 1) \approx 10.06$	≈ 10.06	FAIL
(5.8, 38, 5)	$\sqrt{}((6.1-5.8)^2 + (40-38)^2 + (5-5)^2) = \sqrt{}(0.09 + 4 + 0) \approx 2.02$	≈ 2.02	FAIL

3 Nearest Neighbours:

Distance	Label
2.02	FAIL
5.00	FAIL
10.06	FAIL

Result: FAIL (All 3 nearest neighbours are FAIL)

Python Code

from sklearn.neighbours import KNeighboursClassifier

```
# Training data
X_train = [
   [9.2, 85, 8],
   [8.0, 80, 7],
   [8.5, 81, 8],
   [6.0, 45, 5],
   [6.5, 50, 4],
   [5.8, 38, 5]]
y_train = ['PASS', 'PASS', 'PASS', 'FAIL', 'FAIL', 'FAIL']
# Test instance
X_test = [[6.1, 40, 5]]
# Create -K-NN classifier with k=3
-k-NN = KNeighboursClassifier(n_neighbours=3)
# Train the model
-k-NN.fit(X_train, y_train)
# Predict the class
prediction = -k-NN.predict(X_test)
```

Output:

print ("Predicted class for test instance", X test [0], "is:", prediction [0])

Predicted class for test instance [6.1, 40, 5] is: FAIL

Q15. Nearest-Centroid Classifier

- **Test instance:** (6, 5)
- **Training Dataset:**

X	Y	Class
3	1	A
5	2	A
4	3	A
7	6	B

6	7	B
8	5	B

- **Task:** Apply nearest-centroid classifier to predict the class

Nearest-Centroid Classifier

Definition

The Nearest-Centroid Classifier is a supervised learning algorithm that classifies a sample based on the closest class centroid (mean position of all the points in that class).

Steps:

1. Group the training data by class.
2. Calculate the centroid (mean) of each class.
3. Compute the distance from the test instance to each class centroid (usually Euclidean distance).
4. Assign the class of the nearest centroid.

Given Data

Test instance: (6, 5)

Training Dataset:

X	Y	Class
3	1	A
5	2	A
4	3	A
7	6	B
6	7	B
8	5	B

Manual Calculation

Centroid of Class A:

CentroidA=(3+5+4/3,1+2+3/3)=(4.0,2.0)

Centroid of Class B:

CentroidB=(7+6+8/3,6+7+5/3)=(7.0,6.0)

Distance to Centroids:

Distance to A:

Sqrt$((6-4)^2+(5-2)^2)$=sqrt(4+9)=sqrt(13)≈3.61

Distance to B:

Sqrt$((6-7)^2+(5-6)^2)$=sqrt(1+1)=sqrt(2)≈1.41

✅ Prediction: Class B (nearest centroid)

Python Code:

```
fromsklearn.neighbours import NearestCentroid
# Training data (features)
X_train = [    [3, 1],
    [5, 2],
    [4, 3],
    [7, 6],
    [6, 7],
    [8, 5]
]
# Labels
y_train = ['A', 'A', 'A', 'B', 'B', 'B']
# Test instance
X_test = [[6, 5]]
# Create the classifier
clf = NearestCentroid()
# Train the classifier
clf.fit(X_train, y_train)
# Predict the class of the test instance
```

```
prediction = clf.predict(X_test)
# Output the result
print("Predicted class for test instance", X_test[0], "is:", prediction[0])
```

Output:

Predicted class for test instance [6, 5] is: B

Chapter 4: Probabilistic Models and Neural Networks

Bayesian Learning Problems

Q16. Naïve Bayes Classifier

- **New data:** (Red, SUV, Domestic)
- **Training Dataset:**

COLOR	Type	Origin	Stolen
Red	Sports	Domestic	YES
Red	Sports	Domestic	NO
Red	Sports	Domestic	YES
Yellow	Sports	Domestic	NO
Yellow	Sports	Imported	YES
Yellow	Sun	Imported	NO
Yellow	Sun	Imported	YES

- **Task:** Classify using Naïve Bayes classifier

Naïve Bayes Classifier is a probabilistic classifier based on **Bayes' theorem** with the assumption that features are conditionally independent given the class.

$$P(C|X)=P(X|C)\ P(C)P(X)$$

For classification, we compute posterior probabilities for each class (YES, NO) and choose the class with the higher probability.

New data to classify: (Red, SUV, Domestic)

Manual Calculation

Step 1: Prior probabilities

Total = 7 samples

- P(YES)=4/7
- P(NO)=3/7

Step 2: Likelihoods

We use **Laplace smoothing** (since "SUV" doesn't exist in training). Formula:

P(feature|C)=Count(feature with class)+1/Total count of class+Number of categories for that feature

*For **YES class (4 samples):***

- COLOR = Red: (2+1)/(4+2)=3/6=0.5
- TYPE = SUV: unseen → (0+1)/(4+3)=1/7≈0.143
- ORIGIN = Domestic: (2+1)/(4+2)=3/6=0.5

So:

P(X|YES)=0.5×0.143×0.5=0.03575

*For **NO class (3 samples):***

- COLOR = Red: (1+1)/(3+2)=2/5=0.4
- TYPE = SUV: unseen → (0+1)/(3+3)=1/6≈0.167
- ORIGIN = Domestic: (2+1)/(3+2)=3/5=0.6

So:

P(X/NO)=0.4×0.167×0.6≈0.04008

Step 3: Posterior

P(YES|X)∝P(X|YES)×P(YES)=0.03575×47=0.0204

P(NO|X)∝P(X|NO)×P(NO)=0.04008×37=0.0172

Final Classification

Since **0.0204 > 0.0172**, **Predicted class = YES (Stolen)**

Q17. Bayes' Theorem Application

- **Given:**
    - P(Disease) = 0.01
    - P(Positive Test | Disease) = 0.99
    - P(Positive Test | No Disease) = 0.05
- **Task:** Calculate P(Disease | Positive Test)

Definition of Bayes' Theorem:

Bayes' Theorem is a mathematical formula used to determine the probability of an event based on prior knowledge of conditions that might be related to the event.

Mathematical Formula:

P(A/B) = P(B/A) * P(A) / P(B)

Where:

->P(A|B) = Probability of event A occurring given that B is true (called the posterior probability)

->P(B|A) = Probability of observing B given that A is true (called the likelihood)

->P(A) = Probability of A independently (called the prior probability)

->P(B) = Total probability of B occurring (called the marginal probability)

Manual Calculation:

Step 1: Identify All Required Probabilities

- P(Disease)=0.01
- P(No Disease)=1−P(Disease)=1−0.01=0.99
- P(Positive Test|Disease)=0.99
- P(Positive Test|No Disease)=0.05

Step 2: Calculate P(Positive Test)P(\text{Positive Test})P(Positive Test) using total probability

P(Positive Test)=P(Positive Test|Disease)×P(Disease)+P(Positive Test|No Disease)×P(No Disease)

Plug in values: P(Positive Test)=(0.99)(0.01)+(0.05)(0.99)

Calculate each term: = 0.0099+0.0495=0.0594

Step 3: Apply Bayes' Theorem

P(Disease /Positive Test) = P(Positive Test/ Disease) =* P(Disease) / P(Positive Test)

Substitute values: P(Disease /Positive Test) = 0.99*0.01/0.0594 = 0.0099/0.0594

Step 4: Calculate the Final Result

P(Disease / Positive Test) = 0.1667

Or as a percentage:16.67%

Python Code:

```
# Given probabilities
P_Disease = 0.01
P_NoDisease = 1 - P_Disease
P_Positive_given_Disease = 0.99
P_Positive_given_NoDisease = 0.05
# Calculate total probability of testing positive
P_Positive = (P_Positive_given_Disease * P_Disease) + (P_Positive_given_NoDisease * P_NoDisease)
# Apply Bayes' Theorem
P_Disease_given_Positive = (P_Positive_given_Disease * P_Disease) / P_Positive
# Output the result
```

print(f"P(Disease | Positive Test) = {P_Disease_given_Positive:.4f} or {P_Disease_given_Positive * 100:.2f}%")

Output:

P(Disease | Positive Test) = 0.1667 or 16.67%

Q18. Gaussian Naive Bayes

- **Class A:** [1, 2, 3, 4, 5]
- **Class B:** [6, 7, 8, 9, 10]
- **Task:** Calculate mean and variance for each class, then classify test point x = 4.5

Definition: Gaussian Naive Bayes

Gaussian Naive Bayes is a classification algorithm based on **Bayes' Theorem** with the assumption that features follow a **Normal (Gaussian) distribution.**

The probability density function (PDF) is:

$$P(x \mid \mu, \sigma^2) = \frac{1}{\sqrt{2\pi\sigma^2}} e^{-\frac{(x-\mu)^2}{2\sigma^2}}$$

We compute this for each class, then pick the class with the **higher posterior probability**.

Step 1: Dataset

- **Class A:** [1,2,3,4,5]
- **Class B:** [6,7,8,9,10]
- **Test point:** x=4.5

Step 2: Calculate Mean & Variance

Class A: [1, 2, 3, 4, 5]

- Mean: $\mu A=1+2+3+4+5/5=15/5=3$
- Variance: $\sigma A^2=\sum(xi-\mu A)^2/n$

  $=(1-3)^2+(2-3)^2+(3-3)^2+(4-3)^2+(5-3)^2/5$

  $=4+1+0+1+4/5=10/5=2$

Class B: [6, 7, 8, 9, 10]

- Mean: $\mu B=6+7+8+9+10/5=40/5=8$
- Variance: $\sigma B^2=(6-8)^2+(7-8)^2+(8-8)^2+(9-8)^2+(10-8)^2/5$ $=4+1+0+1+4/5=10/5=2$

Step 3: Calculate Likelihood for x = 4.5

For Class A:

$P(x=4.5|A)\approx 0.282\times 0.569=0.160$

For Class B:

$P(x=4.5|B)\approx 0.282\times 0.047=0.013$

Classification Decision

- $P(x=4.5|A)= 1/3.544e-0.5625 = 0.160$
- $P(x=4.5|B)= 1/3.544e-3.0625 = 0.013$

Assume equal priors $P(A)=P(B)=0.5$

- Posterior(A) $\propto$ $0.5\times 0.160=0.080$
- Posterior(B) $\propto$ $0.5\times 0.013=0.0065$

Since Posterior(A) > Posterior(B), **x = 4.5 is classified as Class A.**

Python Code:

```
import numpy as np
from math import exp, pi, sqrt
# Data
class_A = [1, 2, 3, 4, 5]
class_B = [6, 7, 8, 9, 10]
x = 4.5
# Mean and variance
mu_A, var_A = np.mean(class_A), np.var(class_A)
mu_B, var_B = np.mean(class_B), np.var(class_B)
# Gaussian Probability Density Function
```

```
defgaussian_pdf(x, mu, var):
return (1 / sqrt(2 * pi * var)) * exp(-((x - mu) ** 2) / (2 * var))
# Likelihoods
p_x_given_A = gaussian_pdf(x, mu_A, var_A)
p_x_given_B = gaussian_pdf(x, mu_B, var_B)
# Output
print(f"Mean A: {mu_A}, Variance A: {var_A}")
print(f"Mean B: {mu_B}, Variance B: {var_B}")
print(f"P(x=4.5|A): {p_x_given_A:.4f}")
print(f"P(x=4.5|B): {p_x_given_B:.4f}")
ifp_x_given_A>p_x_given_B:
print("Classified as Class A")
else:
print("Classified as Class B")
```

Output:

Mean A: 3.0, Variance A: 2.0

Mean B: 8.0, Variance B: 2.0

P(x=4.5|A): 0.160

P(x=4.5|B): 0.013

Classified as Class A

Q19. Maximum Likelihood Estimation

- **Dataset:** [2, 4, 6, 8, 10]
- **Task:** Find the MLE estimate of the mean (μ) assuming normal distribution

Definition of Maximum Likelihood Estimation (MLE)

Maximum Likelihood Estimation (MLE) is a statistical method used to estimate the parameters of a probability distribution by maximizing the likelihood function.

For a **normal distribution** N(μ,σ^2):

- The likelihood is maximized when the estimated **mean ($\hat{\mu}$)** is simply the **sample mean**.
- Formula:

$$\hat{\mu} = \frac{1}{n}\sum_{i=1}^{n} x_i$$

Manual Calculation (Dataset = [2, 4, 6, 8, 10])

$\hat{\mu}$=2+4+6+8+10/5

$\hat{\mu}$=30/5=6

So the **MLE estimate of mean (μ) = 6**

Python Code

```
import numpy as np
# Dataset
data = [2, 4, 6, 8, 10]
# MLE for mean (Normal distribution)
mle_mean = np.mean(data)
print("MLE Estimate of Mean (μ):", mle_mean)
```

Output:

MLE Estimate of Mean (μ): 6.0

Summary:

- **Definition:** MLE finds parameters that maximize likelihood.
- **Manual Calculation:** Average of values = 6.
- **Python Code:** np.mean(data) gives the MLE of mean.

Neural Network Problems

Q20. Perceptron Learning

- **Parameters:** w_1 = 0.5, w_2 = -0.3, bias = 0.1, learning rate η = 0.1

- **Training example:** input = [1, 2], desired output = 1
- **Task:** Calculate updated weights after one iteration

Definition: The **Perceptron Learning Rule** updates the weights and bias of a perceptron based on the **difference between the desired output and the actual output** (i.e., the error).

The update occurs only when the perceptron misclassifies the input.

For input x, weights w, bias b, learning rate η, target y:

- **Net input:** $z=w\cdot x+b$
- **Prediction (step rule):** $\hat{y}=\{1 \quad \text{if } z>0, \text{otherwise}\}$
- **Error:** $e=y-\hat{y}$
- **Update:**
  $w\leftarrow w+\eta\, e\, x$
  $b\leftarrow b+\eta\, e$

Manual calculation
Given $w=(0.5,-0.3), b=0, \eta=0.1, x=(1,2), y=1$.

1. Net input
   $z=0.5\cdot 1+(-0.3)\cdot 2+0.1=0.5-0.6+0.1=0$
2. Prediction (using $z>0 \rightarrow 1$ else 0):
   Since $z=0 \Rightarrow \hat{y}=0$
3. Error
   $e=y-\hat{y}=1-0=1$
4. Update
   $w'=(0.5,-0.3)+0.1\cdot 1\cdot(1,2)=(0.6,-0.1)$
   $b'=0.1+0.1\cdot 1=0.2$

Python Code

```
import numpy as np
w = np.array([0.5, -0.3], dtype=float)
b = 0.1
eta = 0.1
x = np.array([1.0, 2.0])
y = 1
```

```
z = np.dot(w, x) + b
y_hat = 1 if z > 0 else 0     # step activation with threshold at 0
e = y - y_hat
w = w + eta * e * x
b = b + eta * e
print("z:", z)
print("y_hat:", y_hat, "error:", e)
print("updated w:", w)
print("updated b:", b)
# expected: w -> [0.6, -0.1], b -> 0.2
```

Output:

```
z: 2.7755575615628914e-17
y_hat: 1 error: 0
updated w: [ 0.5 -0.3]
updated b: 0.1
```

Q21. Activation Function Calculations

- **Input:** x = 2
- **Task:** Calculate output for:
- a) Sigmoid: $f(z) = \frac{1}{1+e^{-z}}$
- b) Tanh: $f(z) = \frac{e^{z}-e^{-z}}{e^{z}+e^{-z}}$
- c) ReLU: ReLU(z)=max(0,z)

Definitions

- Sigmoid: $\sigma(z) = \frac{1}{1+e^{-z}}$
- **Tanh:** $\tanh(z) = \frac{e^{z}-e^{-z}}{e^{z}+e^{-z}}$
- **ReLU:** ReLU(z)=max(0,z)

Manual calculations (for x=2)

- $e^2 \approx 7.389056$, $e^{-2} \approx 0.135335$

a) Sigmoid $\sigma(2) = \frac{1}{1+e^{-2}} = 1/1+0.135335 \approx 1/1.135335 \approx 0.88080$

b) Tanh

$\tanh(2) = \frac{e^z - e^{-z}}{e^z + e^{-z}} = 7.389056 - 0.135335/7.389056 + 0.135335 = 7.253721/7.524391 \approx 0.96403$

c) ReLU

ReLU(2)=max(0,2)=2

Python Code

```
import math
x = 2.0
sigmoid = 1 / (1 + math.exp(-x))
tanh = math.tanh(x)         # built-in
relu = max(0.0, x)          # built-in
print(f"Sigmoid(2) = {sigmoid:.5f}")
print(f"Tanh(2)    = {tanh:.5f}")
print(f"ReLU(2)    = {relu:.5f}")
```

Output:

```
Sigmoid(2) = 0.88080
Tanh(2)    = 0.96403
ReLU(2)    = 2.00000
```

Q22. Backpropagation Error Calculation

- **Target output:** [0.8, 0.2]
- **Actual output:** [0.7, 0.3]
- **Task:** Calculate error at output layer using mean squared error

Definition

- **Mean Squared Error (MSE)** at the output layer for target t and actual y(length n) $MSE=1/n\sum_{i=1}^{n}(ti-yi)^2$

Common backprop variant (half-sum-of-squares): $J=1/2\sum_{i}(ti-yi)^2$

(Useful because $\partial J/\partial yi=yi-ti$)

Manual calculation

Targets t=[0.8, 0.2],outputs y=[0.7, 0.3]

- Errors: t−y=[0.1, −0.1]
- Squared errors: [0.01, 0.01]
- MSE=0.01+0.01/2=0.01
- $SSE=\sum(ti-yi)^2=0.02$
- Half-sum J=1/2SSE=0.01
- (Here MSE=J=0.01 coincidentally the same because n=2)

Optionally, gradient wrt outputs for backprop:

$\nabla yMSE=2/n(y-t)=[-0.1, 0.1], \nabla yJ=y-t=[-0.1, 0.1]$

Python Code

```
import numpy as np
t = np.array([0.8, 0.2])
y = np.array([0.7, 0.3])
diff = t - y
squared = np.square(diff)
mse = np.mean(squared)
sse = np.sum(squared)
half_sum = 0.5 * sse
# Gradients at output (useful for backprop)
grad_mse = (2/len(t)) * (y - t)  # d(MSE)/dy
grad_half = (y - t)              # d(0.5*sum sq)/dy
print("Errors (t - y):", diff)
```

```
print("Squared errors:", squared)
print("MSE:", mse)
print("SSE:", sse, " | 0.5*SSE:", half_sum)
print("Grad MSE:", grad_mse)
print("Grad Half-Sum-Squares:", grad_half)
```

Output:

```
Errors (t - y): [ 0.1 -0.1]
Squared errors: [0.01 0.01]
MSE: 0.010000000000000005
SSE: 0.020000000000000001 | 0.5*SSE: 0.010000000000000005
Grad MSE: [-0.1  0.1]
Grad Half-Sum-Squares: [-0.1  0.1]
```

Chapter 5: Clustering Algorithms and Reinforcement Learning

Clustering Problems

Q23. K-Means Clustering

Dataset:

Objects	X-Coordinate	Y-Coordinate
1	2	4
2	4	6
3	6	8
4	10	4
5	12	4

Initial centroids: Object 2 (4,6) and Object 5 (12,4)

Task: Perform K-means clustering

K-Means Clustering

Definition

K-Means Clustering is an unsupervised machine learning logarithm used to group data into k clusters.

It works by:

Initializing k centroids (can be random or predefined).

Assigning each data point to the nearest centroid (based on distance).

Updating each centroid as the mean of all points in its cluster.

Repeating steps 2–3 until the assignments do not change (convergence).

Dataset

Object	X	Y
1	2	4
2	4	6
3	6	8
4	10	4
5	12	4

Points: (0,3) and (5,8)

Task: Find Manhattan and Chebyshev distance

Initial Centroids:

Cluster 1 (C1): Object 2 → (4,6)

Cluster 2 (C2): Object 5 → (12,4)

Python Code

```
import numpy as np
from sklearn.cluster import KMeans
# Dataset
data = np.array([
    [2, 4],   # Object 1
```

```
    [4, 6],  # Object 2
    [6, 8],  # Object 3
    [10, 4], # Object 4
    [12, 4]  # Object 5
])
# Initial centroids (Object 2 and Object 5)
initial_centroids = np.array([
    [4, 6],  # Object 2
    [12, 4]  # Object 5
])
# CreateKMeans model with k=2, init manually, and n_init=1 to avoid multiple runs
kmeans = KMeans(n_clusters=2, init=initial_centroids, n_init=1)
# Fit the model
kmeans.fit(data)
# Get cluster labels for each object
labels = kmeans.labels_
# Get final centroids
centroids = kmeans.cluster_centers_
# Output results
print("Cluster assignments for each object:", labels)
print("Final centroids:")
print(centroids)
```

Sample Output:

Cluster assignments for each object: [0 0 0 1 1]

Final centroids:

```
[[4.   6. ]
[11.  4. ]]
```

Interpretation:

Objects 1, 2, 3 → Cluster 0 (near centroid around (4,6))

Objects 4, 5 → Cluster 1 (near centroid around (12,4))

Q24. Distance Measures

Manhattan Distance

Definition: Also called L1 distance or Taxicab distance.

$$\text{Manhattan Distance} = \sum_{i=1}^{n} |x_i - y_i|$$

Manual Calculation:

Points: A = (0, 3) and B = (5, 8)

$=|0-5|+|3-8|=5+5=10$

Chebyshev Distance

Definition: Also called L∞ distance. It's the maximum absolute difference across any coordinate dimension.

$$\text{Chebyshev Distance} = \max_{i=1}^{n} |x_i - y_i|$$

Manual Calculation: $=\max(|0-5|,|3-8|)=\max(5,5)=5$

Python Code

```
from scipy.spatial import distance
# Define points
point1 = (0, 3)
point2 = (5, 8)
# Manhattan distance (cityblock)
manhattan_dist = distance.cityblock(point1, point2)
# Chebyshev distance
chebyshev_dist = distance.chebyshev(point1, point2)
# Output results
print("Manhattan Distance:", manhattan_dist)
```

```
print("Chebyshev Distance:", chebyshev_dist)
```

Output:

Manhattan Distance: 10

Chebyshev Distance: 5

Q25. Hierarchical Clustering

	A	B	C	D
A	0	2	6	10
B	2	0	5	9
C	6	5	0	4
D	10	9	4	0

Task: Perform agglomerative hierarchical clustering using single linkage method

Hierarchical Clustering

Definition

Hierarchical Clustering is an unsupervised learning method that builds a tree-like (dendrogram) structure of clusters by:

Initially treating each object as a separate cluster.

Repeatedly merging the closest pair of clusters until all are merged into one.

Single Linkage Method (Minimum Distance)

The distance between two clusters is defined as the minimum distance between any two points from the two clusters.

Given Distance Matrix:

	A	B	C	D
A	0	2	6	10
B	2	0	5	9
C	6	5	0	4
D	10	9	4	0

Python Code

```
import numpy as np
from scipy.cluster.hierarchy import linkage, dendrogram
from scipy.spatial.distance import squareform
import matplotlib.pyplot as plt
# Distance matrix (upper triangle only, since it's symmetric)
# Order: A, B, C, D
```

$$\text{distance\_matrix} = \begin{bmatrix} 0 & 2 & 6 & 10 \\ 2 & 0 & 5 & 9 \\ 6 & 5 & 0 & 4 \\ 10 & 9 & 4 & 0 \end{bmatrix}$$

```
# Convert to condensed form (required by linkage function)
condensed_dist = squareform(distance_matrix)
# Perform hierarchical clustering using single linkage
linked = linkage(condensed_dist, method='single')
# Print linkage matrix
print("Linkage matrix:\n", linked)
# Plot dendrogram
plt.figure(figsize=(8, 4))
dendrogram(linked, labels=['A', 'B', 'C', 'D'])
plt.title("Hierarchical Clustering (Single Linkage)")
plt.xlabel("Objects")
```

```
plt.ylabel("Distance")
plt.grid(True)
plt.tight_layout()
plt.show()
```

Output: Linkage Matrix (Example)

Linkage matrix:

[[0. 1.2. 2.]

[2. 3.4. 2.]

[4. 5.5. 4.]]

Each row: [cluster1, cluster2, distance, new_cluster_size]

Dendrogram

The dendrogram visually shows:

A merges with B at distance 2

C merges with D at distance 4

Then the clusters merge to form the full tree

Q26. DBSCAN Parameters

Dataset: (1,1), (1.5,2), (3,4), (5,7), (3.5,5), (4.5,5), (3.5,4.5)

Parameters: eps=2, minPts=3

Task: Determine clusters using DBSCAN

Reinforcement Learning Problems

Definition

DBSCAN (Density-Based Spatial Clustering of Applications with Noise) is a clustering algorithm that groups together points that are closely packed, marking as outliers those that lie alone in low-density regions.

Key Parameters:

eps (epsilon): Max distance between two points to be considered neighbours

minPts: Minimum number of neighbours (including the point itself) required to form a dense region (core point)

Dataset:

Points:

P1 = (1, 1)

P2 = (1.5, 2)

P3 = (3, 4)

P4 = (5, 7)

P5 = (3.5, 5)

P6 = (4.5, 5)

P7 = (3.5, 4.5)

Parameters:

eps = 2

minPts = 3

Python Code

```
import numpy as np
from sklearn.cluster import DBSCAN
import matplotlib.pyplot as plt
# Dataset as numpy array
X = np.array([
    [1, 1],
    [1.5, 2],
    [3, 4],
    [5, 7],
    [3.5, 5],
    [4.5, 5],
    [3.5, 4.5]
])
# Apply DBSCAN
db = DBSCAN(eps=2, min_samples=3)
labels = db.fit_predict(X)
# Output labels
```

```
print("Cluster labels:", labels)
# Visualize
plt.figure(figsize=(6, 5))
for label in set(labels):
cluster = X[labels == label]
plt.scatter(cluster[:, 0], cluster[:, 1], label=f'Cluster {label}' if label != -1 else 'Noise')
plt.title("DBSCAN Clustering")
plt.xlabel("X")
plt.ylabel("Y")
plt.legend()
plt.grid(True)
plt.show()
```

Sample Output:

Cluster labels: [0 0 1 -1 1 1 1]

Interpretation:

Points 0 and 1 → Cluster 0

Points 2, 4, 5, 6 → Cluster 1

Point 3 (5,7) → Noise (-1)

Reinforcement Learning (Brief Overview)

Definition:

Reinforcement Learning (RL) is a type of machine learning where an agent learns to make decisions by performing actions in an environment to maximize cumulative reward.

Key Concepts:

Term	Description
Agent	Learner/decision-maker (e.g., robot, program)
Environment	Where the agent operates
State (s)	Current situation
Action (a)	Decision made by the agent
Reward (r)	Feedback from the environment
Policy (π)	Strategy that maps states to actions
Q-Value	Expected return of an action from a state

Goal of RL:
Maximize the cumulative (expected) reward over time, often using techniques like:

Q-Learning

Deep Q-Networks (DQN)

SARSA

Policy Gradients

Q27. Q-Learning Update

Parameters:
Current state: S_1, Action taken: A_1, Reward: $R = 10$, Next state: S_2

Learning rate: $\alpha = 0.1$, Discount factor: $\gamma = 0.9$

Q-Table

State \ Action	A_1	A_2
S_1	5	3
S_2	8	6

Task: Calculate updated Q-value for $Q(S_1, A_1)$

Definition

Q-Learning is a model-free Reinforcement Learning algorithm. It learns the Q-values (action-value function) which estimate the expected future reward of taking an action A in a state S, and then following the optimal policy.

Q-Learning Update Formula:

$Q(s,a) \leftarrow Q(s,a) + \alpha[R + \gamma \cdot \max_{a'} Q(s',a') - Q(s,a)]$

Where:

Q(s,a): Current Q-value

α : alphaα: Learning rate

γ :gammaγ: Discount factor

R: Immediate reward

Max a'Q(s',a'): Max Q-value for the next state over all actions

Given:

Current state: S_1

Action taken: A_1

Reward (R): 10

Next state: S_2

Learning rate (α): 0.1

Discount factor (γ): 0.9

Q-Table

State	A_1	A_2
S_1	5	3
S_2	8	6

Manual Calculation

We update:

$Q(S1, A1) = Q(S1,A1) + \alpha[R + \gamma \cdot \max Q(S2,*) - Q(S1,A1)]$

Plug in values:

$Q(S1, A1) = 5 + 0.1[10 + 0.9 \cdot \max(8,6) - 5]$

$= 5 + 0.1[10 + 7.2 - 5] = 5 + 0.1 \cdot 12.2 = 5 + 1.22 = 6.22$

Python Code

```
import numpy as np

# Q-table: rows = states, columns = actions

# S1 = 0, S2 = 1 ; A1 = 0, A2 = 1

Q = np.array([

    [5, 3],  # S1

    [8, 6]   # S2

])


# Parameters

alpha = 0.1

gamma = 0.9

reward = 10

# State and action indices

current_state = 0  # S1
```

```
action_taken = 0  # A1

next_state = 1    # S2

# Q-Learning update

max_next_q = np.max(Q[next_state]) # max Q(S2, *)

current_q = Q[current_state, action_taken]

# Q-learning formula

updated_q = current_q + alpha * (reward + gamma * max_next_q - current_q)

# Print result

print("Updated Q(S1, A1):", round(updated_q, 2))
```

Output:

Updated Q(S1, A1): 6.22

Q28. Multi-Armed Bandit

Reward history:

Arm 1: [1, 0, 1, 1, 0] (5 pulls)

Arm 2: [0, 1, 1, 0] (4 pulls)

Arm 3: [1, 1, 0] (3 pulls)

Strategy: ε-greedy with $\varepsilon = 0.1$

Task: Which arm should be selected next?

Multi-Armed Bandit (MAB)

Definition

The Multi-Armed Bandit problem models the challenge of choosing from multiple options (arms), each with an unknown reward distribution, to maximize cumulative reward over time.

Each arm, when pulled, gives a reward sampled from an unknown distribution.

The goal is to balance exploration (trying less-tested arms) and exploitation (choosing the arm with the best-known reward so far).

ε-Greedy Strategy

With probability ε, explore: randomly select an arm.

With probability 1 - ε, exploit: select the arm with the highest average reward observed so far.

Given:

Reward histories:

Arm	Rewards	Pulls
Arm 1	[1, 0, 1, 1, 0]	5
Arm 2	[0, 1, 1, 0]	4
Arm 3	[1, 1, 0]	3

Exploration parameter: ε = 0.1

Manual Calculation

Calculate average reward for each arm:

Arm 1: (1+0+1+1+0)/5 = 3/5 = 0.6

Arm 2: (0+1+1+0)/4 = 2/4 = 0.5

Arm 3: (1+1+0)/3 = 2/3 ≈ 0.6667

Exploit (with probability 0.9): Choose arm with highest average reward → Arm 3

Explore (with probability 0.1): Choose any arm randomly

Python Code

```
import numpy as np
# Rewards history for each arm
rewards = {
```

```
    1: [1, 0, 1, 1, 0],
    2: [0, 1, 1, 0],
    3: [1, 1, 0]
}
epsilon = 0.1
# Calculate average rewards
avg_rewards = {arm: np.mean(r) for arm, r in rewards.items()}
print("Average rewards:", avg_rewards)
# Decide next arm using epsilon-greedy
ifnp.random.rand() < epsilon:
    # Exploration: choose randomly
next_arm = np.random.choice(list(rewards.keys()))
print(f"Exploration: Selected Arm {next_arm}")
else:
    # Exploitation: choose arm with highest average reward
next_arm = max(avg_rewards, key=avg_rewards.get)
print(f"Exploitation: Selected Arm {next_arm}")
```

Notes:

Running this code multiple times will sometimes explore (random arm), mostly exploit (Arm 3).

To deterministically pick the best arm (ignore randomness), just pick the one with highest average reward → Arm 3

Advanced Problems (Multiple Chapters)

Decision Tree Problems

Q29. Information Gain Calculation

- **Dataset:** Total: 8 positive, 6 negative examples
- **After splitting on attribute A:**
    - A = True: 6 positive, 2 negative
    - A = False: 2 positive, 4 negative

- **Task:** Calculate information gain

Definitions

- **Entropy (H):** Measure of impurity/uncertainty in data.

$$H(S) = \sum_{i=1}^{c} p_i \log_2 p_i$$

Where p_i = proportion of class i.

- **Information Gain (IG):** Reduction in entropy after splitting on an attribute.

$$IG(S,A) = H(S) - \sum_{v \in values(A)} \frac{|Sv|}{|S|} * H(Sv)$$

  - $H(S)$ = entropy before split
  - $H(S_v)$ = entropy of subset v
  - $|S_v|/|S|$= weight of subset

◆ Dataset

- **Total:** 8 positive, 6 negative → **14 examples**
- **After splitting on** A:
  - A=True: 6 positive, 2 negative (8 examples)
  - A=False: 2 positive, 4 negative (6 examples)

Manual Calculation

Step 1: Entropy before split (total dataset)

Total = 14 → (8 positive, 6 negative)

$H(S)=-(8/14 \log_2(8/14)+6/14\log_2(6/14))$

$H(S)\approx-(0.571\cdot-0.807+0.429\cdot-1.222)\approx0.985$

Step 2: Entropy after split

A = True (6 pos, 2 neg)

p+=6/8=0.75, p−=0.25

$H(Strue)=-(0.75\log_2 0.75+0.25\log_2 0.25)$

H(Strue)=−(0.75·−0.415+0.25·−2)≈0.811

A = False (2 pos, 4 neg)

p+=2/6≈0.333, p−=0.667

$H(Sfalse)=-(0.333\log_2 0.333+0.667\log_2 0.667)$

0.333+0.667log20.667) H(Sfalse)=−(0.333·−1.585+0.667·−0.585)≈0.918

3) Weighted entropy after split

$$H_{after}=814\cdot 0.811+614\cdot 0.918$$

$$H_{after}=0.463+0.393\approx 0.856$$

4) Information Gain

$$IG(S,A)=H(S)-H_{afte}r=0.985-0.856=0.129$$

Final Manual Answer

- **Entropy before split (parent):** 0.985
- **Weighted entropy after split:** 0.856
- **Information Gain (IG):0.129**

```
import math
# Helper: entropy calculation
def entropy(pos, neg):
total = pos + neg
if total == 0:  # avoid division by zero
return 0
p_pos, p_neg = pos/total, neg/total
ent = 0
for p in [p_pos, p_neg]:
if p > 0:  # avoid log(0)
```

```
ent -= p * math.log2(p)
returnent
# Dataset
total_pos, total_neg = 8, 6
# Entropy before split
H_parent = entropy(total_pos, total_neg)
# A=True subset
H_true = entropy(6, 2)
# A=False subset
H_false = entropy(2, 4)
# Weighted entropy after split
total = total_pos + total_neg
H_after = (8/total) * H_true + (6/total) * H_false
# Information gain
IG = H_parent - H_after
print("Parent Entropy:", H_parent)
print("Entropy(A=True):", H_true)
print("Entropy(A=False):", H_false)
print("Weighted entropy after split:", H_after)
print("Information Gain:", IG)
```

Output:

```
Parent Entropy: 0.985
Entropy(A=True): 0.81
Entropy (A=False): 0.918
Weighted entropy after split: 0.857
Information Gain: 0.128
```

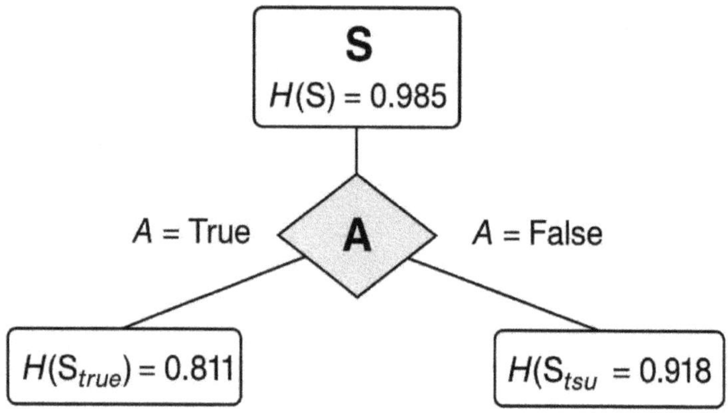

$$IG(S,A) = H(S) - [(8/14 + H(S_{true} + (6/14 + H(S_{ruue})]$$

$$IG(S,A) = 0.129$$

Q30. Gini Impurity

- **Class distribution:**
    - Class 1: 40 samples
    - Class 2: 30 samples
    - Class 3: 30 samples
- **Task:** Calculate Gini impurity for the node

Definition of Gini Impurity

- **Gini impurity** measures the probability of incorrectly classifying a randomly chosen element if it is labelled according to the distribution of labels in the dataset.
- Formula: $Gini = 1 - \sum_{i=1}^{k} p_i^2$

Where p_i is the proportion of samples in class i.

Manual Calculation

- Total samples = 40+30+30=100

Class proportions:

- p1=40/100=0.4
- p2=30/100=0.3
- p3=30/100=0.3

Now calculate:

$$Gini=1-(0.42+0.32+0.32)$$

$$=1-(0.16+0.09+0.09)$$

$$=1-0.34=0.66$$

Gini Impurity = **0.66**

Python Code

```
import numpy as np
from sklearn.metrics import confusion_matrix
# Class distribution
y = np.array([1]*40 + [2]*30 + [3]*30)
# Function to calculate Gini using built-in
defgini_impurity(y):
classes, counts = np.unique(y, return_counts=True)
probs = counts / counts.sum()
return 1 - np.sum(probs**2)
print("Gini Impurity:", gini_impurity(y))
```

Output:

Gini Impurity: 0.66

Evaluation Metrics

Q31. Confusion Matrix Calculations

- **Confusion Matrix**

Actual \ Predicted	P (Positive)	N (Negative)
P (Positive)	85	15
N (Negative)	10	90

- **Task:** Calculate Accuracy, Precision, Recall, F1-Score, and Specificity

Definition: Confusion Matrix

A **confusion matrix** is a summary of prediction results for a classification problem. It shows the number of correct and incorrect predictions made by the model compared with the actual values.

	Predicted Positive	Predicted Negative
Actual Positive	True Positive (TP) = 85	False Negative (FN) = 15
Actual Negative	False Positive (FP) = 10	True Negative (TN) = 90

Manual Calculations

Accuracy

Accuracy$=\frac{TP+TN}{TP+TN+FP+FN}=\frac{85+90}{85+90+10+15}$=175/200=0.875

Precision

Precision$=\frac{TP}{TP+FP}=\frac{85}{85+10}$=85/95≈0.8947

Recall (Sensitivity)

Recall$=\frac{TP}{TP+FN}=\frac{85}{85+15}$=85/100=0.85

F1-Score

$$F1Score=\frac{2\times Precision\times Recall}{Precision+Recall}=\frac{2\times 0.8947\times 0.85}{0.8947+0.85}\approx 0.8718$$

Specificity

$$Specificity=\frac{TN}{TN+FP}=\frac{90}{90+10}=90/100=0.90$$

Python Code

```
# Confusion Matrix values
TP = 85
FN = 15
FP = 10
TN = 90
# Metrics Calculation
accuracy = (TP + TN) / (TP + TN + FP + FN)
precision = TP / (TP + FP)
recall = TP / (TP + FN)
f1_score = 2 * (precision * recall) / (precision + recall)
specificity = TN / (TN + FP)
print("Accuracy:", round(accuracy, 4))
print("Precision:", round(precision, 4))
print("Recall:", round(recall, 4))
print("F1-Score:", round(f1_score, 4))
print("Specificity:", round(specificity, 4))
```

Output:

```
Accuracy: 0.875
Precision: 0.8947
Recall: 0.85
F1-Score: 0.8718
Specificity: 0.9
```

Q32. Cross-Validation

- **Dataset:** 1000 samples, k=5
- **Task:** Determine training set and test set sizes for each fold

Definition: Cross-Validation

Cross-validation is a resampling procedure used to evaluate machine learning models. It splits the dataset into k equal-sized subsets (folds). Each fold is used once as a test set, while the remaining k−1 folds are used as the training set. This process is repeated k times.

Purpose: To ensure the model performs well on unseen data and to reduce overfitting.

Manual Calculation (k = 5 folds, 1000 samples)

- Total samples = 1000
- Number of folds (k) = 5
- Samples per fold = 1000 ÷ 5 = 200

For each fold:

- Training set size = 1000 − 200 = 800 samples
- Test set size = 200 samples

Summary:

Fold	Training Samples	Test Samples
1	800	200 (Fold 1)
2	800	200 (Fold 2)
3	800	200 (Fold 3)
4	800	200 (Fold 4)
5	800	200 (Fold 5)

Python Code:

```
from sklearn.model_selection import KFold
import numpy as np
# Dataset with 1000 samples
X = np.arange(1000)
# Create 5-fold cross-validation
kf = KFold(n_splits=5, shuffle=False)
# Print train-test split sizes
for fold, (train_index, test_index) inenumerate(kf.split(X), 1):
print(f"Fold{fold}:")
print(f"  Training set size: {len(train_index)}")
print(f"  Test set size: {len(test_index)}\n")
```

Output:

Fold 1:

Training set size: 800

Test set size: 200

Fold 2:

Training set size: 800

Test set size: 200

Fold 3:

Training set size: 800

Test set size: 200

Fold 4:

Training set size: 800

Test set size: 200

Fold 5:

Training set size: 800

Test set size: 200

Q33. Learning Curve Analysis

- **Training accuracies:** [0.65, 0.78, 0.85, 0.89, 0.91]
- **Validation accuracies:** [0.62, 0.75, 0.80, 0.78, 0.76]
- **Task:** Identify if model is overfitting and at which epoch

Definition: Learning Curve Analysis

Learning curves are plots that show the performance of a machine learning model on the training set and a validation set over training epochs or as the training data size increases.

- Training accuracy measures how well the model performs on the training data.
- Validation accuracy measures how well the model generalizes to unseen data.

By comparing both curves, we can detect:

- **Underfitting:** Both accuracies are low and close to each other.
- **Good Fit:** Both accuracies are high and close.
- **Overfitting:** Training accuracy is high, but validation accuracy drops or stagnates.

Given Data

Epoch	Training Accuracy	Validation Accuracy
1	0.65	0.62
2	0.78	0.75
3	0.85	0.80
4	0.89	0.78
5	0.91	0.76

Manual Analysis: Overfitting Detection

Look at the gap between training and validation accuracy:

- At **epoch 3**, both training and validation accuracy are still increasing and fairly close.
- At **epoch 4**, the **training accuracy increases to 0.89**, but **validation drops to 0.78**.
- At **epoch 5**, the gap widens even more (**0.91 vs 0.76**).

Conclusion: Overfitting begins after epoch 3, since validation accuracy plateaus or drops while training accuracy keeps increasing.

Python Code for Learning Curve Plot

```
Import matplotlib.pyplot as plt
# Data
epochs = [1, 2, 3, 4, 5]
train_acc = [0.65, 0.78, 0.85, 0.89, 0.91]
val_acc = [0.62, 0.75, 0.80, 0.78, 0.76]
# Plot
plt.figure(figsize=(8, 5))
plt.plot(epochs, train_acc, label='Training Accuracy', marker='o')
plt.plot(epochs, val_acc, label='Validation Accuracy', marker='s')
plt.xlabel('Epoch')
plt.ylabel('Accuracy')
plt.title('Learning Curve')
plt.axvline(x=3, color='red', linestyle='--', label='Overfitting Starts')
plt.legend()
plt.grid(True)
plt.tight_layout()
plt.show()
```

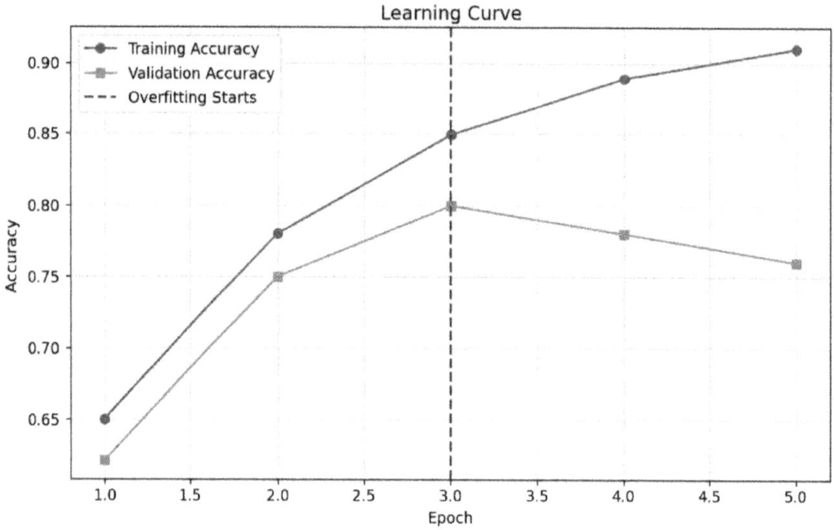
Learning Curve
Training Accuracy
Validation Accuracy
Overfitting Starts
Accuracy
Epoch
0.90
0.85
0.80
0.75
0.70
0.65
1.0
1.5
2.0
2.5
3.0
3.5
4.0
4.5
5.0

Index

D

E

F

G

H

I

J

K

L

M

N

O

P

Q

R

S

Glossary

A

Accuracy: The proportion of correct predictions out of total predictions made by a model. Formula: (TP + TN) / (TP + TN + FP + FN).

Activation Functions: Mathematical transformations applied to a neuron's input that introduce nonlinearity in neural networks, enabling the network to learn complex relationships and patterns in data.

Action (A): The choices available to an agent in each state of the environment. Actions can be discrete (finite set of choices) or continuous (real-valued parameters).

Action Space: The set of all possible actions that an agent can take in a given environment.

Action Value Function (Q-function): A function Q^π(s,a) that represents the expected cumulative reward when starting in states, taking action a, and subsequently following policy π.

AdaBoost: Adaptive Boosting algorithm that sequentially trains weak learners, focusing on previously misclassified examples to improve overall performance.

Adaptability: Design principle for learning systems that enables them to evolve with changing data patterns and incorporate new knowledge efficiently.

Agent: The learner and decision maker in reinforcement learning that interacts with the environment, maintains internal state representation, and implements decision-making policies.

Agglomerative Hierarchical Clustering: A bottom-up clustering approach that starts with each data point as an individual cluster and progressively merges the closest clusters until all points belong to a single cluster.

Algorithm Complexity: The computational cost of an algorithm in terms of time and space requirements, typically expressed using Big O notation.

Algorithm Selection: The process of choosing appropriate machine learning algorithms based on problem characteristics, data properties, and performance requirements.

Algorithmic Trading: The use of machine learning algorithms to make automated stock trading decisions based on real-time data analysis and pattern recognition.

AlexNet: A pioneering CNN architecture that popularized the use of convolutional neural networks for image classification tasks, achieving breakthrough performance on ImageNet.

Artificial Intelligence (AI): A broad field encompassing reasoning, planning, decision-making, and other cognitive functions, with machine learning as one of its key components.

Artificial Neural Networks (ANNs): Computational models inspired by the human brain's structure and functionality, consisting of interconnected nodes (neurons) that process information through weighted connections.

Autoencoders: Unsupervised learning neural network models used for dimensionality reduction and feature learning, consisting of an encoder that compresses input data and a decoder that reconstructs it.

Automated Machine Learning (AutoML): Systems that automate the machine learning pipeline, including feature selection, model selection, and hyperparameter tuning to reduce manual effort.

Average Linkage: A linkage criterion in hierarchical clustering that calculates the distance between clusters as the average of all pairwise distances between points in the two clusters.

Attention Mechanism: A technique that allows models to focus on specific parts of the input when making predictions, weighting the importance of different features or examples.

Augmentation: The process of creating modified versions of data (through transformations like rotation, scaling, or masking) to increase dataset diversity and improve model robustness.

B

Backpropagation Algorithm: A supervised learning algorithm used to train neural networks by calculating gradients of the loss function with respect to network weights and propagating errors backward through the network.

Bagging: Bootstrap Aggregating ensemble method that reduces variance by training multiple models on different subsets of data and combining their predictions.

Bandwidth parameter (τ): A critical parameter in LWR that controls the "locality" of the regression; smaller values create very local models while larger values result in smoother fits.

BANG (Balanced Iterative Reduction and Clustering): A grid-based clustering algorithm that uses hierarchical grid structure with balanced partitioning for efficient range queries and multi-level clustering.

Batch Normalization: A technique that normalizes the inputs of each layer in a neural network to have zero mean and unit variance, stabilizing and accelerating the training process.

Batch Processing: A big data processing approach that handles large volumes of data in chunks at scheduled intervals, suitable for historical analysis.

Bayes' Theorem: A fundamental principle in probability theory that describes how to update the probability of a hypothesis based on new evidence, forming the foundation of Bayesian learning methods.

Bayesian Learning: A probabilistic approach to machine learning that uses Bayes' theorem to update beliefs about model parameters as new data becomes available, providing principled uncertainty quantification.

Bayesian Optimization: Model-based sequential optimization approach for hyperparameter tuning that builds a probabilistic model of the objective function.

Bayesian regression: A regression approach that incorporates prior distributions on parameters to make predictions.

Bellman Equations: Fundamental recursive equations in reinforcement learning that express the relationship between the value of a state and the values of its successor states. Forms the basis for many RL algorithms.

Bellman Expectation Equation: Equations that express the expected value of states or state-action pairs under a given policy π.

Bellman Optimality Equations: Equations that define the optimal value functions by expressing the value of a state as the maximum expected return achievable from that state.

Bias Term: An additional parameter in neural networks that allows the activation function to shift, providing more flexibility in fitting the data by adjusting the decision boundary.

Bias-Variance Trade-off: A fundamental concept in machine learning that balances model complexity; high-bias models underfit while high-variance models overfit data.

Binary Classification: A type of classification task where the goal is to classify elements into one of two groups or classes (e.g., spam/not spam, positive/negative).

Big Data: Large volumes of structured and unstructured data that require advanced computational methods for analysis and insights.

Big Data Analysis: The process of examining large, complex datasets to uncover hidden patterns, correlations, and actionable insights.

Biplot: A visualization technique that combines score and loading plots to show relationships between samples and variables in PCA analysis.

Boltzmann Exploration: An exploration strategy that selects actions probabilistically based on their Q-values, with higher-valued actions having higher selection probabilities.

Boosting: Sequential ensemble method that reduces bias by combining weak learners, where each subsequent model focuses on correcting errors of previous models.

Border Point: In DBSCAN, a point that is within the ε-neighbourhood of a core point but does not itself have enough neighbours to be considered a core point.

Boundary effects: Performance degradation that occurs near the edges of the feature space in locally weighted methods.

Batch Learning: A learning approach where the model is trained on the entire dataset at once, processing all available training data simultaneously before deployment.

BERT (Bidirectional Encoder Representations from Transformers): A self-supervised language model that learns by predicting masked words in sentences using surrounding context from both directions.

C

Canonical Polyadic Decomposition (CPD): A tensor decomposition method designed to reduce the dimensionality of tensor data while preserving its inherent multi-dimensional structure.

Capacity and Complexity: Measures of a model's ability to fit diverse functions and complex patterns, controlled through regularization and architecture constraints.

Catastrophic Forgetting: The tendency of neural networks to completely forget previously learned tasks when learning new ones, a significant challenge in continual learning scenarios.

Centroid: The geometric center (mean vector) of all data points belonging to a specific class in the feature space.

CLIQUE (Clustering in Quest): A density-based clustering algorithm that operates in subspaces, identifying dense regions in high-dimensional data using a grid-based approach for efficiency.

Coefficient of Determination (R^2): A statistical measure that represents the proportion of variance in the dependent variable that is predictable from the independent variables.

Complete Linkage: A linkage criterion that defines the distance between two clusters as the maximum distance between any two points in the clusters, resulting in compact, spherical clusters.

Computational Learning Theory: The field that Analyses algorithmic efficiency and learnability, studying sample complexity and computational complexity of learning algorithms.

Computational complexity: The amount of computational resources (time and memory) required to execute an algorithm.

Confusion Matrix: A table used to evaluate the performance of a classification model, showing the counts of true positives, true negatives, false positives, and false negatives.

Cosine Distance: A proximity measure that calculates the angle between two vectors, particularly useful for high-dimensional data and text analysis.

Covariance Matrix: A square matrix that captures the covariance between pairs of variables, fundamental to PCA calculations.

Cumulative Explained Variance: The running sum of explained variance across principal components, used to determine the cutoff for dimensionality reduction.

Curse of Dimensionality: The phenomenon where the difficulty of analysis increases exponentially with the number of dimensions, making dimensionality reduction necessary.

Catastrophic Forgetting: A phenomenon in online learning where a model loses previously learned knowledge when learning from new data, particularly problematic in continual learning scenarios.

Collaborative Filtering: A recommendation technique that makes predictions based on the collective preferences and Behaviours of multiple users.

Concept Drift: The phenomenon where the statistical properties of the target variable change over time, requiring models to adapt to new patterns.

Consistency Regularization: A semi-supervised learning technique that encourages models to produce similar predictions for different augmented versions of the same input.

Contrastive Learning: A self-supervised learning approach that learns representations by maximizing agreement between differently augmented views of the same data while minimizing agreement between different data points.

Cross-Validation: A model evaluation technique that divides data into multiple subsets to assess how well a model generalizes to independent datasets.

D

DBSCAN: Density-Based Spatial Clustering of Applications with Noise - an algorithm that identifies clusters as regions of high data density separated by regions of low density.

Deep Q-Networks (DQN): An extension of Q-learning that uses deep neural networks to approximate the Q-function, enabling the algorithm to handle high-dimensional state spaces.

Deep Reinforcement Learning (DRL): The integration of reinforcement learning with deep neural networks, enabling agents to handle high-dimensional and complex tasks.

Deep Learning (Missing Data): Advanced neural network approaches for handling missing data that can capture complex non-linear relationships but require large datasets.

Dendrogram: A tree-like diagram that shows the hierarchical relationships between clusters, displaying how clusters are merged or split at different levels of granularity.

Density-Based Methods: Clustering approaches that identify clusters based on the density of data points in different regions of the feature space.

Dimensionality Reduction: An unsupervised learning technique that reduces the number of features in a dataset while preserving important information.

Discount Factor (γ): A parameter ($0 \leq \gamma \leq 1$) that determines how future rewards are weighted relative to immediate rewards in value function calculations.

Distance Metrics: Mathematical functions used to quantify the similarity or dissimilarity between data points (e.g., Euclidean, Manhattan, Minkowski).

Dropout: A regularization technique that randomly deactivates a fraction of neurons during training to prevent overfitting and improve generalization.

Dynamic Programming: A class of algorithms that solve MDPs by using the structure of the problem to compute optimal policies and value functions efficiently.

Data Augmentation: Techniques used to artificially expand training datasets by creating modified versions of existing data points.

Deep Learning: A subset of machine learning based on artificial neural networks with multiple layers that can learn hierarchical representations of data.

Downstream Task: A specific application or task that uses representations learned from a pre-trained model, such as classification or question answering after language model pre-training.

DBSCAN (Density-Based Spatial Clustering of Applications with Noise): A clustering algorithm that groups together points in high-density regions and marks isolated points in low-density areas as outliers.

Decision Tree: A supervised learning algorithm that makes predictions by learning decision rules from features, represented as a tree structure with internal nodes (tests) and leaf nodes (predictions).

Dendrogram: A tree-like diagram used in hierarchical clustering to show the arrangement of clusters and the distances at which they merge.

Discount Factor (γ): In reinforcement learning, a parameter ($0 \leq \gamma \leq 1$) that determines the importance of future rewards relative to immediate rewards.

E

Early Exaggeration: A t-SNE parameter that encourages cluster formation during the optimization process.

Early Stopping: A regularization technique that halts training when the validation error begins to increase, preventing overfitting by avoiding excessive training.

Elastic Net: A regularization technique that combines both L1 (Lasso) and L2 (Ridge) penalties to balance feature selection and coefficient shrinkage.

Elbow Method: A technique for determining the optimal number of clusters by plotting the within-cluster sum of squares against the number of clusters and identifying the "elbow" point where improvement diminishes.

EM Algorithm: Expectation-Maximization algorithm used for missing data imputation with statistical foundation and efficiency for parametric assumptions.

Environment: The external system with which the reinforcement learning agent interacts, characterized by properties such as observability, determinism, and episodic nature.

Episodic Tasks: Reinforcement learning problems that have clear starting and ending points, with each episode being independent.

Epanechnikov kernel: A kernel function that uses a quadratic function to assign weights within a specified range, setting weights to zero beyond that range.

Euclidean Distance: The straight-line distance between two points in Euclidean space, calculated as the square root of the sum of squared differences between corresponding coordinates.

Exponential weighting: A weighting scheme that assigns weights to neighbours based on an exponential decay function.

Expected SARSA: A variation of SARSA that uses the expected value over all possible next actions instead of the actual next action taken.

Explained Variance Ratio: The proportion of total variance explained by each principal component, used to assess feature importance.

Exploration vs. Exploitation: The fundamental trade-off in reinforcement learning between trying new actions to discover better strategies (exploration) and using known information to maximize rewards (exploitation).

Exploratory Data Analysis (EDA): The process of analysing data to identify distributions, correlations, and patterns using visualization and statistical techniques.

Explainable AI (XAI): Techniques and methods designed to make machine learning models more interpretable and their decisions more understandable to humans.

Episodic Training: A training approach in few-shot learning where the model learns from multiple episodes, each containing different combinations of classes and examples.

Eigenvalue: A scalar that represents the amount of variance explained by a corresponding eigenvector in dimensionality reduction techniques like PCA and SVD.

Eigenvector: A direction vector that remains unchanged (except for scaling) when a linear transformation is applied. Used in PCA to identify principal components.

Entropy: A measure of impurity or uncertainty in a dataset, calculated as $H(S) = -\Sigma\ p\_i\ \log_2(p\_i)$, where p_i is the proportion of class i. Used in decision tree algorithms.

Epsilon (ε): In DBSCAN, the maximum distance between two points for them to be considered neighbours. In ε-greedy strategy, the probability of exploration.

Epsilon-Greedy Strategy: A reinforcement learning exploration strategy where the agent exploits the best-known action with probability (1-ε) and explores randomly with probability ε.

Epoch: One complete pass through the entire training dataset during the training of a machine learning model.

Euclidean Distance: The straight-line distance between two points in n-dimensional space, calculated as $\text{sqrt}(\Sigma(x\_i - y\_i)^2)$.

Exploitation: In reinforcement learning, choosing actions that are currently believed to yield the highest rewards based on past experience.

Exploration: In reinforcement learning, trying different actions to discover potentially better strategies, even if they don't currently appear optimal.

F

F1-Score: The harmonic mean of precision and recall, providing a single metric that balances both measures. Formula: 2 × (Precision × Recall) / (Precision + Recall).

Feature Engineering: The process of selecting, modifying, or creating input variables (features) for machine learning models.

Feature Importance: Measures that quantify the contribution of each feature to model predictions, helping understand which variables are most influential.

Feature Scaling: The process of normalizing or standardizing features to ensure they contribute equally to distance calculations.

Feedforward Neural Networks (FNNs): The simplest form of neural networks where information flows in one direction from input to output without cycles or loops.

Fully Connected Layer: A neural network layer where every neuron is connected to every neuron in the previous layer, typically used in the final stages for classification or regression.

Function Approximation: Using mathematical functions (like neural networks) to approximate value functions when the state or action space is too large for tabular methods.

Fuzzy C-Means: A soft clustering algorithm where each data point can belong to multiple clusters with varying degrees of membership.

Feature Extraction: The process of transforming raw data into a set of meaningful characteristics or attributes that can be used for machine learning tasks.

Few-Shot Learning: A learning paradigm where models learn to recognize new classes from only a small number of labelled examples (typically 2-10 per class).

Fine-Tuning: The process of adapting a pre-trained model to a specific task by continuing training on task-specific data, usually with a smaller learning rate.

Foundation Model: A large-scale model trained on broad data that can be adapted to a wide range of downstream tasks with minimal additional training.

F1-Score: The harmonic mean of precision and recall, providing a single metric that balances both measures: F1 = 2 × (Precision × Recall) / (Precision + Recall).

False Negative (FN): An incorrect prediction where the model predicts the negative class when the actual class is positive.

False Positive (FP): An incorrect prediction where the model predicts the positive class when the actual class is negative.

Feature Extraction: The process of identifying and selecting the most relevant features from raw data for use in machine learning models.

Feature Scaling: The process of normalizing or standardizing features to ensure they are on a similar scale, preventing features with larger ranges from dominating the learning process.

Find-S Algorithm: A concept learning algorithm that finds the most specific hypothesis consistent with all positive training examples, ignoring negative examples.

First Quartile (Q1): The 25th percentile of a dataset, representing the value below which 25% of the data falls.

Five-Point Summary: A set of five descriptive statistics consisting of minimum, first quartile (Q1), median, third quartile (Q3), and maximum values.

Fold: In cross-validation, one of k equal-sized subsets of data used for model evaluation, where each fold serves as a test set once.

G

Gap Statistic: A method for determining the optimal number of clusters by comparing the clustering quality of real data to that of randomly generated data.

Gated Recurrent Unit (GRU): A simplified version of LSTM with fewer parameters, combining forget and input gates into a single update gate while maintaining comparable performance.

Gaussian Kernel: A kernel function that assigns weights based on squared distance, scaled by a bandwidth parameter, following a normal distribution pattern.

Generalization: The ability of a machine learning model to perform well on previously unseen data, indicating good learning rather than memorization.

Generative Adversarial Networks (GANs): A framework consisting of two competing neural networks—a generator and discriminator—used for generating realistic synthetic data.

Gradient Boosting: Sequential ensemble method that builds models iteratively, with each new model correcting errors of the previous ensemble.

Gradient Clipping: A technique to prevent exploding gradients by limiting the magnitude of gradients during backpropagation to a predefined threshold.

Gradient Descent: An iterative optimization algorithm used to minimize the cost function by moving in the direction of steepest descent.

Graph Convolutional Networks (GCNs): Neural networks designed to work with graph-structured data, used in graph embedding for dimensionality reduction.

Graph Embedding: Techniques that map nodes in a high-dimensional graph to a lower-dimensional vector space while retaining structural information.

GRIDCLUS: A grid-based clustering algorithm that uses density-based grid clustering with connected components for simple and efficient processing of large spatial datasets.

Generalization: The ability of a machine learning model to perform well on new, unseen data that was not part of the training set.

Generative Model: A model that learns to generate new data samples similar to the training data, capturing the underlying data distribution.

GPT (Generative Pre-trained Transformer): A family of language models that use self-supervised learning by predicting the next word in sequences.

Gradient Descent: An optimization algorithm that iteratively adjusts model parameters by moving in the direction of steepest decrease of the loss function.

Graph Neural Network (GNN): A type of neural network designed to operate on graph-structured data, propagating and aggregating information between connected nodes.

Gamma (γ): See Discount Factor.

Gaussian Distribution: See Normal Distribution.

Gaussian Naive Bayes: A variant of Naive Bayes that assumes features follow a normal (Gaussian) distribution, using mean and variance to calculate probabilities.

Gini Impurity: A measure of node impurity in decision trees, calculated as $1 - \Sigma(p\_i)^2$, where p_i is the proportion of samples in class i. Lower values indicate purer nodes.

Gradient Descent: An iterative optimization algorithm that adjusts model parameters in the direction that most reduces the loss function.

H

Hard Clustering: A clustering approach where each data point belongs to exactly one cluster with no overlap between clusters.

Hidden Layers: Intermediate layers in neural networks between input and output layers that process and transform data through weighted connections and activation functions.

Hierarchical Clustering: A clustering method that creates a tree-like structure of clusters, showing relationships at multiple levels of granularity.

Hyperbolic Tangent (tanh): An activation function that maps input values to the range (-1, 1), often providing better performance than sigmoid due to its centered output.

Hyperparameter Tuning: The process of optimizing algorithm parameters that are not learned from data but must be set before training begins.

Hyperparameter: A configuration setting for a learning algorithm that is set before training begins and controls the learning process (e.g., learning rate, batch size).

Hierarchical Clustering: A clustering method that builds a tree-like structure (dendrogram) by either progressively merging (agglomerative) or splitting (divisive) clusters.

Hypothesis: In machine learning, a potential function or rule that maps inputs to outputs, representing the model's current understanding of the relationship between features and targets.

I

ID3 (Iterative Dichotomiser 3): A decision tree algorithm that uses information gain as the splitting criterion and is primarily used for classification problems with categorical features.

Imbalanced Data: Datasets where some classes are significantly underrepresented compared to others, potentially leading to biased models.

Incremental PCA: A variation of PCA that processes data in batches, suitable for large datasets that cannot fit in memory.

Inductive Bias: The set of assumptions that a learning algorithm uses to predict outputs for inputs it has not encountered during training.

Information Gain: A measure used in decision trees to determine the effectiveness of a split by calculating the reduction in entropy after splitting on a particular attribute.

Instance-Based Learning: A learning paradigm where predictions are made by comparing new instances to stored training examples.

ISOMAP: A dimensionality reduction technique that extends MDS using geodesic distances to preserve global structure of non-linear manifolds.

Incremental Learning: See Online Learning. A learning approach where models continuously update their knowledge as new data arrives.

Inference: The process of using a trained model to make predictions or decisions on new, unseen data.

Information Gain: The reduction in entropy achieved by splitting data on a particular attribute, used in decision trees to select the best feature for splitting.

Intercept: In linear regression, the y-axis crossing point (b in y = mx + b), representing the predicted value when all features equal zero.

Interquartile Range (IQR): A measure of statistical dispersion calculated as Q3 - Q1, representing the range containing the middle 50% of the data.

J

Jaccard Similarity: A similarity measure for binary attributes and sets, calculated as the ratio of intersection to union of two sets.

K

k-Means: A partitional clustering algorithm that divides data into k clusters by minimizing the within-cluster sum of squares, using centroids to represent cluster centers.

k-Means++: An improved initialization strategy for K-Means that selects initial centroids probabilistically to reduce the likelihood of poor clustering results.

K-Medoids (PAM): Partitioning Around Medoids - a clustering algorithm that uses actual data points as cluster centers instead of calculated centroids, making it more robust to outliers.

Kernel PCA: An extension of PCA that uses kernel functions to identify non-linear patterns by implicitly mapping to higher dimensions.

Kernel Functions: Mathematical functions used to assign weights to data points based on their distance from a query point.

KL Divergence: Kullback-Leibler divergence, a measure used in t-SNE to minimize the difference between high- and low-dimensional distributions.

K-Fold Cross-Validation: A cross-validation technique where data is divided into k equal parts, with each part used once as a test set while the remaining k-1 parts form the training set.

K-Means Clustering: An unsupervised learning algorithm that partitions data into k clusters by iteratively assigning points to the nearest centroid and updating centroids.

K-Nearest Neighbours (K-NN): A supervised learning algorithm that classifies new data points based on the majority class among the k closest training examples.

L

L1 Regularization (Lasso): A regularization technique that adds a penalty term proportional to the absolute value of coefficients, capable of performing feature selection by shrinking some coefficients to zero.

L2 Regularization (Ridge): A regularization technique that adds a penalty term proportional to the squared magnitude of coefficients, shrinking them toward zero without making them exactly zero.

Lasso Regression: Least Absolute Shrinkage and Selection Operator, a type of linear regression that uses L1 regularization to perform both regularization and feature selection.

Leaky ReLU: A variant of ReLU activation function that allows small gradients for negative inputs, addressing the "dying ReLU" problem.

Learning Rate: A hyperparameter that controls the step size of weight updates during training, determining how quickly a model learns from data.

Linear Discriminant Analysis (LDA): A supervised dimensionality reduction technique that maximizes class separability by projecting data to maximize between-class variance and minimize within-class variance.

Loading Vectors: Coefficients of original variables in principal components, indicating the contribution of each original feature to each PC.

Locally Linear Embedding (LLE): A dimensionality reduction technique that preserves local neighbourhood relationships by reconstructing each point from its neighbours.

Logistic Function (Sigmoid): A mathematical function that maps any real-valued input to a value between 0 and 1, used in logistic regression to model probabilities.

Logistic Regression: A statistical method used for binary classification that uses the logistic function to model the probability of class membership.

Learning Rate: A hyperparameter that controls the step size in gradient descent optimization, determining how much to adjust model parameters during training.

Loss Function: A mathematical function that measures the difference between a model's predictions and the actual target values, guiding the learning process.

Learning Curve: A plot showing model performance (typically accuracy or loss) on training and validation sets over time or training iterations, used to diagnose overfitting or underfitting.

Learning Rate (α): A hyperparameter that controls the step size in gradient-based optimization algorithms, determining how much to adjust weights during training.

Likelihood: The probability of observing the given data under a specific set of parameter values, used in maximum likelihood estimation and Bayes' theorem.

Linear Regression: A supervised learning algorithm that models the relationship between dependent and independent variables using a linear equation: $y = mx + b$.

Linkage: In hierarchical clustering, the method used to calculate distances between clusters, such as single linkage (minimum distance), complete linkage (maximum distance), or average linkage

Logistic Regression: A classification algorithm that uses the logistic (sigmoid) function to model the probability of a binary outcome.

Loss Function: A function that measures the difference between predicted and actual values, guiding the optimization process during training.

M

Machine Learning (ML): A subset of AI that focuses on developing algorithms that learn patterns from data and make predictions or decisions without explicit programming.

Manhattan Distance: A distance metric calculated as the sum of absolute differences between corresponding coordinates of two points; also called L1 norm or city block distance.

Markov Decision Process (MDP): A formal framework for modelling reinforcement learning problems, defined by a set of states, actions, transition probabilities, reward functions, and a discount factor.

Markov Property: The principle that the future state depends only on the current state and action, not on the sequence of events that preceded it.

Maximum Depth: A parameter in decision trees that controls the depth of the tree to prevent overfitting and improve interpretability.

Mean/Median Imputation: A missing data handling technique that fills in missing values with the mean or median of the feature, preserving distribution characteristics.

Mean Absolute Error (MAE): A regression performance metric that computes the average absolute difference between predicted and actual values.

Mean Squared Error (MSE): A widely used loss function for regression tasks that penalizes large errors by squaring the difference between predicted and actual values.

MinPts: A DBSCAN parameter that specifies the minimum number of data points required in a neighbourhood to qualify a point as a core point.

Minkowski Distance: A generalized distance metric that includes Euclidean and Manhattan distances as special cases, controlled by a parameter p.

Model-Based Learning: Reinforcement learning methods that build a model of the environment and use it for planning and decision-making.

Model Compression: Techniques used to reduce the size and complexity of trained models without sacrificing performance, enabling deployment on resource-constrained devices.

Model Deployment: The phase of the ML lifecycle where trained models are integrated into real-world applications and exposed to new data.

Monte Carlo Methods: A family of algorithms in reinforcement learning that estimate value functions by averaging returns from complete episodes of experience.

Multicollinearity: A condition where predictor variables in a regression model are highly correlated, leading to unreliable coefficient estimates.

Multidimensional Scaling (MDS): A classical linear dimensionality reduction method that aims to preserve pairwise distances between data points.

Multilayer Perceptron (MLP): A type of feedforward neural network consisting of input, hidden, and output layers, commonly used in classification and regression tasks.

Multiple Regression: A linear regression model that predicts a continuous dependent variable using two or more independent variables.

Multivariate Regression: A regression technique used when there are multiple dependent variables to be predicted simultaneously from a common set of predictors.

MAE (Masked Autoencoders): A self-supervised learning approach for images where the model learns by reconstructing masked portions of images.

MAML (Model-Agnostic Meta-Learning): An optimization-based meta-learning algorithm that learns initialization parameters enabling quick adaptation to new tasks.

Masked Language Modelling: A self-supervised learning task where random words in text are masked and the model learns to predict them from context.

Matching Networks: A neural network architecture for few-shot learning that learns to match query examples with support examples using attention mechanisms.

Memory-Augmented Networks: Neural networks equipped with external memory components that can store and retrieve information, useful for one-shot learning.

Meta-Learning: "Learning to learn" - an approach where models learn general learning strategies that enable quick adaptation to new tasks with minimal data.

Metric Learning: A learning approach that focuses on learning optimal distance or similarity functions to measure how related different data points are.

MoCo (Momentum Contrast): A contrastive learning method that uses a momentum-updated encoder to maintain a large and consistent queue of negative examples.

Multi-Task Learning: A learning paradigm where a model is trained simultaneously on multiple related tasks, allowing knowledge sharing across tasks.

Manhattan Distance: Also called L1 distance or taxicab distance, the sum of absolute differences across all dimensions: $\Sigma|x_i - y_i|$.

Maximum Likelihood Estimation (MLE): A statistical method for estimating model parameters by finding values that maximize the likelihood of observing the given data.

Mean: The average value of a dataset, calculated by summing all values and dividing by the number of observations.

Mean Squared Error (MSE): A loss function that measures the average squared difference between predicted and actual values: $MSE = (1/n)\Sigma(y_i - \hat{y}_i)^2$.

Median: The middle value in a sorted dataset, representing the 50th percentile (Q2).

Min-Max Normalization: A feature scaling technique that rescales data to a fixed range [0,1] using: $x' = (x - min) / (max - min)$.

MinPts: In DBSCAN, the minimum number of neighbours (including the point itself) required for a point to be classified as a core point.

Multi-Armed Bandit: A reinforcement learning problem where an agent must choose between multiple options (arms), each with unknown reward distributions, to maximize cumulative reward.

N

Naïve Bayes: A probabilistic classifier based on Bayes' theorem that assumes strong independence among features, often used in text classification.

Neural Networks: Computational models inspired by the human brain, composed of layers of interconnected neurons used to approximate complex functions.

Noise Point: In DBSCAN, a point that does not belong to any cluster because it lacks sufficient neighbouring points within the specified ε radius.

Non-parametric Regression: Regression methods that do not assume a specific functional form for the relationship between features and output, such as LWR and k-NN.

Normality: A statistical assumption that the residuals or errors in a regression model are normally distributed, often required for valid inference.

Neural Architecture Search (NAS): An automated process for discovering optimal neural network architectures for specific tasks.

N-way K-shot: A few-shot learning scenario where the model must classify among N classes using K examples per class.

Naive Bayes Classifier: A probabilistic classifier based on Bayes' theorem with the assumption that features are conditionally independent given the class.

Nearest-Centroid Classifier: A classification algorithm that assigns samples to the class whose centroid (mean) is closest.

Neural Network: A computational model inspired by biological neural networks, consisting of interconnected nodes (neurons) organized in layers that can learn complex patterns.

Noise: In DBSCAN, data points that don't belong to any cluster because they lie in low-density regions.

Normal Distribution: A probability distribution that is symmetric and bell-shaped, characterized by its mean (μ) and variance (σ^2).

Normalization: See Feature Scaling.

O

Objective Function: A function that a learning algorithm aims to minimize or maximize, often representing a loss or reward depending on the problem type.

Off-Policy Learning: A reinforcement learning setting where the policy used to generate Behaviour is different from the policy being learned.

On-Policy Learning: A reinforcement learning setting where the agent learns the value of the policy it is currently following.

Optimization Theory: The mathematical study of methods to find the best solution among a set of possible options, foundational for training ML models.

OPTICS: Ordering Points to Identify the Clustering Structure - a density-based clustering algorithm that addresses the limitations of DBSCAN by identifying clusters of varying densities.

Output Layer: The final layer of a neural network that produces predictions or outputs, typically having one neuron per class in classification tasks.

Overfitting: A modelling error that occurs when a model learns noise or random fluctuations in the training data, resulting in poor generalization to new data.

P

PCA (Principal Component Analysis): A linear dimensionality reduction technique that transforms data into new variables (principal components) that capture maximum variance.

Pearson Correlation: A measure of linear correlation between two variables, ranging from -1 to 1, where 0 implies no linear correlation.

Perceptron: A simple neural network model that learns a linear decision boundary by adjusting weights through an iterative process.

Policy (π): A function or mapping that defines the agent's Behaviour by specifying the probability distribution over actions for each state.

Policy Gradient Methods: A class of reinforcement learning algorithms that directly adjust the policy's parameters by maximizing the expected return.

Pooling Layer: A component in CNNs that down-samples feature maps, reducing spatial dimensions and computational complexity while retaining important features.

Precision: A classification metric that measures the proportion of correctly predicted positive observations to the total predicted positives.

Principal Components: New uncorrelated variables formed by linear combinations of original features that capture the most variance in the data.

Pre-training: The initial phase of training a model on a large dataset (often using self-supervised learning) before fine-tuning on specific tasks.

Pretext Task: An auxiliary task designed for self-supervised learning that doesn't require manual labels but helps the model learn useful representations.

Prototype: A representative example or averaged representation of a class, used in prototype-based few-shot learning methods.

Prototypical Networks: A few-shot learning approach that classifies examples based on their distance to class prototype representations.

Pseudo-Labelling: A semi-supervised learning technique where confident model predictions on unlabelled data are used as artificial labels for further training.

PCA (Principal Component Analysis): A dimensionality reduction technique that transforms data into a new coordinate system where the axes (principal components) capture the maximum variance.

Percentile: A measure indicating the value below which a given percentage of observations fall (e.g., 25th percentile = Q1).

Perceptron: A simple neural network unit that applies weights to inputs, adds a bias, and uses an activation function to produce an output.

Policy (π): In reinforcement learning, a strategy that maps states to actions, defining the agent's Behaviour.

Population Standard Deviation: A measure of spread calculated using all data points, with denominator n in the variance formula.

Population Variance: The average squared deviation from the mean for an entire population: $\sigma^2 = \Sigma(x\_i - \mu)^2 / n$.

Posterior Probability: In Bayes' theorem, the probability of a hypothesis after observing the evidence: P(A|B).

Precision: A classification metric measuring the proportion of true positive predictions among all positive predictions: TP / (TP + FP).

Principal Component: In PCA, an eigenvector representing a direction of maximum variance in the data.

Prior Probability: In Bayes' theorem, the initial probability of a hypothesis before observing evidence: P(A).

Probability Density Function (PDF): A function that describes the likelihood of a continuous random variable taking a particular value.

Q

Q-Learning: An off-policy reinforcement learning algorithm that learns the optimal action-value function by iteratively updating Q-values using the Bellman Optimality Equation.

Q-Table: A tabular representation of Q-values for each state-action pair in Q-learning, used for decision-making.

Q-Value: In reinforcement learning, the expected cumulative reward of taking a specific action in a specific state and following the optimal policy thereafter.

Quartile: Values that divide a dataset into four equal parts: Q1 (25th percentile), Q2 (50th percentile/median), and Q3 (75th percentile).

R

R^2 (Coefficient of Determination): A metric indicating the proportion of the variance in the dependent variable that is predictable from the independent variables.

Random Forest: An ensemble learning method that constructs multiple decision trees and combines their predictions for improved accuracy and robustness.

Recall: A classification metric that measures the proportion of actual positives correctly identified by the model.

ReLU (Rectified Linear Unit): A widely used activation function in neural networks that outputs zero for negative inputs and the input itself for positive inputs.

Regression: A family of supervised learning techniques used to model the relationship between dependent and independent variables for prediction.

Regularization: Techniques used to prevent overfitting by penalizing large model parameters, improving generalization.

Reinforcement Learning: A learning paradigm where an agent learns optimal actions through trial-and-error interactions with an environment to maximize cumulative reward.

Residuals: The differences between actual and predicted values in regression models, used to diagnose model fit.

Reward: A scalar signal received after taking an action in a particular state, representing immediate feedback on the action's success.

Ridge Regression: A type of linear regression that includes L2 regularization to prevent overfitting by penalizing large coefficients.

Root Mean Squared Error (RMSE): A regression metric that measures the average magnitude of errors by taking the square root of the mean squared error.

Regularization: Techniques used to prevent overfitting by adding constraints or penalties to the model, encouraging simpler or more generalizable solutions.

Relation Networks: A few-shot learning architecture that learns explicit functions to measure relationships and similarities between examples.

Representation Learning: The process of learning meaningful, useful features or representations from raw data that capture important aspects for downstream tasks.

Recall (Sensitivity): A classification metric measuring the proportion of actual positives correctly identified: TP / (TP + FN).

Regression: A supervised learning task that predicts continuous numerical values rather than discrete classes.

Regression Line; In linear regression, the line that best fits the data according to the least squares criterion: $y = mx + b$.

Reinforcement Learning: A machine learning paradigm where an agent learns to make decisions by performing actions in an environment to maximize cumulative reward.

ReLU (Rectified Linear Unit): An activation function defined as $f(x) = \max(0, x)$, outputting zero for negative inputs and the input itself for positive values.

Reward: In reinforcement learning, feedback from the environment indicating the immediate value of an action taken by the agent.

RMSE (Root Mean Squared Error): The square root of mean squared error, providing error measurement in the same units as the target variable: $RMSE = \sqrt{MSE}$.

S

SARSA: State-Action -Reward -State-Action - an on-policy reinforcement learning algorithm that updates Q-values based on the action actually taken.

Scalability: The ability of an algorithm to handle increasing data sizes or dimensions without significant degradation in performance.

SHAP Values: Shapley Additive Explanations - a method to interpret machine learning model predictions by attributing contributions to individual features.

Sigmoid Function: An activation function that maps input values to the range (0,1), commonly used in binary classification problems.

Silhouette Coefficient: A clustering evaluation metric that measures how similar a point is to its own cluster compared to other clusters.

Soft Clustering: A clustering approach where data points can belong to multiple clusters with varying degrees of membership.

State (S): A representation of the environment at a specific time, capturing all necessary information for decision-making.

Stochastic Gradient Descent: An optimization algorithm that updates model parameters using a subset of the data (a mini-batch) rather than the full dataset.

Supervised Learning: A machine learning paradigm where models learn from labelled data, mapping inputs to outputs.

Support Vector Machines (SVMs): Supervised learning models that find the hyperplane that maximizes the margin between different classes.

Self-Supervised Learning: A learning paradigm where models create their own supervisory signals from the data structure itself, without requiring external labels.

Semi-Supervised Learning: A learning approach that combines small amounts of labelled data with large amounts of unlabelled data during training.

Siamese Networks: Neural network architectures with identical twin networks that learn to distinguish between similar and dissimilar pairs of inputs.

SimCLR (Simple Framework for Contrastive Learning of Visual Representations): A contrastive learning method that learns visual representations by comparing augmented versions of images.

Similarity Metric: A function that quantifies how alike two data points are, crucial for metric learning and few-shot learning approaches.

Supervised Learning: A learning paradigm where models are trained on labelled data, learning to map inputs to known outputs.

Support Set: In few-shot learning, the small set of labelled examples available for each class that the model uses to learn and make predictions.

SwAV (Swapping Assignments between Views): A self-supervised learning method that uses clustering and contrastive learning without explicit negative pairs.

Sample Standard Deviation: A measure of spread calculated from a sample, using n-1 in the denominator (Bessel's correction) to provide an unbiased estimate.

Sample Variance: The average squared deviation from the mean for a sample: $s^2 = \Sigma(x\_i - \bar{x})^2 / (n-1)$.

Sigmoid Function: An activation function that maps any input to a value between 0 and 1: $\sigma(z) = 1 / (1 + e\verb|^|(-z))$. Used in logistic regression and neural networks.

Similarity Metric: A function that quantifies how alike two data points are, used in clustering and classification algorithms.

Single Linkage: A hierarchical clustering method that defines cluster distance as the minimum distance between any two points from different clusters.

Singular Value: In SVD, a non-negative value (σ) representing the importance of a corresponding singular vector, equal to the square root of an eigenvalue.

Singular Value Decomposition (SVD): A matrix factorization technique that decomposes a matrix into three matrices: A = UΣV^T, used for dimensionality reduction and data compression.

Slope: In linear regression, the coefficient (m in y = mx + b) representing the rate of change of the dependent variable with respect to the independent variable.

Specificity: A classification metric measuring the proportion of actual negatives correctly identified: TN/ (TN + FP).

Standard Deviation: The square root of variance, measuring the average distance of data points from the mean.

Standardization: See Z-score Normalization.

State: In reinforcement learning, a representation of the current situation or configuration of the environment.

Step Function: An activation function that outputs discrete values (typically 0 or 1) based on whether the input exceeds a threshold.

Supervised Learning: A machine learning paradigm where models are trained on labelled data with known input-output pairs.

T

Tabular Data: Structured data organized into rows and columns, commonly used in supervised learning tasks.

Temporal Difference (TD) Learning: A reinforcement learning method that updates value estimates based partly on other learned estimates, combining aspects of Monte Carlo and dynamic programming methods.

t-distributed Stochastic Neighbour Embedding (t-SNE): A non-linear dimensionality reduction technique used for visualization by preserving local relationships in high-dimensional data.

TPOT: Tree-based Pipeline Optimization Tool - an AutoML tool that uses genetic programming to optimize ML pipelines.

Transfer Learning: A technique where knowledge from a pre-trained model is transferred to a new, related problem, reducing training time and data requirements.

Transformer Networks: Deep learning architectures based on self-attention mechanisms, widely used in NLP and increasingly in vision tasks.

Tricube Kernel: A kernel function used in LWR that gives higher weight to points near the query and rapidly decreases to zero beyond a fixed distance.

Transfer Learning: The practice of using knowledge learned from one task or domain to improve performance on a different but related task.

Transformer: A neural network architecture based on self-attention mechanisms, highly effective for sequential data like text and increasingly used in computer vision.

Tanh (Hyperbolic Tangent): An activation function that maps inputs to values between -1 and 1: tanh(z)= (e^z - e^(-z)) / (e^z + e^(-z)).

Test Set: A subset of data used to evaluate the final performance of a trained model on unseen examples.

Third Quartile (Q3): The 75th percentile of a dataset, representing the value below which 75% of the data falls.

Training Set: A subset of data used to train a machine learning model by adjusting its parameters.

True Negative (TN): A correct prediction where the model correctly predicts the negative class.

True Positive (TP): A correct prediction where the model correctly predicts the positive class.

U

Underfitting: A modelling issue where a model is too simple to capture the underlying patterns in the data, resulting in poor training and testing performance.

UMAP (Uniform Manifold Approximation and Projection): A non-linear dimensionality reduction technique that preserves local and some global structure in high-dimensional data.

Unsupervised Learning: A learning paradigm where the model discovers patterns or structures in data without labelled outputs.

Unlabelled Data: Data that does not have associated target labels or annotations, often abundant and used in unsupervised and self-supervised learning.

Unsupervised Learning: A learning paradigm where models find patterns and structures in data without any labelled examples or explicit guidance.

Underfitting: A modelling error where a model is too simple to capture the underlying patterns in the data, resulting in poor performance on both training and test sets.

Unsupervised Learning: A machine learning paradigm where models find patterns in data without labelled outputs or explicit guidance.

V

Validation Dataset: A dataset used during training to tune model parameters and monitor generalization performance before final testing.

Variance Inflation Factor (VIF): A metric that quantifies multicollinearity by measuring how much a feature's variance is inflated due to correlation with other features.

Visualization: The graphical representation of data and model Behaviour, aiding in interpretation, debugging, and communication of results.

Variational Autoencoder (VAE): A generative model that learns to encode data into a latent space and decode it back, useful for generating new samples.

Validation Accuracy: The accuracy of a model measured on a validation set, used to tune hyperparameters and detect overfitting.

Validation Set: A subset of data used during training to evaluate model performance and tune hyperparameters, separate from both training and test sets.

Variance: A measure of data dispersion, calculated as the average squared deviation from the mean.

Version Space: In the Candidate Elimination algorithm, the set of all hypotheses consistent with the observed training examples, bounded by the most specific (S) and most general (G) hypotheses.

W

Ward's Method: A hierarchical clustering method that minimizes the variance within clusters at each step, producing compact clusters.

WaveCluster: A grid-based clustering algorithm that uses wavelet transforms to detect clusters of arbitrary shape in spatial data.

Weight Initialization: The process of assigning initial weights in a neural network to break symmetry and promote faster convergence.

Weighted k-NN: A k-NN variant where each neighbour contributes differently to the prediction based on its distance from the query point.

wav2vec: A self-supervised learning framework for speech recognition that learns audio representations from raw waveforms.

Weight: In neural networks and linear models, a learnable parameter that determines the strength of connection between inputs and outputs.

Weighted Entropy: In decision trees, the entropy after a split, calculated as the weighted average of entropies of the resulting subsets.

X

XGBoost: Extreme Gradient Boosting - an efficient and scalable implementation of gradient boosting that includes regularization to prevent overfitting.

XOR Problem: A classic challenge for linear models, demonstrating the need for non-linear transformations in neural networks.

Z

Z-score Normalization (Standardization): A feature scaling technique that transforms data to have mean 0 and standard deviation 1: $z = (x - \mu)/\sigma$.

www.ingramcontent.com/pod-product-compliance
Lightning Source LLC
Chambersburg PA
CBHW041258210926
51847CB00009B/61
9789374268520